Bug
Music

ALSO BY DAVID ROTHENBERG

Is It Painful to Think?

Hand's End

Sudden Music

Blue Cliff Record

Always the Mountains

Why Birds Sing

Thousand Mile Song

Survival of the Beautiful

Bug
Music

HOW INSECTS
GAVE US
RHYTHM
AND NOISE

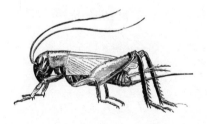

David Rothenberg

ST. MARTIN'S PRESS
NEW YORK

ILLUSTRATION CREDITS: Public domain: contents page, epigraph page, 14, 16, 17, 60, 84, 85 (and title page), 123 (and half title page), 133, 135, 148, 150, 151, 152; from the author: 20, 27, 32, 77, 91, 124 157, 195, 196, 197, 217, 224, 231; Umru Rothenberg: 5; Anderson Design Group, Inc.: 19; Richard Alexander: 24, 25; Jin Yoshimura: 46; Adam Brimer: 72; Alexander Tyrrell, Creative Commons: 75, 76; Curtis Roads: 87, Richard Karban: 96; Frej Ossiannilsson, *Insect Drummers* (Lund: Entomological Society, 1949), 116 (both), 117; H. Autrum, "Über Lautäusserungen und Schallwahrnehmung bei Arthropoden," *Z. vergleich. Physiol.* 23 (1936): 118; J. W. S. Pringle, "A physiological analysis of cicada song," *Journal of Experimental Biology,* 31 (1954): 119; H. Risler, "Das Gehörorgan der Männchen von *Anopheles stephensi,*" *Zool. Jahrb., Abt. Anat. u. Ontog. Tiere.* 73 (1953): 120; T. G. Forrest: 122; Reginald Cocroft: 126; Peter Marting: 128; Holger Gröschl: 143; Heiko Bellmann: 153; the estate of Gyorgyi Ligeti: 154; Patricia Pantaleoni: 160; Georges Meurant: 198; Irene Moon: 207; the estate of Charles Burchfield: 219; Charles Lindsay: 223, 234; Emily Denis: 228, 229; *Bug Music* CD cover, design by Martin Pedanik, used by permission: 253.

www.stmartins.com

Library of Congress Cataloging-in-Publication Data

Rothenberg, David, 1962–
    Bug music : how insects gave us rhythm and noise /
David Rothenberg.
        p. cm.
    Includes bibliographical references and index.
    ISBN 978-1-250-00521-2 (hardcover)
    ISBN 978-1-250-01826-7 (e-book)
  1. Sound production by insects.   2. Insect sounds.   3. Nature
sounds.   4. Nature in music.   I. Title.
    QL496.5.R68 2013
    595.7159—dc23

                                                    2012037394

St. Martin's Press books may be purchased for educational, business, or promotional use. For information on bulk purchases, please contact Macmillan Corporate and Premium Sales Department at 1-800-221-7945 extension 5442 or write specialmarkets@macmillan.com.

First Edition: April 2013

10 9 8 7 6 5 4 3 2 1

Contents

	Prologue	1
One	The Seventeen-Year Pitch	5
Two	Mr. Fung's Cricket Orchestra	54
Three	What Makes Them Dance?	84
Four	Listen Outside the Ear	115
Five	From *El Grillo* to Das Techno	147
Six	Throat-Singing with the Katydids of Glynwood	189
Seven	Sax and Cicadas	214
Epilogue	The Opposite of Terrorism	235
	For Further Reading	243
	The Bug Songs Playlist	247
	Bug Music: *The CD*	249
	Acknowledgments	255
	Notes	259
	Index	269

Mushi kiku to

Honashi na kiku to

Betsu no mimi

Some hear bug music

Some hear people music

All depends on your ears

—Wâfu, 1866, Kyoto

Bug
Music

Prologue

All around us the sounds of the world emerge as music. It's not just that all sound is sound, take it or leave it, but real music is sung by the creatures of this planet, who have evolved to communicate with structures and patterns of mystery. It's nothing like a simple give or take, on or off, win or lose, games people sometimes imagine that animals play. The music of nature is deeper and far less clear, yet it is in its ambiguity that people are able to reach into it.

I have already delved into the most obvious music out there, the songs of birds, in the first book of this trilogy, *Why Birds Sing,* and then I dove into the deepest and grandest arias of the animal world in *Thousand Mile Song,* trying to make music with the giant cries of humpback whales and the shrieking cries of belugas and orcas. Yet the nearest and most incessant natural music may be one that people are most likely to ignore, the songs of insects.

The stridulation of crickets, the tymbaling of cicadas, the *tap-tap-tap*-ing of treehoppers, the thrum of bees. As long as we don't feel threatened by them, most people like these sounds. The rhythms of insects bind us to the landscape, the warm weft of early autumn, a smile at the seasons' march. One small sense that ties us to the eternal, for like all animal sounds, they have been around for millions of years longer than anything human. And the most important thing about them is that they may be the very source of our interest in rhythm, the beat, the regular thrum. And noise. Yes noise. Our love of noise.

Love? Noise? What mean you by that? Noise is unwanted sound, what we cover our ears to avoid, what we shun, what we run from and scream about in our relentless search for *silence*. It's not so simple. We humans love noise, we seek out the trill, the thrum, the resonant, the mangled, the mashed. We amplify our guitars through fuzz and feedback, we have always accented the beat with the rustle of a snare drum or the loud crash of cymbals. Insects make scores of wild percussion sounds. They attract each other with strange tones that may entrance us as well. Bug music—people music. Choose your ears. One animal's racket is another's delight. One person's dolorous melody is another's saccharine Muzak.

Noise rules the day, in a world guided by machines. We either praise or damn those sounds, depending on our mood, our pessimism, or our optimism. These days enough people prefer the exact tones of drum machines to the flexibility of real drummers; indeed, whole genres of music have evolved based on the range of sounds technology can make. The more we get into such artificial sounds the more intriguing the songs of insects sound, who made similar sounds for millions of years before we humans appeared on the scene. In a musical world that celebrates noise, we may seek ever greater noises. We have become connoisseurs of the ruckus, lovers of the strange patterns of unallied sounds.

This journey will take us from the tiny chirps of creatures that might just be simple enough to be like the meticulous machines that science often wants animals to be. Still it is damn hard for us to make a model of the cricket brain sophisticated enough to explain what the bug will and can do. Certainly birds and whales, for those who spend time with them, are very much individuals and not predictable representatives of species who behave the way they are supposed to. But insects? They are supposed to make sense as a swarm, to overwhelm us in the millions, and their music has great group qualities as well. They respond reliably, like little computer routines, waking up to sounds and silences, filling in the spaces between. They clearly listen from one species to another—something birds, whales, and even humans are not so used to doing. The whole insect chorus is many species interacting in intriguing patterns. Their rhythms thrum intensely at us like the early noise musics of Luigi Russolo and Edgard Varèse; they challenge the gentle advice of John Cage to simply listen, threatening to overwhelm us with the great crackle and buzz of a prehistoric Earth. What could be more gigantically sublime than a huge sound made by thousands of singing creatures, each a tiny part of a giant noise, with hardly a room for any human to get a sound in?

My method, as always, is *not* to peacefully listen, but to insist on joining in. Arrogant like most humans, I want to believe my own music can matter as a tiny line amid these ancient tones. From crickets and katydids to treehoppers and finally cicadas, I will strive to make my own music together with the stridulating hordes. The culmination will be the grandest, deepest, and slowest of animal rhythms, way beyond the one-beat-every-four-minutes precise rhythm of the giant fin whale. Yet it is a bug that has the longest beat in the animal world—the great sound of the *Magicicada* comes out so rarely that many forget they've ever heard it, since it emerges only once every seventeen years. When this book arrives in print the periodical cicadas will soon climb out of the ground in the New York environs. This time, you will be ready for them.

But this trip is a tough one for me, as it has taken me some effort to learn to love these sounds. I appreciate their incessance, I am amazed by their tenacity, but I don't immediately hear all this insect noise as music. Instead, I ask you to follow me on this journey to learn an appreciation of bug music. Here I have undertaken the very adventure I have been asking readers of these music/nature books to do for years . . . to listen wider, to expand your sense of music to more than human sounds, and to thereby take in a world of greater beauty and of greater meaning. At the end of the trip, I promise you will be living and listening in a better place.

How to convey this search for enthusiasm? Mine is in some ways a narrow quest. I want you all to consider insect sound as music, the arrangement of tones and rests into patterns that must be repeated endlessly to get its message across. The message, usually having to do with attracting a mate or defending a territory, is not really the point, since that is all the same throughout the animal world. It is the music that differs, its qualities evolved to make each species have its own identity and stand out from the fray. The diversity of life is what is most interesting about evolution, not the simple rules that explain what each strange sound is for. We may decode the purpose of all we hear, but we cannot explain away the love for sound itself that emerges once we accept the alien as worthy of the name "music."

So I won't tell you everything there is to know about the world of insect sound. I will strive to convince you that it is music, and try to get you to love it, and then to take the noisy and the humming and the scratching and the beating part of human music just a little more seriously, all around.

ONE

The Seventeen-Year Pitch

It's the slowest sonic beat in the animal world. It's a sound that can be used to mark the phases of a human life. It's a mathematical conundrum, an unearthly wonder of animal sound. The cloud of insect music you can barely recall. When you last heard it, you were just settling down. The time before that, you were a teenager. Before that it was the year you were born. The next time you will hear it you might be a grandfather.

This time the song arrives, you are smack in the middle of your journey through life.

"You are a Cicada Boy," my friend John P. O'Grady insists. Once an English professor, he is now a photographer, flaneur, and part-time astrologer. "Believing that the stars affect us is a useful fiction," he smiles. "One might also believe the appearance of cicadas every seventeen years touches us in a similar way." He looks up the year 1962. It was one of those years that the great thrumming insects arrived en masse in the trees of late spring in the Northeast. One month later I was born in July. The cicadas were back when I graduated high school, and again when I moved from the city to the country. That last time back in 1996, O'Grady took me out to the Mohonk Mountain House to experience the great emergence. At the time I wrote these lines about them, part of a longer poem that dealt with my own inability to rigorously mark the passing of time:

Seventeen years
to those that note the passing of time:
They're back!
The crunching of footsteps over carapaces underfoot
The slow swelling, the rhythms of the one-time forest
Crzzzzzzzzzzhh Chrzzzzzaahhh . . .
What are these insects for?
They sit, bewildered, on fence posts, with glaring red eyes.
They can barely fly, like puffins falling from rocks,
Sparrows try to catch them but can't get their beaks around 'em. . . .

Every seventeen years I'll check in on what happens.
I'll trace the memories of their return.
Seventeen years from now it may all make sense.
Certain situations will be resolved.
There will be other, outward problems to face.
I will not be able to solve them alone.

There will be low soft whooms in the trees.
Fluttering wings struggling to lift us between the trees.
We will stare up again and wonder:
who else has had to wait so long to face the air?
No reason to go on except the only reason that matters:
there is nothing else to do
this is the plan
this is our place in the plan
this is the sound.

In the years since then I have been making music together with all kinds of animals. It has humbled me a bit and taught me to appreciate many more kinds of sounds. Now I am even more in awe of this longest animal rhythm, a great beat that emerges out of silence only once every seventeen years. It is only a North American thing, nowhere else has this kind of wave of cicada appearances, following these strange great cycles of prime-numbered years.

Most cicadas all over the world come out in large enough numbers every year to enthrall people with their volume, energy, and roughness of sound, and annoy us as well, especially those who would wish that nature was closer to silence. Anacreon, in the first century BC, was fascinated by this great energy from the top of the trees:

We praise thee auspicious Cicada, enthroned like a king
On the tree's summit, thou cheer'st us with exquisite song . . .
Old age does not oppress thee O good little animal,
sprung from the bosom of the earth, loving song,
free from suffering, that hast neither blood nor flesh—
What is there prevents thee from being a god?

The earliest naturalists knew that this insect was an amazing symbol of love and music. The cicadas having eaten enough underground emerge for just a few weeks for nothing but revelry, music, and sex. They party on thinking nothing of their rapid, impending doom. Leave it to the great poet Bashō to make deepest sense of that in 1690:

Cicadas sing—
know not how soon
They all will die.

Each shrill, whining, or whooshing song is a call to the endless nature of love. However fast love goes we know it will return, the one sure thing that will never be exhausted as all the rest of nature gets spent, used up, or destroyed. Cicadas on the branches, eternal optimists, lovers of the moment.

Most species of cicadas, even those that come out every year, grow underground for at least two to five years, and many non-periodic species may have longer life cycles, whose length we know little about because this is information very hard to find out without these big, coordinated emergences. We cannot easily watch what these larvae do underground for so many years. We might never know.

Too many people confuse cicadas with locusts and fear some great scourge upon the crops at once when they appear. But cicadas hardly eat at all, having stored up enough energy to live after all those years underground. What modest damage they do to leaves on trees comes when the females lay their eggs near the end of branches, and the branches split and die after the eggs hatch.

So inhabit the mystery, even as you try to delve deep. Do not shun science as you listen to the swarm. Why not imagine they are talking to us, pleading for their lives? A ninth-century anonymous Greek wrote this:

A man wanted to eat a cicada but the insect suddenly spoke up: "O human I beg you, don't kill me so vainly for nothing. I harmed no corn crop and did no insult to anyone; By uttering sounds, I entertain you travelers, and you will find no voice as fine as mine." And so the man let the cicada go free. . . .

Let us praise not only the cicada but the great entomologist Keith Kevan, director for many years of the Lyman Entomological Museum at McGill Unversity in Montreal, who in his spare time compiled and self-published five 300-page volumes of every reference to singing insects he could find in the classical and modern literature of many languages, from ancient Chinese, Japanese, Greek, and Latin to Sanskrit and Russian as well. It is the best compendium in existence on references to the sounds of insects in the world's literatures, and I was surprised to discover that hardly anyone seems to know about it. I found an old obituary online that said "copies of these volumes may still be found in the basement of the Lyman Entomological Museum," so immediately I wrote to the current director, Stéphanie Boucher, and she was suspicious.

"How do you know about those books?" she asked.

"Like most of us, I waste a lot of time on the Internet. I found all the old issues of a 1980s journal called *Cultural Entomology* on a website somewhere, and just read through them one by one, looking for something on the music of bugs. The obituary for Keith Kevan was so fascinating I read it all the way to the end. And there, the five mysterious volumes were mentioned. So I want them. As soon as possible," I said.

That sounded like a good enough reason for Ms. Boucher, and now I've got those big books on the floor of my office, and that's where I found most of these incredible cicada and cricket poems.

Possibly the greatest poetic work on cicadas in all of Kevan's thousands of pages is the "Song of the Cicada," composed in the Year of the Great Flood 1056 at the Wine Spring Temple by Ou-Yang Hsiu, where he was doing his best to pray for better weather. These excerpts were translated by Arthur Waley nearly a century ago:

Here was a thing that cried upon a treetop,
sucking the shrill wind
To wail it back in a long whistling note—
That clasping in its arms
A tapering twig perpetually sighed,
Now shrill as flute, now soft as mandolin;
sometime a piercing cry
Choked at its very uttering, sometimes a cold tune
Dwindled to silence, then suddenly flowered again,
a single note, wandering in strange keys,
An air, yet fraught
With undertone of hidden harmony.

Are you not he, cicada,
of whom I have heard told you can transform
Your body, magically molding it
To new estate?

Are you not he who, born
Upon the dung-heap, coveted the sky,
Found wings to mount the wind?

Again your voice, cicada
Not grave, not gay, part Lydian,
part Dorian, your tune that,

as suddenly as it began
suddenly ceases.

Now there is a great paean to the wildness of insect music, all tunes and tones we cannot quite place, of melodies and harmonies beyond the scales and chords of human sense. It's not Lydian, it's not Dorian, whatever those ancient Greek modes were really sounding like we really don't know, but any musician who has tried to jam along with insects knows we struggle to place the sounds we like together with this essential but alien noise.

Throughout history, we humans have wanted to embrace these sounds as music, however they differ from our own rules and structures of melody. It is as if we have always intuitively known that the sonic declarations of animals make much more sense to us humans if we consider them to be music rather than language. Music is immediately meaningful even if we cannot translate it, so once heard as music, the world of animal communication is immediately accessible, emotional, and interesting.

When did people first notice the prime-numbered cycles of cicadas, something that only happens in the New World of North America? Certainly the early Pilgrims experienced an emergence a few years after Plymouth Rock. They were not always sure just what to call the insects they were astonished by. William Bradford wrote in 1633: "all the month of May, there was such a quantity of a great sort of flyes like for bigness to wasps or bumblebees, which came out of holes in the ground and replenished all the woods, and ate the green things, and made such a constant yelling noise as made all the woods ring of them, and ready to deaf the hearers." Music indeed. He goes on: "They have not by the English been heard or seen before. But the Indians told them that sickness would follow, and so it did in June, July, August, and the chief heat of summer."

Naturalist Paul Dudley was the first to study the emergence in detail. His research took a very long time to get going. He incorrectly called them locusts, and first observed them in 1699, then again in 1716, but he waited until 1733 to *make sure* they really were emerging every seventeen years, when he submitted his results to the Royal Society of London. Science papers had a somewhat different tone in those days, and rather creative spelling:

. . . They are in great numbers in our woods, the noise is loud to the degree that our farmers have not been able to hear their cowbells tho in sight. I have myself been traveling thro the midst of thousands of them, and the noise was such that there was no conversing for some miles together, & it carried even some terror with it. That which seemed to me some what strange was that tho the Locusts were close by, and all around me, yet their noise was, as tho it had been distant & come from far.

This agrees with the Prophet Joel when he alludes to the noise made by this animal (*Joel* ch. 2 v. 5: As the noise of the chariots upon the tops of mountains shall they leap, like the noise of a flame of fire). Here it must be noted, That 'tis only the male makes the noise, & it is not formed with the mouth as some of our People at first imagined, nor yet is it by the percussion of the air, or meer vibration of the wings, as Pliny & the Poets would have it (*Tanto volant permarum stridore*), but by the striking of the upper wings upon two tender drums, as I may call 'em, situated between the neck and the body, where there is an opening, and a tremulous fold of a whitish purple color . . .

So, detailed observation dovetails with scripture and classical literature in the words of one of the colonies' first scientific naturalists. What wonders of nature did God prepare for us to puzzle over! The great Finnish–Swedish naturalist Pehr Kalm felt the same way in 1749. He thought they were grasshoppers:

> It was unbelievable how many there were of them now. There had not been anything like it in 17 years. The many holes in the earth that you can find all over in this country, of the size that you can put a finger in them, now became the haunt for the nymphs of these grasshoppers before they came out. I saw several of these nymphs sitting in the opening of these holes, but I did not know what kind of animal would come out of them. Mostly they came creeping out during the night, wandered up trees, branches and plants, took off their nymphal skins which split on the top. After they had crept out, they sat for a while and dried their wings and started then trying to fly. The nymphal skin remained sitting on the tree or plant, where the grasshopper left it. It was then blown to the ground or swept away by rain. . . . Hens were very clever catching the grasshoppers as they came out of their holes. They ate them with pleasure, and so did other birds. This might be the reason for the Creator to make them come out at night, so they will not be all eaten by birds before they hatch and are able to fly . . .

The Creator, in this century before the idea of evolution, must have thought of everything. Today we are still trying to find out why and how this strange periodic rhythm has evolved. And even though these tasty morsels seem to be a gustatory gift for whoever dares to taste them, some biologists believe the simplest way to understand this occurrence as a strategy is that there are just so many cicadas that they will simply exhaust any predators' attempts to consume them. Too many chickens and dogs get sick to their stomachs by not knowing when to stop eating this sudden periodic feast!

Observe how they emerge from wingless nymph to flying adult:

In 1839, Nathaniel Potter, professor of medicine from Maryland, scoffed at the notion that this noisemaker could have anything to do with the musical insects praised by the ancient Greeks. There must have been some mistake:

> The cicadae of Greece must have been highly gifted with musical powers to have been celebrated by Homer, who compares the strains of his orators to the sweetness of their notes. How differently would the ear of the imperial poet have decided had he been condemned to listen to the monotonous, protracted *twang* of the American locust! He would have been as much pleased with the scraping of a scissor grinder, or the grading of a file.

I beg to disagree. I still believe people like the sound of all this white noise in the forest. It is like begging to listen to the call of the ocean in a conch shell, or the repeating peal of waves on the shore, or even the pleasing flow of traffic on the highway below the city window. We have long appreciated the washes of pitchless rhythms crashing in from this noisy world. And now more than ever we can praise the musical value of noise as never so much loved before. Think of it, Potter, Homer actually loved this noisy sound of the cicada, as it is clamorous and whirring all over the world, never a pure or calm cricketesque tone. The bard loved noise, arrhythmic noise, a wash of sound that could confound his beats. Inside all that noise he must have heard the potential for beauty, as a wash of sound contains all perceptible sounds, as a solid block of marble contains all sculptures that could be honed out of it.

D. L. Phares in 1845 had another theory: "The sound produced by the commingled notes of the whole tribe of cicada *seems* loud and harsh, but on closer examination, and distinguishing one individual voice from the whole mass it will be found the softest, sweetest, languishing notes of true love ever produced." *This* must be why the Greeks kept them in cages! Not only to enjoy their songs passively, but to practice along, to "improve their own voices by imitating the sounds of their insectile teachers."

And let us not forget that ancient legend of Eunomos and Ariston, competing for a prize in playing the harp. Eunomos broke a string during the contest, and a cicada, who had been listening to the whole thing, flew right to the instrument and attached itself to the soundboard, *shwooming* exactly the note that was required in place of the missing string. Of course he won the prize. There is an ancient illustration of this legend below:

No wonder that in 2011 a group of Columbia, Missouri, alternative musicans released a compilation album called *Cicada Summer* with eighteen tunes inspired by the emergence of the Brood XIX thirteen-year cicadas, with titles like "The Great Southern Brood," "Still in Love in 2024," and "Why Do You Keep Me Up at Night?"

By the end of the nineteenth century, scientists were getting most meticulous in their observations of periodical cicadas. First Benjamin Walsh with Charles Riley, and then later C. L. Marlatt,

had finalized the list of the various "broods" of periodical cicada that come out at very definite times over 17- and 13-year intervals, in very specific locations only in the Eastern United States. Nowhere else in the world has evolution organized such a pattern of vast cicada emergences. There were originally fourteen 17-year broods, numbered I to XIV. Today brood XII is extinct. There were four 13-year broods, numbered XIX to XXIII. Today brood XX is extinct. The most extensive broods are II, X, XIV, and XIX, which will next emerge in 2013, 2021, 2025, and 2024 respectively. So if you don't catch 'em this year in the Northeast it may be a while before you get to see them. However, intrepid periodic cicada hunters can find Brood III in Iowa in 2014, Brood IV in western Missouri and eastern Kansas in 2015, and Brood V in eastern Ohio in 2016, and you might run into me there if I get addicted to this rare and total wash of sound. Now here's where to look and listen this year for the great Brood II cicada emergence of 2013, as noted by Marlatt ninety years ago:

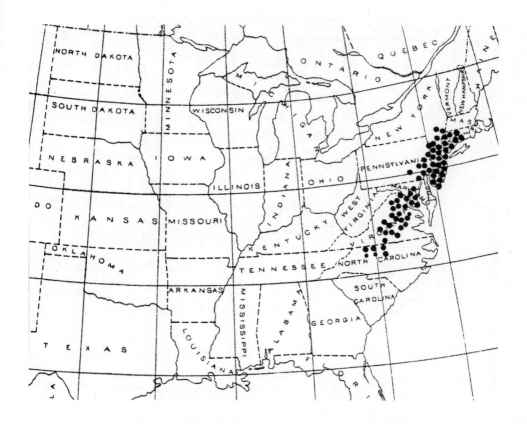

Since Brood II is the one that is most prevalent in the New York metropolitan area, it is no surprise that this is the one that has gotten most attention in the last 130 or so years of the *New York Times*, that venetable institution with all the news fit to print. These days it takes but a few strokes at a computer to pull up everything the paper has ever published on singing periodical cicadas, and there is much interesting stuff. Every seventeen years the same fears of mass destruction, loud annoyance, and the occasional voicing of love for this wonderful phenomenon comes through the old, scanned letterpress pages.

The overwhelming din of a forest full of *phaaaaaaarohhh*-ing seventeen-year cicadas seems to frustrate all journalists who write about them while usually barely remembering the last time they heard such a sound. In 1894 a *New York Times* editorial hoped we could find a use for these creatures:

> Nervous people who become exasperated by its ceaseless drone during the hottest part of the day will hail with savage delight any discovery that may allow them to "get even" with an insect that adds to the injury of our ornamental woodlands the insult of a noise peculiarly shrill and mechanical. There *are* people who keep cicadas in cages and ask them to sound their rattles, notably Spaniards, but it is evident that Spaniards must lack American nerves—to stir them properly they need bullfights, and to keep them from sleeping all day they require cicadas in their darkened rooms to "stab the noon silence with a sharp alarm."

The article goes on to suggest we find some use for this boon of protein . . . cicada biscuits perhaps for dogs and cats? Would the ASPCA approve?

Already in 1885 the famous cicada biologist Charles Riley was spotted breakfasting on the tasty freshly emerged morsels. "The visitor was served with a spoonful of dark objects like very small fried oysters . . . 'Don't be afraid of them,' stated Riley, 'They are only the quintessence of vegetable juices, and everything in nature feeds upon then ravenously.'" So why not us?

In fact, in 2011 the Missouri Department of Conservation whipped up a feast for humans featuring four cicada-heavy dishes. Cicada pizza. Cicada-portobello quiche. "El chirper" tacos, and Emergence Cookies. Mike Arduser, conservation biologist, suggests this approach if you are adventurous in your food gathering: "You want the cicadas that are just emerging, the tenerals. They're soft for just a few hours. Go out early in the day and find cicadas at the bases of trees. They will be white or pale yellow. Ideally you want females. They have more meat. Female cicadas will have a sharper, pointier bottom. That's the appendage they use to lay eggs."

The Anderson Design Group of Nashville offered up a special cicada invasion Web page with the following self-explanatory banner:

© Anderson Design Group, Inc. Used by permission. www.andersondesigngroup.com

Sing, fly, mate, die—all those reasons we admire them so much. These guys recommend cicada satay, or stir fry, and present their taco recipe for our testing:

Ingredients:
    2 tablespoons butter or peanut oil
    1½ pounds of cicadas
    1 onion, finely chopped
    1 teaspoon chili powder
    1 tomato, finely chopped
    1½ tablespoons ground pepper
    1½ tablespoons cumin
    1½ tablespoons oregano
    taco shells
    1 handful cilantro, chopped
    sour cream
    shredded lettuce
    shredded cheddar cheese

Cooking instructions:

1. Heat the butter or oil in a frying pan and fry the cicadas for 10 minutes, or until cooked through.
2. Remove from pan and roughly chop into ¼-inch cubes and place back in pan.
3. Add the chopped onions, chili powder, and tomato. Season with salt and fry for another 5 minutes on medium-low heat.
4. Sprinkle with ground pepper, cumin, and oregano to taste.
5. Serve in taco shells and garnish with cilantro, sour cream, lettuce, and cheddar cheese.

Again, make sure you use freshly gathered, white young morning nymphs. And if that all sounds like too much work for you or you've already eaten dinner, cicada ice cream is available once in a while at Sparky's in Columbia, Missouri:

The Missouri Board of Health advised them against making a second batch . . . they had no rules about how to deal with the public safety of cicadas as a protein source. But they can't stop you from serving your own freshly emerged cicadas at home. Get 'em while they're white and juicy, don't wait until they start to sing and get crunchy!

A lavish, two-page illustrated spread by Donald Prattie from a 1936 issue of the *New York Times* maintains that the periodical cicada is "still the most misunderstood insect on our continent." He reminds us, as the newspapers always seem to do every thirteen or seventeen years, that these cicadas are not locusts, they do not eat crops, they do not sting babies to death, and they will not harm your fruit trees excessively. He urges us to respect the cicada, to think of all the dangers it must face in its short, few weeks of life aboveground: being chased by birds, eaten by dogs, cats, and foxes; struggling to have a chance to mate; and get the most out of their brief time singing and breathing in air. At the time it was believed, even by the naturalist Jean-Henri Fabre, that cicadas couldn't even hear this incredible din. But today we know they just hear with organs we weren't able to recognize back then as being able to take in sound. But Prattie sure hears the giant, swirling noise: "To me the din is one of the most depressing and unnerving ever heard, not only because of its monotony but because of its suggestion that something terrible is going to happen."

Something terrible? What? One day, all of a sudden, the sound will stop, and we will have seventeen years of *Magicicada* of silence. It is a humbling thought, with a touch of the sublime. The great entomologist H. A. Allard had this to say after the emergence of Brood XIX in eastern Virginia in 1920:

I felt a *positive* sadness when I realized that the great visitation was over, and there was silence in the world again, and all were dead that had so recently lived and filled the world with noise and movement. It was almost a painful silence, and I could not but feel that I had lived to witness one of the great events of existence, comparable to the occurrence of a notable eclipse or the visitation of a great comet.

This is truly the writing of a great scientist, who, while trying to rationally explain a mysterious phenomenon of nature, is not afraid to reveal to us, in a scientific journal, his true feelings on being in the midst of such an awesome experience. Would that more science as it's written today retain this quality! I get the sense Allard is not far from the view of the Maori, who tend to speak of their native Aotearoa/New Zealand cicadas as "the insect people." In a well-known chant first written down in 1853 they speak of what it means to connect to these other beings:

Ki ouru
Ki owhawha
Kia kata noa mair to Kikitara

To join
To feel
The cicada's cry

All of us who have tried to make sense of this awesome sonic phenomenon have wanted to find a way inside the sound, to become part of it or make it a part of us. And yet it is so hard to remember, so many years in between these emergences, to know what it means to live deep inside of noise. To know it, not to fear it. To find it wonderful, and not be afraid.

Even Bob Dylan caught a whiff of this as he was picking up an honorary degree at Princeton University in 1970, smack in the middle of Brood X, New Jersey's greatest cicada moment. While the Princeton Alumni Bulletin described the incident as nearly biblical in proportion, Dylan wrote the song "Day of the Locusts" that appeared on his *New Morning* album. Over a high, distant organ sound that resembles the high whine of the seventeen-year cicada, Dylan calls their song chilling, sweet, and—like so many of us human commentators on nature—he felt the sound of the insect orchestra was there just for him. Like all those early scientists, he called these critters "locusts." Sure, "locusts" scans much better than "cicadas," and is all the more ominous, too. Who can blame Dylan for making the same mistake that most who encounter the great emergence do? He thought they were a plague of crop-destroyers, as opposed to harmless lovers and performers.

As we move closer toward the present day, the science of periodical cicadas gets more precise. In 1925, William T. Davis decided these strange beasts deserved their own genus, which he named *Magicicada* to distinguish them from the more prosaic annual *Cicadae* who come out dutifully every year, usually later in summer, at least in the temperate Northern Hemisphere. It is a perfect name for a being whose behavior still seems like magic, no matter how often scientists enjoy the rare opportunities they have to study them.

The three basic sounds made by the magic cicadas were first enumerated by Charles Riley in 1885. By the twentieth century these were identified as belonging to three distinct species of *Magicicada,* all of whom emerge simultaneously when their seventeen or thirteen years are up.

Magicicada septendecim	Phaaaaaarraoooooooh!
Magicicada cassini	Tshtke-EHHHHH-ou!
Magicicada septendecula	mch mch mCH mCH mCH Ch ch ch ch!

The sounds described in mnemonic words are nothing like a birdsong. I am impressed by entomologist Richard Alexander's very elegant schematic sonogram drawing of the differences, where he tries to symbolically draw the structure of the three main sounds abstracting from the sonograms scientists were just beginning to use in the 1960s, images that graph frequency on the vertical axis and time on the horizontal. Such technical pictures give drawn shape and form to the sort of unpitched noise that is impossible to transcribe in musical notation.

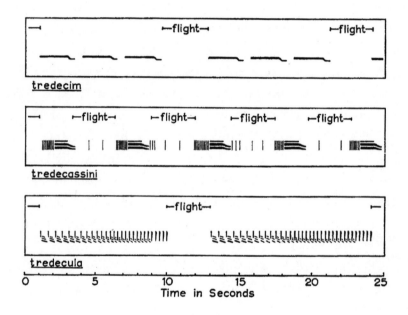

You may note these species' names are slightly different. Why? Alexander determined that, in those very rare occurrences when thirteen-year and seventeen-year populations appear simultaneously, the different-cycled insects would not mate with each other in sufficient numbers to suggest that they are all one species. He and his collaborator Thomas Moore put a bunch of these overlapping bugs in a cage and tried to get them to mate, but most of the time they refused. So Alexander named three more species of

Magicicada: tredecim, tredecassini, and *tredecula,* who sound exactly like their seventeen-year counterparts. (I know it can get confusing, but that's what happens when you start to listen closely to the insect world.) Alexander and Moore also noted that the different species tend to vocalize at different hours of the day:

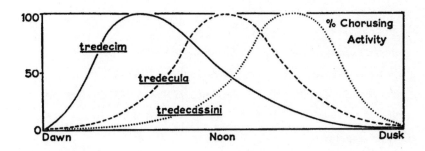

This might also help you identify which type of *Magicicada* you're hearing, though I'm not sure this pattern works universally with different emergences in different regions. *Tredeculas* and *septendeculas* are far less common than the others, and also much quieter.

Studying such a creature is quite a curious vocation. Think how long you have to wait for them to turn up once more. Or, you roam the country year by year, looking for their next appearance. At least such things are well documented for the last century, and regularly updated online, on websites such as www .magicicada.org and www.insectsingers.com. But the world of science, and especially those bodies that fund research, often question the validity of such an obsession. Nevertheless, the two leading former students of Alexander, John Cooley and David Marshall, have a fantastic track record of coming up with more discoveries during the more recent *Magicicada* emergences. In 2000, they found yet another species of thirteen-year cicadas with a higher-pitched *phaaarooooah* song, which were attracting specific females. They are genetically very similar to the seventeen-year cicadas, suggesting that in the course of evolution some part of a population may have made the leap from seventeen to thirteen years, then distinguishing themselves into a separate species. The new species with a higher-pitched tonal call was named *Magicicada neotredecim*. So, for all the latest details, here we go:

17-year species:

Magicicada septendecim	Phaaaaaarraoooooooh! *[1.2–1.5 kHz]*
Magicicada cassini	TshtkeTchtke-EHHHHH-ou!
Magicicada septendecula	mch mch mCH mCH mCH Ch ch ch ch!

13-year species:

Magicicada tredecim	Phaaaaaarraoooooooh! *(1–1.25 kHz)*
Magicicada neotredecim	Phaaaaaarraoooooooh! *(1.4–1.7 kHz)*
Magicicada trecassini	TshtkeTchtke-EHHHHH-ou!
Magicicada tredecula	mch mch mCH mCH mCH Ch ch ch ch!

Even more significant a discovery by Marshall and Cooley was deeper insight into the extremely complex mating behavior of the periodic cicadas. As with most insect species, in the case of periodic cicadas only the males do the singing. It used to be thought that the male cicadas gathered in great numbers to sing in trees to attract the females en masse, the lek model of mating that's like a giant dance club where the females approach, attracted by the whole great music of the males. This is why frogs sing in large choruses, crickets as well. The females were supposed to select males with specific visual cues. But Cooley and Marshall discovered, after years of observing the insects at work in the field, that at the very end of the male's call, the female makes a tiny, wing-flick sound, and if the male hears that, he moves just a bit closer and responds with a slightly different song. If the female gives another wing-flick, the male gets closer with yet a third song, and if he reaches the female while she's still interested mating begins. Far more complicated than we originally thought. Here is a schematic diagram of the process in *Magicicada septendecim*, adapted from Marshall's dissertation of 2000:

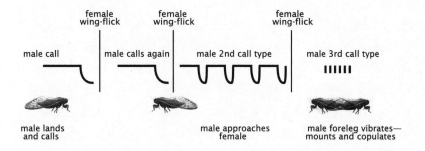

Through a series of experiments, Cooley and Marshall were able to determine that the precise timing of the wing-flick is the crucial bit of signal information:

> Only simulated wing-flicks produced right after the downslur caused male *M. septendecim* to respond positively. Males usually responded to such stimuli by walking toward the stimulus while calling. In this behavior, termed "callwalking," males stopped walking for approximately one second immediately following each downslur. This pattern is distinct from chorusing behavior, which involves bouts of stationary calling alternating with flights or silent walks.

An absolutely amazing advance in insect-mating studies, cutting through the fear of all this cicada noise and confusion in the midst of the great *whoosh* of sound to discover a courtship process that is the most complex known in any acoustical insect. When you go out to listen to the vast chorus of cicada song armed with this knowledge of the subtle differences in courtship song, the whole thing sounds like a complex orchestra, not just a wash of white noise. The beauty of nature seems all the more intricate and amazing once science gives you some details to make sense of the strange and the rare.

In addition to these three different songs, there are nonacoustic anomalies, like a special male foreleg vibration that occurs right before the moment of mating. Marshall and Cooley achieved something quite significant with their tandem thesis research: finding a new species of periodical cicada, and revealing complexities of mating in insects hitherto unimagined, a magnificent display that has been made famous by David Attenborough's *Life in the Undergrowth* on the BBC and many other television productions.

And yet, neither of these intrepid researchers has a tenured job as a scientist today. I find this truly shocking, and I was fortunate to spend some days together with Cooley and Marshall during the latest emergence of thirteen-year cicadas in Missouri in 2011. I ask Marshall how he decided to devote so many years of his life to a creature so anomalous.

"I used to joke when I first finished my thesis, that I had spent so many years, a really embarrassingly large number of years, studying an organism from which one can generalize nothing. Because it was arguably this unique, one-off thing that happened in the corner of the world. But of course that is not true. Because evolution occurs so slowly, over such large time scales, the kinds of evolutionary processes that lead to complex adaptation occur too slowly to be observed in the lab. Most of what we have learned about evolution has come from examining correlations of traits of organisms and their environments across the broad spectrum of living things. This is the comparative method. . . . It might be the strange species, the apparently odd things that are the most valuable to study because they might be most likely to falsify our pet theories and really move us along," he replies.

"And what do you think of all this noise? Do you truly appreciate this sound now that you've found out so much from studying it?" I ask.

"It is almost a nostalgic sound to me by now, because I have experienced more than a full seventeen-year generation worth of cicada emergences. But just the other day I almost felt intimidated by them. Two days ago down in southern Illinois, coming up through a road through Paducah, I came back from town during the peak time of activity for the *cassini*, the ones that are really loud. And the road kind of closed in so the trees were right in close to this small, two-lane road, and even though I am whipping along at sixty with the windows open, these things were synchronizing and they're just at peak right now down there, *swiiiiiishhhh swiiiiiiish swiiiiish*, all swelling and fading in unison like a great wave. With the heat in the air, and the sunlight perfect, no wind, they were just surging. I think it was louder than I have ever heard it, and I got this little jolt of almost this primal fear, like—this is a scary sound. It was intense enough to make me kind of just clench up a little bit inside. Even though of course I know exactly what this sound is all about, the sound can get so strong, there is a hint of that primal fear that sneaks up even on me," he says.

A little hint of the primal scream perhaps. "Now, do you think these sounds are *music*?" I ask.

"Music for whom? I don't know what music is for people. What are people doing with music in the first place? People are using music in courtship, aren't they? Look at how the young women swoon over rock stars. It just seems to be tied up in the mating game and we can get technical about the songs of cicadas and crickets and katydids and say, 'Oh, this is species recognition,' but what it boils down to is an individual of a particular species trying to convince, in a sense, another individual to mate and trying to mess around with its sensory responses and push the buttons in the right way that it will induce the response that it is after: mating success. So certainly in a biological sense it is music."

Why do they all need to be together in one tree? Wouldn't it be easier for a female to find one alone somewhere? Why are they all together?

"Because they gain from being in close proximity to as many other cicadas as possible, because it is safety in numbers. It is just a selfish herd. A female who flies into a group of males, is not going to have to wait as long to be found when she is ready, she can flick and pretty soon she gets that business over with and gets on to the lengthy task of laying her eggs in the trees. There are costs to it as well. We don't yet know enough about the movements of the females after mating—it could be that there is some dispersion somewhat away from those choruses because the females don't want to be harassed by the males all the time, either. And the males will pester them while they are done mating, lying in wait to lay their eggs. He will walk up and give it a try, try to climb on. A female might have to bat her wings to dislodge the male and say, 'Go away, I'm no longer interested, and am on to the next step here.'"

"Do you remember how you felt when you first discovered the female's wing flick?" I ask.

"How could I forget my surge of excitement? Actually at that point, as is often the case in science, I was looking for something else, trying to figure out if older females, those a few weeks old, mated more vigorously than younger ones. When they get two weeks old they do start doing very bizarre things, like laying unfertilized eggs or trying to mate with other females. I introduced a male to a cage with several females in it, and closed the bag, and began watching with my notebook and pencil. 'Time three thirty-eight: male approaches a certain female and is looking, "Oh, what's going on here, do I see the female doing anything, what is going on?"' And I remember after having written some notes about a particular male, that he suddenly turned in the cage while singing and went straight across the cage and mated with a female in the far side of the cage. It was completely startling because he had other females right near him—they were all unmated, why did he choose that one that was further away?

"What was going on? I did it again, and the second time exactly the same thing happened in no time whatsoever. And then it became obvious to me. I could see that the female twitched quite obviously right after each of several songs as he moved across the cage toward her. I realized *it was precisely timed,* and that was the critical thing. If you watch periodical cicadas in cages or whatever, you can see them flicking their wings constantly and it is usually a negative sign. A flicking of the wings, whether it is a male or female, means, *Go away get off me.* A male trying to climb on another male gets wings flicked at him. But what I saw here was a positive, encouraging response. I told John Cooley right away and he immediately grasped the significance," Marshall says.

On the next page is a mating pair, oblivious to the photographer's intruding lens.

"Right away we reorganized what we were doing and started looking at the other species and figured out what we had to do to demonstrate this well enough, with the timing and acoustical and visual components. Just a little simple fact like that, and that was before we could even begin to appreciate the doors that would open for looking at other aspects of behavior with these cicadas and other cicada species as well. We never would have found any of it if we weren't tuned into these little timed clicks."

"And how long did it take you to figure out that precise timing was essential?" I ask.

"I could see that right away. One of the things I began doing was making my own little flick signals, just by flicking pieces of paper. John, who is more mechanically inclined, was inventing devices that make exact, repeatable clicks. So we did experiments, clicking during songs and during long durations after the end of songs, just to demonstrate what was obvious from watching the cicadas. First we had to realize that the wing-flick didn't always mean, *go away,* that, if timed precisely, it means, *come here.*"

"So, when you hear these cicadas, what do you hear that other people don't hear? Are you some kind of cicada music connoisseur?" I ask.

"Before I studied these things I was screening them out as well. We learn to pay attention to the sounds that we decide are important to us. Insect sounds don't matter to people, so it is remarkable how effectively we screen them out. I was pulled over by a policeman in central Illinois during one of these emergences, somewhere near Champaign. I was mapping, working out details of the distribution. I am in my little car that is not from Illinois, putzing along, slowing down in front of people's houses. So of course the cop pulls me over, 'Whatchya doin?' he says, and I say, 'Oh, I am mapping these periodical cicadas that are out right now.' He could see I am for real, with all this recording equipment, maps everywhere, so he was just sort of bemused. But he did say, 'Oh, there are cicadas out around here?' And half a mile back is this screaming population of thousands of thirteen-year *cassinis,* like you hear around here now, and he hadn't even noticed them."

So what exactly can we learn about evolution from these three concurrent species and their distinct songs?

"I am interested in what those different songs mean, because those different songs mean different species, and it means different species that are in the very earliest stages of evolving apart from one another. Behavior seems to change faster than morphology. It is common for us to find populations that have some geographic coherence and distinctive songs, distinctive in some minor way but still diagnostic. When we put specimens next to each other we can't find anything in the morphology that clearly separates them. I don't know if it is technically correct to say that the behaviors have all evolved faster or it is just that the sounds come in such nice, conveniently packaged, and measurable units that they facilitate diagnosis. Where average, complex morphology doesn't. The songs are really valuable to those biologists interested in what drives diversification. I want to see where diversification is happening, so I have to travel all over the country and observe what is different, what is the same."

Marshall and his wife, Kathy Hill, a cicada biologist from New Zealand, have actually traveled all over the planet searching for the sounds and rules guiding the world's cicadas' behavior. He does not laugh when I ask him if insect sounds might influence human music. Instead, he plays me two recordings—one from Argentina, another from China—intense cicada soundscapes that resemble nothing I have ever heard. "I don't know if Chinese music has overtly learned from cicada sound," Marshall muses, "but something just sounds Asian about them. What do you think?"

The recording has a strange, grating whine; like someone playing a cymbal with a cello bow. It is a jarring, intense sound, though not unlike Peking opera. When I slow it down a few octaves it starts to get beautiful to my human ears, like an unknown species of whale. Marshall's Argentinian recording has rhythmic, shaker-like sounds, just a tiny nod to the rhythmic lilt of Latin music. Though I'm not sure . . . maybe I'm hunting for meaning where I wish there would be some. But how else do we move forward to the next pattern, in science or in art?

That is the same thing that drives Marshall to make use of discoveries in cicada life that surprise: "People usually don't bother checking the things that already make sense, and they are the most insidious studies of all, right? A bad fact can lie there unchallenged for decades." Without questioning assumptions, we'd never learn that a wing-flick can sometimes be positive, not always negative.

And the deep investigation of cicada song and dance goes on. . . .

The voice "ta-te-te":
How do you produce the call?
The cicada's husk—
How can I leave my body?
I do not believe I know!
   —Fusatai Susume, c. 1186

John Cooley arrives a few days later to the International Meeting on Invertebrate Sound and Vibration, the largest gathering of insect acoustics scientists ever attempted, smack dab in the middle of the 2011 Midwestern cicada emergence in Columbia, Missouri. I am honored they've allowed me to speak on the influence of insect sounds on human music (no ornithologists have ever invited me to talk about bird song and music, mind you, so thanks so much to the entomologists). Cooley's been driving across the country keeping tabs on Brood XIX, trying to collect the most accurate data possible on how the range has changed since thirteen years before when he was finishing up his dissertation and discovering the new species and the newly realized mating behavior with his colleague David Marshall. But since neither of them has landed a tenure track job, he is understandably somewhat bitter.

He agrees with Charles Darwin that exceptions in nature often teach us the most important things about evolution. Though mainstream biology has other ideas today. "Nobody in their right mind would try to develop something like a periodical cicada as a model organism. You want to use something safe like a fruit fly, because you can get funding. The fundamental drawback with this kind of work is that it is *cheap*. It does not cost millions of dollars, and generate millions of dollars in overhead for universities. It doesn't generate that kind of excitement or buzz," Cooley explains.

What about David Attenborough and *Life in the Undergrowth?*

"OK, the TV cameras come by, they do a couple of BBC episodes or *Animal Planet* shows up, but that doesn't translate to actual money for the research. Fifteen minutes of exposure and then it's all over. That is why no one does this kind of work anymore," Cooley replies.

And this is why so many of the pioneering works describing animal communication, whether in bird song, whale song, or cicada song, were all done as far back as the 1960s. Cooley is fairly pessimistic about research into the big questions of biology today: "Research today is not driven by the interesting evolutionary questions, but instead by what is fundable. These tend to me more applied kinds of questions. Places like Donald Borror's lab in Ohio in the 1950s, and certainly the Museum of Zoology back in

Michigan. Those were big question places, where they asked about evolution, about origin of species."

"Yes," I look around where we're sitting. "This is the Monsanto Atrium." We're in the middle of the agro-industrial complex. Bugs are something to get rid of, preferably with a copyrighted product that requires corporate-owned seeds that won't germinate so you'll have to buy more from The Man next year. It seems such a shame that corporate interests dictate even what pure scientists choose to study in their noble quest to figure out just how life works.

"I've just about had it," shrugs Cooley. "I'm going to have to leave academia. I have a family to support, I've started business school."

I don't believe it. "Frankly, I'm shocked that you guys don't both have prestigious positions, for the remarkable cicada discoveries you've made."

"Well, thank you, but the academic system is really broken today, especially in the sciences. Academia is broken in this way. It should be encouraging people in their own way to go out on a limb and test hypotheses and take risks. But the way it works now, you apply to NSF for funding, and you better have the project figured out before you submit the grant. If I apply for a research job and say, 'I am going to do something really risky and I don't know whether it is going to work, but it is going to be innovative and interesting,' then you can just kiss the job good-bye. You would never get tenure. It is good to come to a meeting like this and see that there are students coming up in the business, but it is tough to know what is going to happen to them. It is a sad fact. It is a problem I have with academia and maybe that is why I don't have a job, because I sit here and call it like it is."

The Monsanto Atrium looms around us tall and round. Cooley goes on: "That was how I was raised. I came out of Yale, I interacted with Evelyn Hutchinson, who never got a grant in his life. He invented modern ecology. At Michigan I was Richard Alexander's student at the Museum of Zoology—the guy got only one grant in his entire career. The rest of it was just cassette tapes and staples. One of Dick's daily rants was, 'Why the hell are you graduate students going over to the four corners of the world, spending all this money to look at things that are in somebody else's backyard, when there are a million questions right in your own backyard that you could be answering, and nobody has ever bothered to do it?'"

"And didn't Hutchinson spend a lot of time at Linsley Pond right there in Branford, Connecticut?" I remember.

"Exactly. There is so much we hardly know right outside our own homes. Is there any reason for the specific differences in the sounds the concurrent periodic species are making?"

I say that I still want to know.

"The reasons that they tend to have different sounds are to avoid having hybridization. The species groups are old, so if we peel away the question of periodicity in broods and just look at the species groups, they are old on the order of say two-ish million years or so, and the songs change over time. Certainly one scenario is it started out much like this *tredecim-neotredecim* business, where here are two species that are quite recent, no more than ten thousand years old, the songs are different but still quite similar, well imagine as you will a movie, and you play that forward two million years, as those species get pushed into different glacial refugia, and subjected to different conditions and experiences and histories, there is going to be selection or even just drift on their songs, and their songs are going to diverge. So it is possible that say the difference you see between *cassini* and *decim* is really what happens to these subtle difference between the *decim* species two million years later."

"Is it important that the *tredecim* sound of *phaaaroooah* comes through the wash of noise?" I ask.

"Well it does and it doesn't. I don't think anything cuts through the *cassinis*. You know I think that the female cicadas face the same problems that we do—they cannot hear individual males unless they are right on top of them. You are hearing that wash of sound, but they are certainly able to detect the right males. The cicadas that Paulo Fonseca and I have been looking at are extremely sensitive. If you dropped just a pin over here, their peripheral nervous system would respond."

What would it do?

"Well, the cicada would be all wired up—you just get an electrical signal on the nerves. It is glued down to a stick, it is not going to do much. It is going to stay right on the stick. You know if you try to catch normal cicadas, if you are chasing them in the forest and you step on a twig and crack a twig, you have pretty much blown it, because they will stop singing or fly away. Cicadas have very good hearing. They can detect these differences; they can certainly hear the chorus. Whether that has any function in preparing them for mating, I don't know. There is a lot of stuff that is said in literature about the background chorus increasing stimulation, getting the female ready, but that might all be wishful thinking. We really don't know."

Is there a wing-flick behavior in other, nonperiodical cicadas?

"Oh, yes. Much more highly timed. All these New Zealand cicadas the males call and the females answer with a nice little timed wing-flick."

"And nobody knew about this before you and Dave Marshall saw it?" I ask.

"Just little hints of it in literature. Kathy Hill said she had seen it when she was a kid in New Zealand, *'Zip, tick, tick, tick, tick, tick, tick, tick, tick.'* You just get those clicks in there, they all respond, but they don't have the complex courtship that *Magicicada* does. *Magicicada* are unusual. You snap your fingers, and they come to you. I've gotten out of the habit of bringing nets with us when we collect them, because you can just walk the cicada in, walk them in with the clicks. One day I'll take you out in the field and show this to you." (He would show me in Virginia about one year later. And I would have my clarinet ready.)

"Has anyone attempted a complete review of all these connections between sound and clicks, like a whole catalogue of musical phrases, where all the possible relationships are analyzed?" I ask.

"We are working on that with the New Zealand and Australian species, where we are cataloging species and their wing-flick responses. Surprisingly, for something that was discovered and published over a decade ago, every time we tell the whole wing-flick story, it is like new news to people. The story never really got around."

"Maybe that's because cicadas are only on people's radar every thirteen or seventeen years," I suggest.

"Insect songs have always been popular and useful to study because they are *not* learned. The problem with many birdsongs is that they are learned, and the songs are incredibly plastic. In some of them, sexual selection has gone off on this tangent where there is a benefit of having more elaborate and more unusual sounds. In insects the songs are very stereotypical."

"So they are like little devices, little machines or objects of software?" I wonder.

"Well, I do like to think of insects as running basic little computer programs. Their behavior is very simple. You trigger this little routine and that routine goes to completion. It is not the same as the old behaviorists who would talk about learned and innate behavior, but it is a statement that is very stereotypical and broken down into very simple components, even if it looks complex.

Watch the cicadas; you see the program really is a good metaphor for understanding their behavior. If they lose tarsi on their front legs, they have a hard time walking. Why? Because when they walk they kind of go forward and test the surface, and then do it with the next leg. The front tarsi are used for getting information about the nature of the surface they are walking on. If a cicada is missing that claw, it just paws endlessly as if it were stuck in a loop." Cooley moves his hands as if he's swimming the dog paddle. "It is behavior broken down into very simple components."

"So what is the biggest reason to study this kind of simple non-learned behavior?" I ask.

"Often beginning students will ask, or be asked in textbooks, 'What is the most successful group of species?' There actually is only one answer to that. A species is an evolutionary lineage going back to the origins of life. Everything out there that is alive has succeeded in that task. There is an unbroken lineage connecting every one of these species back to the origins of life. Therefore they are successful when that lineage has persisted for four-and-a-half billion years. And all those things that are extinct and so forth, they didn't. Usually textbooks are angling for something else, like a number of species or biomass or something like that. But in the end, if you want to talk about success in the evolutionary sense, it is *what works*."

So Cooley is saying we need to learn as much as possible about those remarkable evolutionary strategies that somehow seem to work.

A loud buzzing is heard to our left, and a cicada alights on my chair. Cooley picks it up.

"See, that is a disturbing cicada." He is not pleased.

"What is wrong with this guy?"

"Well, you see by its size it is a *tredecassini*, but he has got little orangey stripes, like the *tredecula*."

"So this one creature is messing up our neat characterizations," I ask.

"Ah, well, they just get like this out here in the West. You know we like to categorize things and fit them into slots, but nature doesn't always work that way. Not in the least. *Cassinis* are always described as having a black abdomen, but it is not really true—let's call it a black*ish* abdomen."

Somewhat bitter and a bit burnt out, Cooley talks at length about his journey across the Southeastern United States, trying to keep tabs on exactly where his beloved cicadas are and whether they are coming out the way they are supposed to. "My cicada trip is about more than just cicadas. In the course of this I will drive almost twenty thousand miles across all parts of the U.S. I have almost seen everything. A lot of it is thought-provoking. I don't think most people who tune into TV for three hours a night, those who travel only by interstate, I don't think they have any clue that all this exists."

I tell him he should be writing about all that, the human side of his hunt for cicadas. This can only help the public's respect for the research. But it wouldn't be science now, would it? And it might not help him get tenure. But then again, it just might.

Magical cicada
how come I always know
just when you will arrive;
no way to explain it
impossible to divide the years
into each other beyond the primes?
thirteen

seventeen
Only your music counts such beats
no one else alive can feel them.
    —Cicada Boy

Unfortunately there is no ancient Chinese or even Native American poem that talks about the mysterious prime number cycles of the *Magicicada*. This remains a deep part of their magic. Honestly, we really have no idea why these insects come out when they do, why they have such a great inscrutable rhythm that emerges rarely but precisely over the years.

I am trying my best to conceive it as a vast natural rhythm, whose downbeat I can barely remember. It was there when I was born, in 1962. Then I had a pale glimmer of awareness of it in 1979, when I was just starting to care about music in nature. Then in 1996, is swirled around me at my first home in the Hudson Valley and prevented me from thinking about anything else. Then I began to think that by the next round I would write a book about it, since no one had thought of this whole slow measure as music ever before. Now, in 2013 we're here.

In between, I've sought out a few other cicada broods just to practice for this one, but it is hard to prepare for such a thing. It slows down our whole sense of time, makes us wonder if anything in our life connects to these vast cycles of nature. I seem to remember a film on Mark Twain from my childhood where he is born under the reign of Halley's Comet in the sky, and dies exactly seventy-five years later when it next returns. What can we learn from such coincidences? My father suffered a massive stroke on the day of the great blackout in 2003, and died exactly eight years later when the catastrophic Hurricane Irene struck the coast of Connecticut where I grow up. At his funeral the rabbi said it must mean something, and he assured us the power would soon return.

Scientists attempting to explain why periodical cicadas return every thirteen or seventeen years often seem to be doing little more than my examples here—tracking coincidences, tossing out possible explanations, and hoping for the most interesting thing that can be said.

In fact, if you read the popular science literature, sometimes it seems that this issue is completely settled. It even appears as one of the first examples in *The Math Book*, a beautiful, coffee-table volume on what makes mathematics cool. The book proceeds by date, from the earliest to the latest, and the third entry, timed at 1 million BC, is the description of periodical cicadas as nature's prime number generators. There are, it seems, relatively few prime numbers in the world of natural cycles, so the example of the cicadas having cycles of both thirteen and seventeen years is most notable and unusual. A simple explanation is often given, and it is one suggested by biologists for decades, and made popular by Stephen Jay Gould in *Ever Since Darwin,* one of his popular collections of science essays. The idea is simple, and that is to suppose that the cicadas appear in prime number cycles simply because no predators appear in such cycles: Most animals that have cyclical rises and falls of population do so in more regular numbers of seasons like every two, four, six, or eight years. And since prime numbers are defined as numbers that cannot be divided into other numbers, such other cycles would hardly ever line up with the cicadas' emergences. Voilà! A perfectly ingenious and reasonable explanation, one that is repeated in many biology textbooks and all over the media.

Only problem is, there is absolutely no evidence for it whatsoever. No one has *ever* identified even a single predator of the periodical cicada whose population follows such a cycle. Of course such a predator cycle still might exist, but we haven't found it, or even spent much time looking for it. This explanation might fall into that category of "just so" story that science puts forward because it sounds like it should work, and the public is so intrigued by the idea that hardly anyone seems to notice that there is little evidence for the hypothesis in the first place.

Although the predator/prey story sounds pretty cool, there is no predator that follows a periodic cycle of a more even number of years. Besides, there are so many cicadas that emerge during the brood years that the sheer number of the insects overwhelms any possible predators; it is a much simpler strategy that doesn't need prime numbers for it to work. It's a simple situation of the enemy being overrun by the horde!

Much of the work on trying to decode the prime number periodicity has been a kind of bioinformatic mathematical modeling based on theory and running computer models, rather than collecting any evidence. Mathematical biologists have tried to see if there is something *inevitable* about the prime number cycles that appear simply by running the numbers through hypothetical situations of competition. Although such models are basically simulations that depend entirely on their assumptions, it seems that a likely hypothesis is starting to emerge. Whether or not there are actual predators who are foiled by prime number cycles, it seems that when the math is done the predation model alone is not enough to generate prime number cycles. One has to also add the variable that different populations of cicadas inherently contain a mechanism to avoid hybridization, that is, they want to ensure that as a species they are kept separate. This is also coupled with a tendency that a small number of individuals in the seventeen-year broods have of emerging four years early. So it is believed this tendency might have originally led to the establishment of thirteen-year species at the start.

It also appears that the establishment of prime number cycles may have something to do with a population that is nearly decimated, such as the few remnants of a species remaining after a catastrophic ecological event, like the advance of glaciers during an ice age compromising cicada habitat except for a few isolated pockets. It turns out that in such situations of very small populations, the reproduction rate increases with high population density, as opposed to large populations where if things get too dense, there is too much competition for resources and the population is no longer able to increase. This might explain why many animals congregate in leks, or concentrated groups for the purpose of mating, and that this may have evolved especially with very small populations who have to work hard to find each other when their habitat has been stressed.

This situation was identified by ecologist Warder Clyde Allee in the 1920s and is today called the Allee Effect. In a mathematical model devised by Yumi Tanaka and Jin Yoshimura in Japan together with Chris Simon in Connecticut, prime number cycles were observed to develop over just one thousand hypothetical years, only if the Allee Effect is considered. Though still a purely theoretical exercise, it does give some clues for how these cycles might have evolved in a situation where the cicadas became nearly extinct and then had to congregate in order to find enough of each other to survive. In a second paper the authors suggest that "Our results indicate that prime number selection is a very rare event, occurring at the verge of extinction. This is probably why the evolution of prime-numbered periodicity was likely only in what is now the Central and Eastern United States, where glacial advances created many refuges during the uneven Pleistocene glaciation." The model is based on the idea that a small population of insects, sequestered in the few available habitats that remain during glaciation, congregate in order to best survive. The even-year gestation periods tend to disappear because the insects hybridize with each other when they emerge, losing the species' distinctiveness.

After even 150 hypothetical years only prime number years remain, 13, 17, and 19. Perhaps 19 is just too many years of development for an instinct. No matter—keep running the model, and after 500 years only the 13- and 17-year cycles remain. The graphs of the model's runs show some cool images of rhythm. Note that all these other periodical cicada possibilities are completely imaginary, they exist only inside the theory that proves they would not survive:

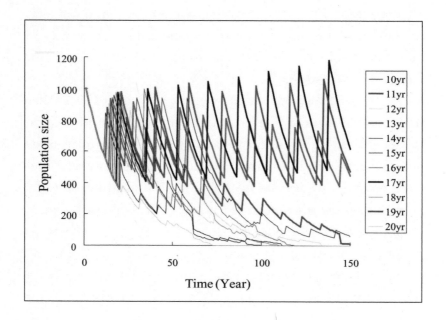

The latest mathematical thinking on the mysterious prime-numbered cicada cycles thus suggests that the predation idea is not enough to lead to such neat prime results. We also have to have competition within the species to avoid hybridization, and then also the Allee Effect of the small, concentrated populations. The specific glaciation situation might help to explain why this phenomenon is only found in Eastern North America, with its peculiar glacial history. Then there is also the strange fact that a certain number of seventeen-year cicadas do emerge four years early, more than two, three, five, six, or any number of years early. Thus the thirteen-year species could have evolved from the seventeen-year species. Mysteries, mysteries.

Think of what it feels like for a cicada to emerge early. Sixteen years underground . . . now where's the party? He's all up on a tree singing alone, and not likely to find a mate. But sing he does, on and on, lonely and continuous, because that is what a cicada does. All dressed up, and nowhere to go. But no sense of futility, no sense of loss. Only humans worry about such things.

> *Singing in the morn from autumn trees it sounds clear.*
> *It wears diaphanous silk*
> *lives in cool air*
> *looks like the shade of a woman's hair*
> *It drinks but the free wind and dew*
> *Morning til night, morning til night.*
> *Occasionally it cries,*
> *and sorrowful it sounds.*
> *Always a tiny sound remains—*
> *All of a sudden*
> *from one tree to another*
> *it will fly.*
> —Chou Yuan, 1230

People want unclaimed sounds to convey the greatest of emotions. Is it not remarkable that mysterious noises can evoke the greatest power? This is why music always has the potential to take us far beyond words, and if we find music in the tones of species far from ourselves, their sounds and their lives become all that much closer to our own.

Really, what do I have in common with a cicada? Well, the

same as so many other living things, we will both be born, grow, eat, survive, mate, reproduce, and die. Is that not enough to share so much of life's joys and troubles? Can I not find immediate emotion in the sounds you make, sounds I know were never destined for my ears? This is what keeps nature close to us, and hearing such things does make us ever more alive. Nature's sounds *are* for us, if we want to understand our world and how it works. You can enter information into mathematical codes, and run the numbers to convince you there is clear reason for the mysteries. The program may satisfy your curiosity. But it won't remove the mystery. The best science opens up clues to deeper mysteries, and the world gets ever more wonderful as we go.

Or, just listen to the cicadas, the white noise of memory and time. Strive to inhabit the sound long after it is gone. Use it to mark the great passages of time. But how to even conceive of being able to keep track of such a long, odd length of time? What would it mean to mark such a long period underground, hidden away, apart from life in the air and the comfort of all the rest of your species, singing so intently in the trees around, a great experience you will only know for the brief few weeks that climax your life? Can any human ever feel what it would be like to experience time in that way? How does one *feel* seventeen or thirteen years as a moment of sudden transformation?

I thought I would pose this question to my friend Tim Blunk, who spent almost exactly thirteen years in prison for being part of the Resistance Conspiracy, an underground group who bombed the Capitol in Washington and the Army War College in Baltimore in the 1980s, part of a general protest against the activities of the U.S. government in Central America and elsewhere during the Reagan years. Blunk was initially sentenced to fifty-eight years in prison for the charge of illegal weapons possession. This is the longest sentence anyone has ever received in the United

States for such a crime. So unlike the cicadas, when he went in he had no idea how long it would be when, or if, he got out.

It was with trepidation that I mentioned to Tim I wanted to connect his terrible ordeal to my entomological story. Since he had accompanied me on some of my earliest forays in playing music with birds at the National Aviary in Pittsburgh (recounted in my earlier book *Why Birds Sing*), I thought he might appreciate the connection. I really wanted to know what it felt like to experience time, both underground, and in incarceration, and especially what it felt like to finally experience the light of day, after seventeen years locked up mostly in the dark.

"I think about that a lot actually. You know, periodicity," he said. "I think one of the problems for me talking about, looking at that period of time was for me, those thirteen years was—I didn't know that there was an end point. Today with determinent sentencing, when most people go to prison they are told, you've got a seventeen-year sentence, or you're going to do thirteen. For them then there is a start and a finish. I don't know what that is like. I was given fifty-eight years, which I could be doing; I have comrades still in prison doing every bit of seventy-five years. How do you get your mind around that?"

"You became a musician when you were in prison, right?" I asked.

"I learned saxophone and actually the thing that was the most compelling for me about learning music had to do with time, and with rhythm. It was another way of marking time, counting time. I wanted to count time in more interesting ways, I wanted to play jazz. I didn't do my time in prison on straight 4/4, I did my time on 5/4. So I wanted to do "Take Five," I wanted to do Paul Desmond and Dave Brubeck, I wanted to do interesting rhythms where the downbeat happens at different measures. So what I mean by that is, I was determined when I got locked up that my life wasn't going to be over, and that I was going to live as full a life as I possibly could, as creative a life as I possibly could."

So much of Tim's life consisted of marking the time, counting the days. To no certain end.

Tim is not the only one imprisoned for his politics to have considered the song of the cicada and hunted for a connection. In 658, Lo-Ping Wang, commonly known as Luo Binwang, wrote the poem "A Political Prisoner Listens to a Cicada":

While the year sinks westwards, I hear a cicada
Bid me to be resolute here in my cell.
Yet it needed the song of those black wings
To break a white-haired prisoner's heart . . .
His flight is heavy through fog,
His pure voice drowns in the windy world.
Who knows if he be singing still?—
Who listens any more to me?

After I showed Tim that poem, he sighed and said, "Now where did you find that, David? We prisoners always look for signs of hope out through our narrow windows."

"Did you ever hear things? What did you see out the window of your cell?" I asked him.

"Paradoxically the most beautiful place of the various prisons I was moved around to was Marion, one of the roughest. It is located in a large swamp in southern Illinois. At the perimeter there would always be deer, especially in the springtime. And then there were the killdeer sandpipers who were always laying eggs and making nests on the yard where we had recreation, so those were two of our most important animals. That was the little bit of nature I could get, because during that period I was in solitary confinement because of my previous infraction revealing an FBI entrapment scheme at Leavenworth where they were trying to coax prisoners into planning an escape. I wasn't going to let that happen. For ratting on the feds I got seven years of solitary confinement, and could only go outside once a week. If only I could have been as resigning as an underground cicada."

Three of Tim's codefendants pleaded guilty to conspiracy and destruction of government property, but charges against Tim and two others were dropped because they were already serving long enough prison terms. In 1999 Tim was released on parole, after years of "good behavior."

How to make sense of those long, solitary years Tim Blunk lived through? How does a person keep track of such hollow time? How does a cicada do it?

"I can look back at my time in prison and it is a very defined, very circumscribed period. I don't think that I am about to write a letter of thank you to the Bureau of Prisons but, I know I became a better person as a result of those experiences, these different prisoners, these different inmates. We were all reduced to a very common level. I don't know, like some vast insect society. The experience of prison eradicates distinctions of class, of race even, although the media does everything it can to come up with the opposite viewpoint, but in my experience it was a very leveling experience.

"I was on a tier with John Gotti, I was on a tier with people who had done hundreds of millions of dollars' worth of business in their lives. Manuel Noriega was downstairs from me. We were all dressed in the same exact uniform, we all ate the same slop every morning, we all had the same bad relationship with the so-called councilor who cuts short our visits. So we end up *not* fighting each other. Instead we fight the same inner struggles. We were there for each other in different ways and we listened to the football games on the radio, and this was us gnawing at the roots of these trees while we were underground, we were all going about the same business. It is when the doors fly open that everybody goes their own which way, everybody goes different directions. I've avoided contact with anyone I was close to when I was inside."

"The first day I got out of prison, I was driven to my parents' home in Cleveland, Ohio, from Pennsylvania. Before I got to my house my one request was to stop at the shores of Lake Erie, a couple blocks from their home. I desperately wanted to go to the lake. At the shore I realized this was the first time I had been able to look out and see a horizon in thirteen years! It was the first time I had seen the moon, or the stars. No matter where I was, either buried in solitary confinement in some dungeon somewhere or in a regular cell with the searchlights around the perimeter of these prisons so bright, they had obliterated any possibility for me to see anything in the night sky. I remember quietly weeping. I still clutch up when I talk about this—I had been so out of touch with the world! I used to camp, climb rocks, go ice climbing. Holy fuck, look at the sky, looking across Lake Erie toward Canada. I can still see this. I feel so sorry for that man on the beach, all those years that he missed. I emerged back to this world with such a *whoosh* of emotions and noise within me, like the hiss of a million cicadas back in the sunlight after thirteen years underground. I don't know how the insects experience this, but I feel after what I went through I might be able to understand it in a way not everyone can."

Tim was lucky to get out before his hair turned white, like the ancient Chinese prisoner in the poem above. He worked for years at the Puffin Foundation to help political artists get their work out in the world. He went on to earn an MFA and develop his own visual and performance projects. He's written a fine screenplay based on his years inside, and he can be found most days at his flower shop in a small New Jersey town. And he remembers the hordes of cicadas as a boy in New Jersey, but seventeen years ago he wasn't around to hear them.

Soon I will take Tim out to hear the cicadas again, since he missed the last round seventeen years ago. Then we'll see what the wash of insect noises and rhythms will mean to someone who has also had to count so many long, dark monotonous years. Those bewitched by the cicadas' call will realize, as H. A. Allard did in the 1920s, that this is one of the great natural cycles we are privileged to find our way within. I may not hear them so many more times in my life, but each time will be important, and special.

To confront the insects on my home ground I had to prepare. So in 2011, I embarked on a journey to make music with the great Brood XIX of the Central States. I needed to get inside the noise of it all. But before that I had to learn as much as I could about what made the sounds of more common insects anything like music at all. What about the far more familiar bug music of crickets? I had to go to Sweden to meet Mr. Fung.

TWO

· · · · · · · · ·

Mr. Fung's Cricket Orchestra

On the Södermalm of Stockholm, the biggest island in a city of islands, I'm climbing up a steep street with a man who goes by many names. Some call him Bolingo, others know him as Mr. Fung. He looks like a Chinese holy man from a whole different era: wrapped in loose clothes, walking barefoot, wearing a Fu Manchu beard and a shaved head. But what about those bright blue eyes? They say his real name is Lars Fredriksson, and he may know more about the ancient Chinese custom of raising crickets for the most beautiful songs than anyone in the Western world. He, too, has this same problem of how to get people interested in these tiny insects' songs. As we amble down the street, he pulls a small, ornately carved wooden box from the folds of his tunic, and slides open a small trap door.

"I must say, it always helps to have live crickets on your person."

Chirp.

My eyes widen. "You always carry one around?" *Chirp chirp chirp.*

Mr. Fung smiles. "This will probably make me burn in cricket hell for the bad karma of keeping insects in small boxes, but if you want to talk about the environment and how important insects are for the planet, it is a good idea to keep one at the ready. Because they will start the conversation; you don't have to. A chirping is heard. *Chirp chirp* you know. 'What is that?' But, 'No, it is not my phone, no it is not that fridge, no it is not the lights. It is that guy over there, it is coming from him!' And then, maybe you pull out a box on the table, and everybody goes: 'What do you have there?' And then it starts. You didn't start it, the singing cricket started it. You answer slowly, questions will become multiple, abundant. The problem is that some will go, 'Oh, no, you have insects, ahh!' And some other will go, 'Oh . . . insects.' Very different reactions. But then of course, 'Why do you have insects?' And my answer is that I prefer the sound of a cricket to that of a bird."

As if on cue a cricket chirps. This time it is a mobile phone—not Mr. Fung's. "Now why do you like cricket sounds better than birds?" I ask him.

"The sounds I like most are those that have a comforting sound that puts me at ease. It does the same for the crickets. Crickets in nature do not sing unless they feel safe. When there is a thunderstorm, or there is low pressure, or there is some bad weather coming, they will not sing. But on the blades of grass that are dried by the sun, you may see a cricket climbing up, announcing that the coast is clear; you can all go on with your lives—and fornicate."

The music of insects has always had a close connection to sex and violence. In fact, many more people in China raise and sell crickets for the practice of fighting with them rather than to simply enjoy their sounds. Perhaps the more contemplative among us prefer the songs of crickets to watching them viciously ready for battle. Or maybe not—the rules of the contest are also noble and deep, as Jia Sidao wrote in the venerable classic *The Book of Crickets* in 1348. These insects, too, are possessed with five solid virtues that only nature can ensure:

> *The First Virtue: When it is time to sing, he will sing.*
>   *This is trustworthiness.*
> *The Second Virtue: On meeting an enemy, he will not hesitate to fight.*
>   *This is courage.*
> *The Third Virtue: Even seriously wounded, he will not surrender.*
>   *This is loyalty.*
> *The Fourth Virtue: When defeated, he will not sing.*
>   *He knows shame.*
> *The Fifth Virtue: When he becomes cold, he will return to his home.*
>   *He is wise, and knows the situation.*

I mention this to Mr. Fung, and he smiles, knowing that humans have long favored war over music—at least in our actions. Yet loving the cricket song is easier, once you learn to attend to it. More virtues are required, but from within us, not in the rules of the bug.

"There is a reason we have two camps, at least two camps in China, for appreciation of crickets. Youth likes an adrenaline kick, they are excited when you put two contestants against each other and the challenger has an opponent. There are no less than seven weight classes in crickets for fighting. There are high-tech electronic scales produced only for fighting crickets. It is kind of odd when you see some of the very tattooed, young mafiosi who are in charge of the betting of the cricket fights, pulling out these extremely modern gadgets in this very old tradition. There are auctions in Shandong beginning around end of August into early September, where male cricket warriors are sold at prices up to two thousand dollars."

"Why would you buy so expensive a cricket? What would you do with him?" I ask.

"Earn a lot of money gambling. When you put this cricket against some other soldier, the stakes are very, very high. The crickets fight to the death. There are more than two hundred fifty different names for bites and hits—we have uppercut, they have two hundred! Jaw bite to second bone, so many different ways to describe how they attack."

The fighting champions themselves have colorful titles. Hugh Raffles gives us the names of some of the most prized competitors: Purple Headed Golden Wing, Bronze Head and Iron Back, Yin Yang Wing, Strong Man That Nobody Can Harm. You irritate the cricket before the fight, you poke them with a small brush, resembling his antennae. Work them up in a frenzy, collect the bets, and toss them into the ring.

There is also a smaller, more sensitive audience who would rather just listen to the music of these creatures. Fung explains why: "You have gentle people of age that turn mellow, maybe after a sour life that didn't always serve them well. You have the composers, the opera singers, you have your occasional calligrapher, or painter. They all appreciate the crickets as scholarly playthings. Bring them inside and they are like hostages of nature—close your eyes, you are outdoors."

Crickets sing long into the autumn as the days and nights

turn cold. After some months they tend to enter our houses of their own accord. This is the time of late autumn melancholia, a looming sense of the passage of time, an advancement toward death. We who may have many more seasons to count as we grow old and wise, attend to the songs of the crickets who will only last a few more weeks. When the first cricket arrives on the ledge of the fireplace, we know late autumn is here, with its lessons for us, as in this excerpt from the "Songs of T'ang," 829 BC, here translated by Ezra Pound:

Cricket in hall, the year runs to its close,
Rejoice and now, ere sun and moon subtract.
Exceed no bound, think what thine office is;
    Enjoy the good, yet sink not in excess.
    Hereto is good knight's true attentiveness.

Cricket in hall, the year is on the wane.
The sun and moon defend no man's delight.
Stretch not thy wish, know where stands outerness,
Right man is light of foot in banquet rite.

Cricket's in hall, the killers' carts put by,
Rejoice and now, tho' suns be insolent.
Too-much sires woe, be mindful of thine extent.
    Enjoy the good, yet sink not in excess.
    True scholar stands by his steadfastness.

Crickets come into houses all over the world, but somehow in China their presence is taken with the greatest seriousness. Perseverance, discipline, and endurance are but a few of the virtues humanity is able to learn from insects in Asian lore. In romantic moments in Chinese feature films insects appear right on-screen, something that Hollywood hardly ever proffers for us. Think of the end of Bertolucci's epic film where the Last Emperor, now a humble old man sweeping the steps of the Forbidden City, brings an aged cricket in a cage to show a small child, all this on the steps of the great palace where he once ruled. The fighting cricket is the sage of order and strength, the singing cricket the sage of melancholy waning of the autumn season and the noble acceptance of impending death, the necessary march of time.

But Fung sees this not as giving up, he loves the pull of that lonely sound, and endlessly wonders at how the Chinese for hundreds of years have been able to pay such attention to the tiny details of the lives of insects with great meticulousness: "There is another ancient cricket manual from the eleventh century that explains how to take care of your aging crickets by boiling pig's liver, mixing it up with very fine chestnut, and yolk of egg, and a little bit of corn starch. The cricket toward the end is no longer able to feed itself, it says. This is so beautiful—you can stroke him a little bit on the beak, and he will sip a tiny bit of liquid during his final days."

We keep the song alive as long as we can.

In the late autumn days outside my own small village home, when the mornings threaten frost and November's already here, I am amazed to still hear a few crickets singing. Their pitch is lower, now that it's become so cold. I can hear each perfect note, a solid rhythm of the tones. It's like those slowed-down birdsongs I've created on the computer, revealing ultrasonic structures just beyond the range of human ears. As winter approaches, the crickets themselves have slo-moed their songs so that we humans can better hear them. The closer the insects come toward death, the more beautiful their songs appear to us.

In the garden of the Natural History Museum in Stockholm, Mr. Fung tells me that those individuals with the lowest-pitched songs are often the biggest, and the strongest, those that command the highest prices. He told me also that it was possible to artificially lower the pitch of some cricket songs by tapping tiny drops of resin onto their stridulating rear legs and wing. As we slow sounds down by machine, they did so with the sticky liquid from pines. Anything goes in the pursuit of the deepest cricket sound.

Lars Fredriksson worked for years as librarian in Sweden's finest Asiatic book collection. After that facility closed down he now works for a literary publishing house, seeking out Asian works to render into Swedish. As Fredriksson he organized the documents of the foreign East with his fluent knowledge of the language. As Mr. Fung he became as Chinese as he could, delving deep into the curious pursuit of insect music because he loved the cricket song. On his website www.bolingo.org he presents this convoluted story in layers of pages, networks within networks, rhythms upon rhythms, and images far and wide. "It's a good thing you came to talk to me," the blue-eyed master smiles. "Everyone else in this business has something to buy or sell: singing cricket war-riors, cages, feeding spoons, guides to this ancient hobby and what it means. Me, I just love the sounds."

Back listening to crickets. Music, but no notes. Rhythms, but no beats. The repeating marks of safety and the longing to mate, to survive, to live. Cricket in hall; cricket in leaves, in branches high in trees often impossible to see.

The most beautiful of insect tones comes from the tallest tree leaves, the tiniest creatures. The snowy tree cricket, with its trans-parent, rounded wings; a cricket that does not seem to be a cricket, a sprite, a sylph. You will never see one but will often hear them, and once you mark this sound it will not leave you for life. You will hear its pitch go down as the colder days do come. Its simple beating rhythm is what keeps life on its course, week after week, year after year.

Fung is not content to trade his singers, to laud their virtues, and to keep them haltingly alive for as many weeks as he can. No, he has taken his own radical turn, tried something no Chi-nese traditionalist would do. He has raised an orchestra of singing crickets, 108 individuals to be exact, the number of Buddhist sutras, the number a devout meditator is supposed to count on his rosary beads as he repeats whatever mantra has been chosen for him; a symbolic number, and a resonant number. He keeps all these creatures in a small apartment at the edge of Stockholm, where his family just had to put up with the experiment. Over the years, Fung has arranged a series of celebrated concerts of his cricket orchestra together with noted improvising musicians.

Drummer Adam Rudolph remembers what it was like to play with this insect ensemble: "I loved it, I found it inspiring and soothing at the same time. Their choir sounded complete to me, so it was a matter of tuning in to the timbres I was hearing, and also the rhythms. They would come in and out of sync at certain times, so it was a matter of doing some deep listening to hear where that was. As I would hear certain rhythms pop out, I would play spacious little accents to further bring those existing rhythms out . . . like making an outline in pen upon something already in pencil." Drummer Bengt Berger said, "I felt like an elephant in a porcelain store. However low I kept the volume or however long I paused, I was still playing too much too often. Apart from that it was wonderful."

I asked Fung why he always used a precise number of individuals in his orchestra. "Did you decide on the number one hundred and eight because you are Buddhist in persuasion?"

He thinks for a moment before responding: "I am a very religious person, but I lack a specific belief. I like the way that religions can turn us spiritually inclined, turn us to sort of cultivate our spirit and see if we have some finer fabric. I like that in all religions. Since a lot of religion is there as a relief for the tormented soul, and I am not tormented, I have no need for consolation, and I have no need for prayer since I pray nothing. If I pray, I pray for someone else. I pray for someone else to realize their potential, to find out who they are, I pray for people who are not fortunate enough to even have the basics. But there is nothing I lack. What I need is focus to understand what I already have. And that is so much. It is abundant. Maybe this is a lot of mumbo jumbo, but I think you get what I am saying. Spirituality can easily be coopted by ulterior motives and become a vehicle for greed."

"So we should not use it to trump ourselves up. How does this connect to crickets?" I ask.

"Crickets are very humbling. I don't pretend that I communicate with crickets, I'm no insect Dr. Dolittle. I'm just full of awe that they can be so focused doing their thing while we are so easily sidetracked. Just when we start to understand things, we go off somewhere else."

The crickets are still singing their songs, as they have been since before anyone thought time was something to be measured—no doubt about that. They have no need for us. So why did Fung decide to bring our music to them? It started with flamenco.

"I was walking the streets of Seville, carrying crickets, as usual. I went to the streets where young people were roaming the streets flamencoing here and there." The guitars were strumming, the crickets cheeped in with song. "It was an incredible scene, people were beating on boxes and playing with cards, singing, and dancing.

"There was one very beautiful young woman from Taiwan, and she had come there only to dance flamenco. She hardly spoke any Spanish, but she danced like a queen. Even other women appreciated her—which is rare, right? But, OK, she came from the outside. I spoke proper Chinese with her, which she hadn't spoken to anyone in ages. They saw, 'Oh, this guy is carrying crickets.' So we were hanging out. And one evening we were sitting in a wine bar doing music and I had these crickets with me. I just took them into the light and they began to sing, like some fairytale situation. So it can happen spontaneously, and doesn't have to be planned for months.

"But most of my good concerts were planned for long time. The problem is if you have one gig, these crickets have to be individually fed, three hours a day of feeding! Just opening and closing cases, for months. Yet I am notorious for keeping crickets alive for a very long time. My Chinese friends call me *Xio Xing Lon*— 'Cricket Longevity Star.'"

Fredriksson has released two albums of his cricket orchestra, *Tingqiuxuan Presents . . .* and *Listening to Autumn*. These only feature the insect singers, not the blend with live humans. They are slight bends upon natural possibilities, each species named by the cricket-keepers as if it were a musical instrument: a Heavenly Bell solo upon Bamboo Bell chorus; Small Yellow Bell meets Longevity Bell; Red-legged Ant Bell meets Precious Pagoda Bell. The names are codes to the sound of the music. At first all Fung's recordings sound like incessant ringing and resound too much in our ears, like an electrified cricket remix assembled on a laptop computer. Maybe we are all so jaded that when we hear a luminous cricket sound we're so sure, as I am writing these lines on a moving train, that it's just someone's mobile phone.

Take any sound and we are able to translate it into meaning something else, so fluid can the motion of noises in the electronic ether be today. But Fung is making noble art when he assembles his one hundred and eight insects for a public concert, be it in the Djurgården Park or a Södermalm gallery. I ask again why he's set on a hundred and eight if he doesn't claim to be so Buddhist. "It is a good, auspicious number. It is the number of beads in a rosary. We pray for peace. We like the repetition, the cycle."

Does it sound any better than the wild cricket nights of late August and September, in the fields, in backyards, in everyday suburbia? In Sweden there are but two singing species, the sonic insect palette is not so wide. But here in Northeast America we have nine months of cricket richness to enjoy, more than in China, with dozens of species making sounds.

"A few years ago I was standing in line at a cricket shop in Beijing," says Fung. "I had an iPod with American cricket sounds and I put the headphones on the ears of the man standing behind me, and he was like, 'Wow!' It was as if he was digging a concert. He took them off and said, 'So are there a lot of people in the States who appreciate cricket songs?' And I said, 'No.' And he got so upset that he pulled away, 'Those stupid Americans, they have even better crickets than we do, and they don't appreciate them?!'"

H. A. Allard, the pioneer naturalist, agreed with this sentiment way back in 1929. "We Americans are too busy, too hurried, too mechanized in our moods, to hear what this cricket or that katydid says . . . We are a hurried, worried people." Allard, who even has a species of ground cricket named after him, surmised that the sound of crickets wasn't just some rote communication necessary to the evolved process of mating, but a primitive musical sense. "The proclivity for sound-making by one method or another is a ubiquitous impulse and mood of life. The great insect kingdom has not been backward in following the *same weird organic trend* toward the egotisms of self-expression." *Ego?* In bugs, members of a great swarm? What could Allard be talking about? Well, he explains, think of a human who sings all the time, refusing to shut up. We call such a person the most self-aggrandizing egotist in the room. "If crickets were judged on this basis they would be the most egotistical creatures on earth, obsessed as no other with the sounds of their own wings." He admits honestly that we cannot be certain what the meaning of such sound can be for the insects from within. Maybe noisy self-expression is their prime directive or purpose in life. Maybe they're all after some resounding form of companionship. Or maybe cricket singing "is the elemental impulse of pure art, the love of sound, tone, rhythm of music in some manifestation."

Allard is not at all satisfied with the idea of sex as the explanation. He takes in the beautiful, high, luminous tone of the snowy tree cricket, sylph-like and nearly impossible to see, and he calculates the sheer weight of all that song: "I have heard the snowy tree cricket chirp at the rate of about ninety times per minute all night long. Think what that means; 5,400 chirps per hour, 64,800 chirps in a 12-hour night, nearly 4 million chirps in ninety days, demanding the muscular energy of 16 million wing strokes on the basis of 4 strokes for each chirp. . . . What is it all about? *Sex alone does not explain it. No cricket needs to chirp himself to death.*"

There is no practical need for such music, the weird mystery of the persistence of insect music remains—can it be that it is necessary to keep the insect alive?

It is important to remember that an entomologist of so high esteem as Allard said such things, because it shows that at the very birth of insect song science, there is a belief that it all may be a special kind of music, that purpose and function can never explain. If it wasn't musical, we would never love it or wonder about it so. Crickets *sing* in many human languages—is this because we know the males are doing it to get attention from the females, or because we know that only beautiful music has a reason to be repeated so endlessly? It is beautiful to them and almost beautiful to us, or it is beautiful to us but still can seem excessive, cloying, pealing out from a species ever just beyond our grasp.

What of the fact that it is so hard to tell where in the thicket these insects sing from? The genius of their song consists in part that we are often unable to guess where the faithful musician lies. The great French insect writer Jean-Henri Fabre was onto this more than a century ago. Listen for the true stridulating song—as soon as you approach it is somewhere else. You cannot find the source. "You move across. Nothing. The sound comes from the original place. No, it doesn't, after all. This time, it is coming from over there, on the left, or rather from the right; or is it from behind? We are absolutely at a loss, quite unable to guide ourselves by the ear towards the spot where the insect is chirping." In his frustration at being unable to locate the source of this chirping, and to grab the musician with his hand and take him home to delight his guests with the longing song of the wild captured and put on display in civilization, Fabre ascends into the kind of reverie that all dedicated cricket listeners might wish for:

In addition to this illusion of distance, which, at the faintest sound of footsteps, is constantly taking us by surprise, we have the purity of the note, with its soft tremolo. I know no prettier or more limpid insect song, heard in the deep stillness of an August evening. . . . And, with its clear and charming voice, the whole of this little world is sending questions and responses from shrub to shrub, or rather, indifferent to the hymns of others, chanting its gladness for itself alone. . . . In your company, O my Crickets, I feel the throbbing of life, which is the soul of our lump of clay; and that is why, under my rosemary-hedge, I give but an absent glance at the constellation of the Swan and devote all my attention to your serenade! A dab of animated glare, capable of pleasure and of pain, surpasses in interest the immensity of brute matter.

Fabre was a master of detail, spending decades attending to the minute activities of the insects surrounding his Avignon country home. His dedication and attentiveness is said to have given Charles Darwin inspiration for his own last, most attentive writings. We can long for the closeness Fabre feels for the subject of his researches today, in an era where we are taught to be dispassionate as naturalists and never reveal our love for what we observe.

The simple song of the snowy tree cricket is perfect as is, yet as a musician I am compelled to mess with it. I am sorry—when I hear sounds I hear the potential for other sounds. I think of Brian Eno stuck in bed, unable to move, at the very moment he supposedly invents ambient music by being unable to stop the stuck record from skipping, stuck record from skipping, stuck record from skipping, stuck record from etc., etc., as he settles into the rhythm of the repetition, the phrase that is not a phrase becoming a musical phrase. One sound can thus be enough, but then again, it is never enough. Soon it becomes something else. Such inspirations become direct instructions that we can turn into music. Yet one thing still must come first: love of sounds.

With insects we have simple sounds, machine-like sounds that are surprisingly natural sounds. This may be the great beguiling quality about them. Immanuel Kant wrote famously that we are not critical of a bird that repeats the same tune incessantly; indeed, that is what we expect from a bird. If a human being tries the same strategy we shake our heads in exasperation, so Kant says in his great *Critique of Judgment,* but he may be missing an essential alternate side of music, that it always has a sense of repetition, rhythm, and familiarity about it, those qualities that endear the beat to us, the known pattern that we want to hear again and again and again and again.

Nowhere in nature is such essential repetition more prevalent than in the sounds of insects, each individually singular and simple, but together forming vast choruses of automatic rhythm. The cricket alone on the hearth is a familiar tuneful reminder of the oncoming chill of autumn and then winter, and we welcome the break in our silence. But hear it as someone's mobile phone, and not everyone likes it. Natural meaning has been co-opted, captured, cricketed away. *Cheep?* Cheap.

Is it noise? Is it music? It's the first if you're sick of it, the second if you love to listen to it, if it creates a precise aesthetic feeling of the kind that only art can do. Or perhaps there is more to it than that. Bush crickets are inherently noisier than tree crickets, but they may have more rhythm. There might be the most music in overlapping layers of percussion and flute, buzz and tone, insects all doing their part of some great *plein air* orchestra, a whole more than the hum of its parts. No one is in charge, and the beauty comes to those who choose to take it all in.

Crickets offer a mixture of pure musical tone and archaic buzz. Does the buzz get in the way of making it seem as music? On the contrary, humans have always loved a goosy sound one way or another. The traditional African thumb piano, the mbira, always has little pieces of metal attached to it to add a bit of grit and noise to the sound, at least until musicologist Hugh Tracey purified the sound with his kalimba to make it more palatable to European ears fifty years ago. But today we are back to preferring the noisy version, witness the popularity of groups like Konono N°1's "Congotronics," where a buzzier mbira sound is plugged into classic guitar distortion effects, never mind the digression, when we humans want noise, we love noise. We decide it is the kind of noise we like, somehow the rich harmonics beyond the narrow limits of tonal musical sound grab our attention and lure us in.

It is this inherent lust for noise that leads people to love insect music. In the early writings of the great ethnomusicologist Bruno Nettl appears a remark where he tries to distinguish folk music from art music. The music of the people, he supposedly says, is rough, buzzy, scratchy, celebrating irregularity and the unique, personal voice. The most refined of art music, on the other hand, celebrates pure tone, refinement, order, virtuosity, and exact discipline.

I have heard some recordings of insect sounds so grating they are painful to the ears. And it is true, there is nothing quite like playing soprano saxophone live with *Magicidada* crawling all over your hair and inside your clothes, buzzing in unison swells of broadband, wide-range pulses, a total environment of noise. It is an experience that can be had only once every thirteen or seventeen years. So seek it out, and do your best to remember it once you do. Such are the extreme edges of bug music, we don't have to get there yet. Right now we're still with crickets, the most warming and familiar singing six-leggeds. Deciding that their wingscrapes en masse produce music means entering into a musical aesthetic not just accented by the buzz, but composed of it. What makes a giant assembly of insects sound musical?

I decided to ask people who work with noise on a daily basis: electronic musicians, who form art out of sounds that are ignored or even shunned by most of us. When I play insect sounds for true cognoscenti of noise, their ears often perk up, for they are experts who hear great subtleties and structures in complex sounds that often confuse the rest of us. I've been asking all the electronic musicians I know, some of whom, I confess, make music I have a hard time listening to, how they evaluate the quality of complex sounds far away from the aesthetic mores of tone, form, and even rhythm. There will be much more on this in chapter five, but one thing they often say is that the noise as we hear it must be rich, complex, hard to predict, and offering more depth the more we listen to it.

The music of a thousand insects does the job because there is so much more to it than we can ever hear in a single listen. Or is there too little to hear just once? We are calmed by the familiarity of the quiet, simple cricket tune not only because it stands for autumn moving into winter, or the warmth of the hearth as the out-of-doors gets cold and November brown. The music of insects is one based on texture, and on rhythm, not flamboyance in melody and grand virtuosity. It is not dull or too simple, but nuanced in timbre and texture. To *get* it requires undue sensitivity to what the uninitiated may call noise, or a primitive beat, something on the evolutionary road to music, but not quite there.

Not at all. The most loved and praised of human music is often the simplest kind. We cannot deny that. Aspects of our favorite kinds of music are already present within insect aesthetics, to levels of subtlety that we ought to attend to. Later we will delve deeper into the aesthetics of buzz, swish, swirl, wash, and noise, but first let's stick with the more obvious quality of rhythm. Humans love a beat, to dance, or just to mark time. Scientists are constantly claiming that hardly any animals can keep time, even to the point of deriving whole research programs to test the abilities of a single white cockatoo named Snowball that likes to sway along with the Backstreet Boys, as if this is some unique ability that no other parrot can ever achieve. I can tell you, plenty of large parrots have this same ability, just watch them in aviaries or in the wild. But never mind creatures as advanced and musically appreciated as birds, who appeared a few hundred million years later than bugs. Insects are already singing the roots of complex rhythms, owning up to a sense of beat and time that at first we were loath to admit they could possess.

Listen to a complex insect chorus, think what you can pick out. There are tonal crickets, noisy meadow katydids, rhythmic katydids perhaps, ungodly grating noises of cicadas. Perhaps even the repeating peeps of tree frogs, whose communication systems are similar enough to insects to be often discussed together, as in the fabulously comprehensive book *Acoustic Communication in Insects and Anurans* by Carl Gerhardt and Franz Huber. How do all these sounds fit together? Is each just doing its own thing while we the human listener hunt to find order and pattern? The more we are attuned to searching for music in nature, the more beautiful and evocative we may find it, but do the bugs themselves have a sense of rhythm?

Science didn't want to believe it. Yet they saw the phenomenon themselves, in both sound, and light. For hundreds of years, European travelers reported miles of riverbanks full of synchronizing fireflies, turning their tails on and off in unison. How could they ever keep such exact time? Our musically inclined entomological master H. A. Allard had heard such reports, but he himself only saw it once, in Massachusetts, right after a heavy thunderstorm where huge flashes of lightning had crashed upon the nightscape. Thousands of fireflies emerged in the calm after the storm, and here Allard began to see order in the chaos, as he reported in the journal *Science* in 1916: "From time to time, as if moved by a common impulse, great numbers would flash so closely in unison over the entire field that an extensive sheet of tiny light-point would gleam upon the vision for a moment—and then vanish." It happened only that one night, in 1914, and since then Allard had spent many years watching, hunting, never to see such a rhythmic display again. (Perhaps this explains why he moved over to sound, where rhythm appears all the time.) The entomologist Philip Laurent was less convinced by what he himself saw often in Asia. He responded to Allard in 1917 that this "illusion" must have been caused by the involuntary twitching of his own eyelids! He trusted his own rhythm far more than the supposed beat abilities of any bugs. Fireflies pulsing at night?

What do blinking fireflies have to do with syncing crickets? The sense of irregularity and regularity in light is far easier for humans to grab hold onto than the irregularities of music, and the principle is the same. We are not surprised in the least when we hear rhythms roll in and out of phase in a chorus of nighttime crickets, and like Laurent we tend to question our own senses rather than try to figure out how it might actually happen. The firefly stories and claims of insect musical prowess were oft discussed in entomological and more popular scientific publications in the teens and twenties nearly a hundred years ago, but science really didn't know what to do with the phenomenon because I suspect they were afraid of the consequences . . . we wouldn't want insects to have any more cognitive abilities of rhythmatizing that might lead us to take them too seriously. For humans to follow a rhythm en masse, there is supposed to be one leader, and many followers. Swarms of invertebrates are not supposed to work that way.

Though of course they do. The accomplishments of insects happen because groups do tremendous things, each performing their own little part, with no one actually in charge. Only in the last fifty years have we realized that spontaneous pattern in nature can come without anyone being in charge, through the fact of individuals following only simple rules, which have the remarkable ability to create complex patterns without a guiding intelligence behind them. This is the argument made famous in Steven Strogatz's popular book *Sync,* which begins with the firefly story and expands upon it to introduce the whole new science of emergent order:

> In a congregation of fireflies, every one is continually sending and receiving signals, shifting the rhythms and being shifted by them in turn. Out of the hubbub, *sync* somehow emerges . . . the fireflies organize themselves. No maestro

is required, and it doesn't matter what the weather is like. Sync occurs through mutual cuing, in the same way that an orchestra can keep perfect time without a conductor. . . . Each firefly contains an oscillator, a little metronome, whose timing adjusts automatically in response to the flashes of others. That's it.

In explaining the firefly situation, Strogatz immediately uses a musical example. But doesn't an orchestra need a conductor? If things are complicated enough, yes, but if we want to listen like bugs, no.

Thomas Walker noticed the same thing doing experiments with the mellifluous snowy tree crickets back in 1969. It seemed to Walker, one of the great American insect scientists, with a vast Web page containing a huge amount of information on singing insects, that a snowy tree could hear only two consecutive chirps from a neighboring cricket and then he would synchronize quickly with his neighbors. These singers had two distinct kinds of responses, L (lengthen) and S (shorten). L happens when the cricket hears another chirp toward the end of his own chirp. Then he delays his next chirp slightly, or sometimes lengthens his sound. S happens when he hears another chirp during the beginning of his own chirp, then he shortens the length of his chirp, and sometimes shortens the interval between chirps.

Got that? No one else did, either, until scientists were able to mathematically quantify the process with a simple algorithm. Michael Greenfield calls it an "inhibitory-resetting, phase-delay" mechanism, which does sound complicated, but, as mathematical models go, is pretty simple. Insect chorusing, firefly flashing, and even frog chorusing is supposed to work like this:

The chirp or flash is made by the central nervous system of the creature, which has something in the brain, like an oscillator, that produces periodic electrical impulses that rise on a regular rhythm from zero to one. When it hits one the sound is made, then it returns to zero and rises again. If we hear a regular rhythm, there is a regular constant time between peaks, and that's how an animal can make regular rhythms.

How does he change his rhythm in response to another chirper? He does not have to be conducted, he only has to adjust his oscillator in response to the second cricket's sound, the "external stimulus." If the other chirp occurs toward the beginning of his own chirp, he resets his own clock and starts his own cycle a tiny bit earlier. If the other chirp occurs toward the end of his cycle, he lengthens his own cycle slightly. The exact same phenomenon Walker observed is more mathematically explained and illustrated in the following diagram:

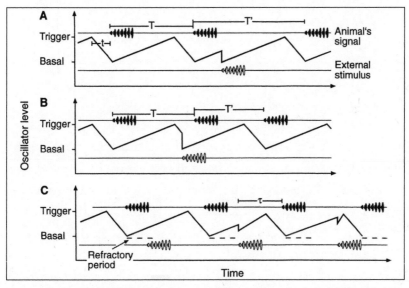

Diagrams showing phase-delay models of varying complexity. (A) Simple phase-delay model, showing a phase delay (T' = black signals) caused by an external stimulus (white signal); t = effector delay; T = free-running period. (B) Simple phase-delay model, showing a phase advance (T') caused by an external stimulus. (C) Inhibitory resetting model with refractory periods (indicated by dashed lines); τ = rebound interval.

I have seen this story very simply demonstrated in an exhibit at the Boston Museum of Science, which combines the sound and light aspects of the story. A giant blinking light simulates the firefly. A person standing next to the light is supposed to clap along with the light. Twenty feet away is another blinking light, slightly out of sync. Someone else claps along with that one, and then a legend on the wall says look at the other light; try to adjust your clap so it is in sync with that one. The lights adjust. Gradually your clap adjusts. Universal rhythm happens. Here's how several out-of-phase chirps or blinks come all into one:

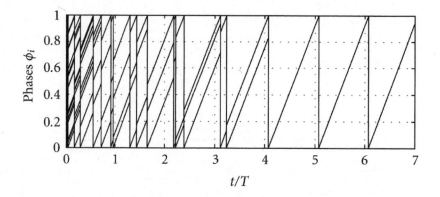

Versions of this model can explain the mechanism of the human heart, which takes about ten thousand oscillators. Or nodes in the brain, or even the great synchronized rumble needed to make an earthquake. The beat goes on when no one leads it. Musically it seems almost too easy. Either we hear rhythm in any chorus of overlapping beats, or else they come into sync all by themselves.

The significance of this phenomenon is enormous, because it shows how a very simple response-mechanism or mathematical model can both produce mass synchronization and rhythm, and also, by detuning it a little, produce interesting rhythms of astonishing complexity. Or, I'm hoping, musically interesting complexity. So I contracted a crack musical software programmer and composer, V.J. Manzo, to invent a piece of software for me that plays with this algorithm to generate overlapping, interesting rhythms emulating a cricket trying to synchronize and hocket (alternate) with other crickets. Here's what it looks like:

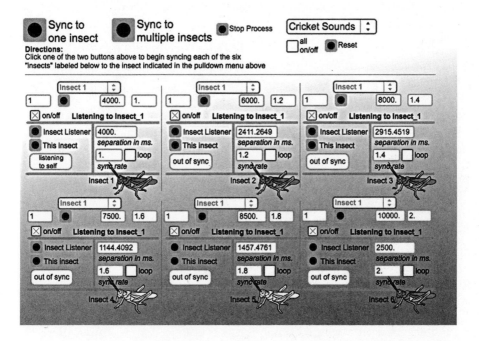

You'll hear this algorithm in use in some of the music on the *Bug Music* CD. The rhythms phase in and out, and the quantization process so prevalent in electronic music, where exactly regular beats are effortlessly produced by machines, is here tuned to go gradually in and out of sync, so we the listeners can strain to grasp the rhythm and enjoy the various bits of unevenness that makes something sound natural, not entirely artificial, even if it is all made by machines. You may download the device for yourself on the www.bugmusicbook.com website. Real or artificial, who are the true musical machines, our software ideas or the actual singing crickets?

Mr. Fung knows the conflict, he gets the paradox. You can assemble your crickets onstage, a few different species, and let them sing their rhythms into being. Or you can bring in the human element, and there, as usual, we have Fung's recollections of the event, not recordings of the actual show. I don't know why that is so often the case—so many musicians have done wonderful things live with birds, whales, and wolves, and so few examples end up being preserved. Maybe this is because the live moment of such interspecies music always ends up being more than the memory, or, more likely, the results are too unusual, or too risky, to be listened to often enough for humans to want to record them. How much easier it is to generate studio creation where the animal and the human may be mixed precisely in an electronic atmosphere of total control? We can turn any sound into any other sound, and as the technology gets ever smaller and easier, more and more people are figuring out these media secrets.

As Junichiro Tanizaki's tale "A Portrait of Shunkin" depicts a Japanese nightingale trapped indoors in the city to turn the wilderness into something we can admit into civilization, so Fung takes his insects into our galleries and onto our stages, placing the music of nature where human music is used to go. He knows there is something disingenuous about the whole project. It is impossible— the wild does not have words, it does not belong with us. Soon he will give up conducting his cricket ensembles and instead spend his days wandering in search of the perfect bug music.

"You think you can find this perfect chorus of crickets in nature?" I ask him.

"I know the place. There's one stone pagoda . . ."

"Where?"

"I'm not giving away all my secrets! It's a round room, its whitewashed walls, slightly sloping inward, have the most beautiful resonances. Speak here and someone else stands there, they can speak to their ear and no one else will hear. Amazing room. The sound travels by walls."

"Still a human building. Must be an ellipse. Still the crickets must wander in. What about in nature?" I ask.

"Soon I will spend my days in search of such places and such sounds. It is futile to imagine I can continue to bring such choruses into our noisy, troubled world."

He who loves the symphony of crickets turns about-face from the rough complexity of our human habitats. And yet he is one to take refuge in a primal noise, a music that has been with us before anyone started keeping track of time. Unlike the bird or whale mysteries, which have captivated me before, the songs of insects are singularly simple, and paradoxically exact. We still long for their simplicity, their tenacity, their calling all along until only death makes them stop. It is the music of the journey that can captivate us right here at home.

Why should the tiny cricket's
tune so sway my heart?
Unsafe outside, it crawls in
beneath my bed to sing at night.

I've wandered long for many years,
my sadness so endures.
The wife at home, asleep alone
will toss and turn til dawn—

No wind or string can move us
like the cricket's faithful song . . .
       —Tu Fu, 759

Nature's music always knows its place far more than any human melody. That's why at times it seems there is little more to say about it other than the call to arms—go outside, slow down, stop, and just listen—but all the same I keep writing about it probably because I believe we can someday understand. Now in retrospect I am studying what this knowledge does to me, since this process of listening to the simple, the "awesomely simple" as Charles Mingus put it, makes me want to know just how knowledge may transform what we hear.

Certainly I have loved the sound of the snowy tree cricket for years without even knowing what it was, and I have heard that their pitch lowers and their tempo slows as the thermometer goes down, but only now that I am fixated on this theme do I start to hear this thing that I have seen only in words until now. And as I take one phrase of tree cricket on my computer and gradually slow it down, spin it on top of itself as a new electronic music, now I will think of the Chinese cricket master dropping sticky resin on his charge's legs, just to bring its pitch down just a tiny bit into a better range for human listening. There are no limits to how far we will go to turn their music into ours. Again we listen only for what we want to hear, something palatable to ourselves. The melancholy, the longing, the song, though fainter, goes on and on, still faithful to our world.

We all know by now that human beings are the only ones who can do something wrong by nature, make things, sing things, that really don't fit in. The rest of nature makes no mistakes. There is no noise that is out of place, it all fits in, as Henry David Thoreau wrote in these extracts from his *Journal,* "Nature makes no noise. The howling storm, the rustling leaf, the pattering rain are no disturbance, there is an essential and unexplored harmony in them. . . . Now I see the beauty and full meaning of that word 'sound.' Nature always possesses a certain sonorousness, as in the hum of insects, the booming of ice . . . which indicates her sound state." No noise, only music, and nothing at all for us to criticize.

Later we shall see what kind of human cultures have praised the thrum of insects as something musical. It may have always been a minority though; or, among those who like such sounds, a simple fact of a culture's life, the familiar background to ways of life, in noisy rainforests or hissing summer meadows. We are used to it, we enjoy it, we rarely notice it. Looking up from his notebook to notice how wonderful nature's sounds can be, Thoreau praises all such natural noise, realizing nothing out there is ever out of place, it is only we, the human, questioning species who can do anything amiss from nature. Or maybe all we do is natural, too; enough ecologists and nature-philosophers have argued as much, but by then, nature loses its ethical weight; there is nothing so right or alluring about it if we decide it includes everything we do, instead of just those things that ally us with our place, our home, our environment, sonic or otherwise.

Some people ask me why I make use of nature's sounds so much and try to consider them as music. I am used to responding with pithy proverbs from the likes of John Cage, announcing that if you learn to hear all sounds as music then the more you listen, the more you will be surrounded by beautiful wind and earth symphonies and will come to love the world. Or I go along with field recordist Bernie Krause and speak of the "great animal orchestra," where each creature has its proper sound that fits into an acoustic niche, a bit like an ecological niche, every instrument and part its place in a vast evolved composition of the diversity of life where no one is in charge, the greatest example of living in sync that evolution can have produced, weaving natural and sexual selection into a fabulous tangled music where all of us have our place to listen in and take part in the wonder.

It's true, when you go out to such places where nature's thrum exceeds anything we humans can approach all musicians will get wind of the vibe. I'm not all that surprised to learn that even Michael Jackson got it right away while visiting the Ivory Coast: "I believe that in its primordial form all of creation is sound and that it's not just random sound, that it's music." So even the King of Pop was a fan of nature's music, no surprise really. The great always know the world is far greater than they will ever be.

Bug music may be among the more humble parts of this grand resonance, but it is one of the easiest pieces of the puzzle to find. Focusing on the buzz, the whirr, the cheep, the saw, the rhythmic splay too hard to pinpoint, I find it all a calming, meditative quest, akin to the glimmers of Zen Buddhism that have fascinated me for years. There is only one bug in the *Blue Cliff Record,* my favorite collection of monk's koans, but it is one that brings the quest easily home. Out of a hundred stories the text offers Case 29, "Just Go Along With It":

Flames will destroy everything
at the end of the universe.
It may already be destroyed.

A cold cricket cries in the pile of wet leaves.
He wanders back and forth, unable to get past regret.

Go along with it
Stumble in rain,
Walk on alone.
At the end of the trail is a warm cabin with a single fire.
There you may dry out those lonely years.

I will not shiver at home, I will not be alone, but will instead travel the world to share the most luminous, rhythmic songs with the most modest of creatures. With such tenacity they will outlast all of us other natural musicians, us mammals, birds, and dinosaurs. Their grounded six-legged noisy rhythms are the origins of all the globe's beats. Dance along with them and you, too, will endure.

THREE

What Makes Them Dance?

think we humans have always heard crickets as being musical. You could go back throughout history and find people who have gathered, as Mr. Fung has done, a whole ensemble of crickets solely for the purpose of enjoying their singing. Search the *New York Times* for such a story, and an article comes up way back on May 29, 1880, with the headline, "Two Hundred Crickets: A Lady Artist's Mania for Capturing the Musical Insects." The paper was so scandalized as to be afraid to reveal the exact details of this mysterious happening. First their offices received this cryptic invitation:

You are respectfully invited to attend a cricket concert on Friday night at the studio of _____ _____, any time most convenient to you, between the hours of 7 and 10, with friend. If you cannot come, send representative. Very respectfully, LUCILLE—, *Don't ring. Second floor. Crickets in full song.*

The reporter who arrived on the scene was a bit chagrined not to find the crickets, who for some reason he imagined would be "an association of young people of both sexes in gorgeous array." Instead he found a young woman, attired in a sundress, who pulled aside a screen to reveal two hundred *Ensifera* in a fern-filled terrarium, consistently rubbing their wings to produce "the sounds so familiar to thousands everywhere, sounds that seemed to be the finest music to her ears." Lucille told tales of traipsing through the Berkshires and Catskills, capturing insects wherever she traveled, coaxing the frightened insects to crawl all over her arms and shoulders. "She has watched their breeding, growth, and death. . . . She thinks that life would be unbearable to her without the chirping of the cricket," that comforting creature whose ears lie on its legs:

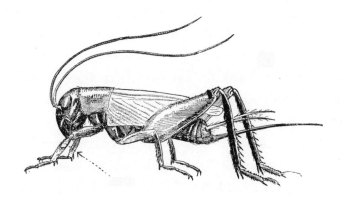

So Mr. Fung, you are not alone. You and Lucille could have created quite a band. The cricket chirps, familiar to all, loved deeply by only a few. Now give me one good reason why the few should convince the many. What more might we hear in bug music?

There is a way to look at all of music as a hierarchy of levels in the experience of time. At one edge is infinity, or nearly there, the whole temporal extent of the universe. Then there are the eons needed for life in general and species specific to evolve. Then there are the grand eras of human cultures and civilizations, replete with their musical traditions. Then you have the time of musical genres, their invention and thrivings and revivals. Then the lifespan of individual composers and performers. Then the time it takes for each of them to compose a musical work, then the much shorter time it takes for the work to be performed. Then you have the structure and sections of the work. Then the rhythm and meter of the work. Then the individual beats that hold that rhythm together. Then the sounds chosen to play each beat, and the tones held out to mark a melody. Then the numbered frequencies vibrating in each held tone, the counting and layering of the waves of sound. Then getting smaller, the tiny fragments of sound all wrapped and repeated together to produce the minute digital repeats of sonic information that emulate smooth analog tone with fast and binary illusion. Sound waves split up into ever finer textures turn, like light, into particle on an instantaneous journey away from wave. Thus all music is rhythm, even continuous tone or complicated noise. All sound exists through the traversing and organizing of time.

This full-on cosmic vision of sound is introduced by Curtis Roads in his fine book *Microsound* from 2001. Here, just twelve years ago, Roads introduces the theoretical basis for granular synthesis, the process of breaking sound into tiny little pieces for recomposing as new musical timbres. It is probably the best digital music technique to analyze, understand, and to emulate insect sounds. Just a theory at the turn of the century, it is now a technology that enables us to work fluently with insect-type noises and make music out of them.

What is great and unique about Roads's book is how he situates this project as a vast philosophical vision of the world as broken down into beats, from the longest possible span of the universe to the most microscopic rhythmic units that make up continuous tone: the whirr of a cicada's wings, the vibration of his tymbal, the fiddle of the crickets' wings, the tiny whirrs that produce sound we hear as a continuum. This massive diagram of all time scales visualized as one is something I have never seen anywhere else:

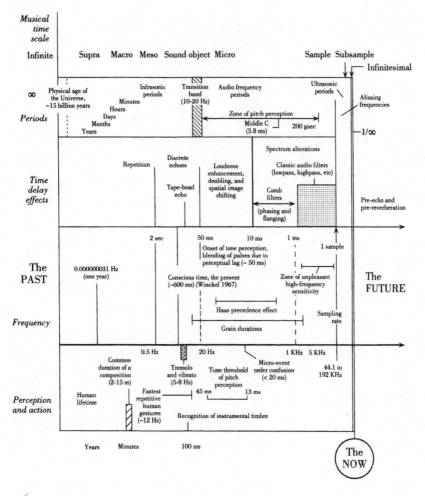

Stare at this diagram a little while and soon you will get it: All is rhythm, everything is time, from the arc of our lifespans through to the beats we can groove to along to the regular vibrations that make up clear pitches and humming textures. Even the possibility that music is nested hierarchies of time fills me with awe . . . never had I thought of rhythm conceived of in such a way that includes all senses of the repetition of moments regular enough to be noticed as a holistic pattern. Insects may understand all swishes around them to be music. People can understand all sounds to be possible music.

Each call a cicada makes easily seemed a musical note to Ou-Yang Hsiu and to many other poets. But what of the whole emergence, the great beat of thirteen or seventeen years? I want you to consider that as a musical note, a grand composition at an ultimate scale. If the particulate thrum of insect noise is microsound, as Curtis Roads wants us to believe, then the seventeen-year beat is *macrosound,* a giant scale of a whole species population swooshing to a different drummer, the mysterious prime number beat of this very unusual number of years. Fabulous! A great natural invention along the lines of composer La Monte Young's Theatre of Eternal Music or Jem Finer's Longplayer, which will run for a thousand years as part of Brian Eno and Stewart Brand's Clock of the Long Now. The periodical cicadas have been performing their music for at least ten thousand years, since the last ice age.

The granular dimension of time is the secret to bug music. I don't just mean the music bugs make, but something wider and deeper, the "bug music" aspect of life, or the bug and the glitch hiding inside all music. The macroscopic can turn into the microscopic, with a single gleam of conception. Roads's mathematical analysis of sound made all these new sonorities computationally possible and musically actual. But his approach is eminently conceptual as well. Ezra Pound hinted at the same already in 1910 with his ideas of the Great Bass, that rhythm can be harmony, that it can ground all music. "Music is pure rhythm, pure rhythm and nothing else, for the variation in pitches is the variation of rhythms of the individual notes, and harmony is nothing but the blending of these individual rhythms." This far-reaching poet got the insight that frequency is also rhythm, the point at which a vibration eases out from steady tone to rapid beat is a key moment in the perception of the highest value of sound. The aesthetic importance of this idea is to figure out how to organize your listening to the environment, or the composing of your music, so that it takes account of all overlapping layers of rhythm and rhythm that turns into pitch. For Pound it was a dream, for Roads it was a theory, and today it's a musical tool available for all of us to use.

The irregular accidents of overlapping metrics are where art appears! The smooth arc of time, of what constitutes a beat. The music of time can be larger or smaller than what we take from it. It is one scale to think that insects *zzhh* in time and then to think that they appear in seventeen-year cycles, or that they have been at it for millions of years. All these things are rhythm; they can all be mapped on the grand scale of total time. From the marking of eons down to the imperceptible slow, drawn-out beat of the fin whale down to the vibrating maracas of the common sword-bearer conehead katydids parsed into finer micrograins, sound at all levels streams at us most sublime.

Musicians who work with electronic sounds often praise the "warmth" they hear in the early electronic synthesizers, which work with analog oscillators to produce pure electronic tones. The ease and precision of digital sound offers meticulous control, but we are able to hear, at the limits of our auditory perception, the digital nature of the sound that makes everything too crisp, too shimmery, too metallic and exact. It is an aesthetic metaphor of something many of us suspect is amiss with the whole one-zero digital world. Precise control, but no dirt, grime, or messiness. A mirroring of nature that denies the fluid irregular *muck* of nature.

According to a digital worldview something like a musical tone is an auditory illusion; it's just an immensely rapid repeating of tiny specific beats, over and over again so we imagine there is a continuous sound. According to an analog worldview all is flow and sweep, continuous variation without any freezing of pitch, beat, or moment: just an imagined dream that time might stop. Well, which is correct? Depends what you want to listen for and how you want to know nature. Is it not best to admit both approaches and pick and choose whichever you want? Aesthetically, yes. Conceptually, sometimes one needs the digital to make sense of what analog can only imagine can be done.

All those experimental composers of the twentieth century from Luigi Russolo to Morton Subotnik dreamed of making music out of pure noise, of turning sounds from one form into something radically different, of going beyond traditional structures and rules and emerging in a whole new place where any sound might be possible. Classical ideas of what makes art work, says Roads, are linked to a "wave-oriented view of sound," where great works of art are built upon certain forms and proportions. Rhythms or beats are divided regularly and calculated upon basic senses of order and pattern. But once you are able to sculpt art out of microsound, dividing musicality into infinitesimal bits that can be woven and recombined at will, at last we can enter a whole new place where the impossible is now easy:

> To think in terms of microsonic materials and procedures is to shift the aesthetic focus away from sharply defined intervals toward curvilinear and fuzzy morphologies. Just as it has become possible to sculpt habitats from fiberglass foam, the flowing structures that we can create with microsound do not necessarily resemble the usual angular forms of musical architecture. On the contrary, they tend toward droplike, liquid, or cloudlike structures.

You may not know where a sound begins, or what pitch it represents. Its rhythm may be a blur. A note may evaporate, coalesce,
mutate into something else. Forget traditional musical ideas of note,
motif, phrase, and rhythm. Now we have sound *clouds*: "evolving
streams of particle morphologies." At last here is a musical vision
that could explain a familiar summer sound whose sonogram looks
like this:

Tibicen chloromera, the swamp cicada, is a common creature you
may hear in the Northeast every August. This sound, a familiar one
to anyone basking in a lazy August afternoon, is hard to categorize
as a traditionally understood musical event. This sonogram shows
visually how such a sound is far away from the normal human
musicality of a clear pitch, a single horizontal line. All the beauty
in this image comes from the fact that it is a tightly structured
instance of beautiful noise. The sonogram shows the growing
intensity of the sound, and the glimmer of a rhythm that emerges

at its heart. Right afterward the noise of this single bug fades away. This cicada sound event takes several seconds; it has form, identity, noise timbre, and shape. We humans hear it and think: cicada. If we know more we may think: swamp cicada. It immediately presents an association with late summer, hot, sticky afternoons. When does it become music? When we smile, sit back, and enjoy it! When we dare to pick up our horns to join in. Or, when we deconstruct the sound into musical anomalies. When we have the sound transformation tools to turn any rhythm into ever smaller rhythms, all the way down to a continuous tone.

Take that sonogram on the previous page, use it as a score as if you sat in a box at the opera. Listen to that infernal bug, and follow along on the time-bounded map of the sound. The picture helps us find some order. When we analyze, we are much more visual than aural. When we move, when we enjoy, the auditory takes over, that sense that makes us love music so much. Accustom yourself to the world of underappreciated bug sounds by hearing in each glimmer the potential for thousands of rhythmic divisions at all levels of pulse and design.

The cicada's song is a wash of complex frequencies. Adult cicadas live for but a few weeks every late summer when they mostly sing and mate, the ultimate libertine hedonistic musicians. What more can we glean from their life story?

Socrates repeated an ancient myth about them to his student Plato in the *Phaedrus,* announcing that these penultimate singers were once, in the age before the Muses, human beings, who got so carried away with music they forgot to eat and drink, and thus they died. Now they have returned to Earth as beings who can live only upon singing, since they have spent years underground building up nourishment in order to spend but a few weeks ensconced in bliss. The Muses have rewarded the cicadas with the gift of never needing food or sleep, so they may sing and mate for a few sweet weeks of aboveground life. But watch out: When they die, they will go and inform the Muses which humans have been honoring them down on Earth. They may not know who has been naughty or nice, but the cicadas know who has been listening, and wondering what all this music might mean. It is best, concludes Socrates, not to sleep, but to philosophize at midday, letting our thoughts unfold in dialogue upon the restless background of swirling, building, pulsing, and waiting that makes up insect music.

Do not waste a life that can make sense of so multifarious a sonic world around us! At least I would like to imagine Socrates would approve of anyone who takes the time to attend to natural mysteries (though the *Phaedrus* is the only dialogue of Plato's that takes place outside the city walls). Most cicada species come out every year, but they all have spent at least a few years feeding and slowly growing underground. We don't even know how many years most species take, the process is so hard to discern. These come out in July and August, as opposed to the periodical seventeen- and thirteen-year cicadas to come out in late May or early June.

In what sense is such a great, regular, seventeen-year beat really a rhythm? Consider the theory of biological clocks, the steady rhythms that guide the life cycles of all living things on this planet, anyone that is born, grows up, procreates, sustains, and finally dies. Living things seem to know when to do the things they need to do. They are attuned to the circadian rhythms of day and night, to the seasons, to the thrum of wingbeats, and to the pulse of heartbeats. Are they all in fact music? Are they all models of music? Those interested in electronic music might be excited to learn that nature is full of oscillators, clocks moving regularly back and forth like a pendulum or the movement of the tides. Each atom inside us oscillates at 10^{16} times per second. Our brain's electrical activity pulses at 10 times a second, or once every tenth of a second.

The heart is at sixty times a minute, or once a second. The daily cycle between sleeping and waking is about 10^5 seconds. Lunar based monthly cycles are 10^6 seconds. The annual molting of a reindeer's horns is about 10^7 seconds. High up near the limit of biological cycles is the mysterious emergence of periodic thirteen- and seventeen-year cicadas, though the longest germination cycle of a living thing is an honor that belongs to the American agave, which can take a hundred years to flower. All of these are regular periods and predictable patterns. The faster ones may even be heard as continuous tones of sound, with the very fastest being far above our range of hearing or even conception. Thus explained, life is a vast music, with irregular rhythms swirling on top of one another, which we can choose to tap into and appraise when we wish.

Take any rhythm and tap it with your feet. Fast or slow, it's smack in the midst of the great overlapping pulses of life. The screeching whines of cicadas are the result of precise and fast vibrations, but the life cycles of these insects represent another rhythm that is far beyond any beat we can musically perceive. Yet in its prime number predictability it is itself a magical and consistent music. We don't call these periodic species *Magicicada* for nothing—such a long and irregular numbered gestation period is indeed a fact of insect magic, suggesting ties to ancient alchemy or numerology.

How can these tiny cicadas count the precise number of years to know when to emerge? The adults live only for several weeks, during which the males are constantly singing and the females listen and wait. When the time for mating comes they make the mysterious wing-flick sound and the males know they are ripe for approach. They eat little during this time of sex and song. There is little else they need to know. The female's ovipositor spears into small tree branches and settles the eggs inside. Each female can lay hundreds of eggs, in up to fifty different tree branches. Eight weeks after being laid in the branch, tiny ant-like nymphs hatch and then burrow into the ground, where they dig about a foot down to begin to feed—*for seventeen years!*

How can they possibly live so long underground gently sucking food out of the roots of trees? Rick Karban at University of California, Davis, organized an ingenious experiment to figure out how the cicada nymphs were counting. He found a bunch that had already been underground for fifteen years and brought them into a controlled laboratory where he attached them to the roots of fruit trees that had been coaxed into flowering twice a year. This led the cicadas to emerge one year early, suggesting that the nymphs were counting changes in the trees that they could sense from deep below. Thus he determined the clockwork creatures were counting seasonal cycles in the trees, and were not hardwired to a fixed duration of seventeen years, or an accumulation of a certain number of total warm days, as some other scientists had hypothesized. They measured cycles of annual time and changing tree physiology, right from underground, and they rarely went wrong. See the next page for how the scientists managed to confuse the cicadas' infallible counting of the years.

This inspired experiment does not explain *how* the little insects keep track of time, but it does suggest they are precisely aware of this giant prime number intervallic rhythm, a grand oscillator at the high end of the big bass drum pulse possible for life.

I try to experience the very preposterousness of this prime number rhythm held and remembered by tiny inscrutable insects. We cannot know what they are thinking because they are not really thinking. They are alive in a far more certain, regular, and machine-like manner than more complex life forms can ever be. They understand complex sounds in a way humans never can. They sense and produce rhythms with absolute certainty in a way questioning beings can only hope and strive for. They know who they are, while we can never be so sure about ourselves.

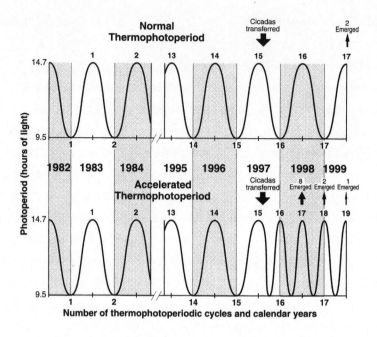

How much work does it take to hear the overlapping strands of cricket, katydid, and cicada rhythms to be a vast kind of necessary natural music? As insects are millions of years older than humans in the scale of evolution, can it be possible that we learned our appreciation of rhythm from these most venerable musicians?

Mark Changizi doesn't think so. This psychologist wrote an intriguing book called *Harnessed* in 2011 that argues that human music is based on human movement, and that's why it more often than not has a beat similar to the gait of human walking: "We humans make a variety of beat-like sounds, including heartbeats, sexual gyrations, breathing, and certain vocalizations like laughing and sobbing. But one of the most salient beat-like sounds we make is when we walk, wherein our legs hit the ground over and over again in a regular repeating pattern. . . . Natural human movement has a beat, and so music must have a beat."

Changizi offers scores of statistics, including numerical analysis of thousands of pages of "familiar melodies" from Western music to bolster his theory that almost all our music makes use of rhythms based on the human speed of walking, more than any kind of natural cycle or rhythm. It is an intriguing idea, and he's got numbers to prove at least an association with a lot of human music and a walking beat, but I am more intrigued by how he brings cicadas into his story. Turns out he grew up in Virginia where once in his childhood he remembered the seventeen-year cicada emergence, how the large insects would sit on his shoulder as he walked all the way to school. If human music is based on our walking gait, of course Changizi believes cicadas preferred music that is based on their strange motions, a mix of awkward buzzing flight and a lumbering creep up and down the crowded stalks of warm spring trees:

> If cicadas were someday to develop culture and invent music that tapped into their auditory movement recognition mechanisms, then their music might have dozens of notes between each beat. With *"Boooom"* as their beat and *"da"* as their wing-flap inter-beat notes, their music might be like . . . *"Boooom-da-da-da-da-da-da-da-da-da-da-da-da-da-da-da-da-da-da-da-da-da-da-da-da-da-da-da-da-da-da-Boooom-da-da-da-da-da-da-da-da-da-da-da-da-da-da-da-da-da-da-da-da-da-da-da-da-da-da-da-da-da-etc."* Perhaps their ear-shattering incessant mating call *is* this sound.

If cicadas were able to develop culture and invent music, eh? Why doesn't Changizi think what they are doing right now *is* music? Many people, scientists and others, believe what animals are doing is rote and programmed and only humans have stepped away from natural evolution to engage in cultural evolution. Fair enough; we are the only species that needs to wonder and comment on our situation, but I have argued for years that the sounds of animals aren't called "songs" innocently . . . we know these utterances, those beautifully, rhythmically formed and evolved, are repeated incessantly and emphatically by all these creatures not because their message hasn't gotten across the first time, but because they enjoy, love, and need their music, sounds sometimes appreciated only by the species who makes them, but sometimes enjoyed by humans, especially when we learn to listen outward and expand our acoustic consciousness.

When I mentioned this to Changizi he immediately, as a good scientist, thought there was a way to *test* this. His mind started spinning: "If you take arbitrary sexually selected plumages or sounds, designs of animal stuff where people tend to think there is no sexual selection at all, just ask naïve human observers how interesting do they think the patterns or sounds are—has anyone done that?" I said I wasn't sure, but I did know that Ellie Ratcliffe at the University of Sussex is leading a project to examine whether or not listening to birdsong is good for people. We'll see what she comes up with.

Is listening to bug music good for people? My intuitive sense is that people enjoy the layers of rhythmic complexity that insects create as a swarm or a hive mind. We hear something alive and wonderful, a musical order that comes not from a guiding musical intelligence, but from an emergent organization that comes out of nature, akin to the aesthetics of the swarm but somehow more inviting, more lovely. *Katy did. Katy didn't. Didn't didn't. Katy katy did. Did did. Did did did.*

Changizi is an adaptationist. He designs experiments to test his novel ideas of possibly practical reasons for the evidently musical qualities in human music and language. He summarizes his theory in his recent book *Harnessed* as follows: "Speech sounds like solid-object physical events, (B) music sounds like people moving, and (C) *Homo sapiens* became modern human by virtue of cultural evolution designing language and music to mimic nature," to harness the way we perceive and travel through the natural world, and in our expression build a model of what we have evolved within. It's an intriguing picture, and he does analyze a lot of data from human music and from the structure of human languages to support it, but there remains something arbitrary in his whole enterprise. Arbitrary in an admirable way, he is a bit like a mad scientist performance artist, operating at the statistical edges of his discipline.

His book makes me want to put forth the hypothethis that we learned our love for rhythm not from the adrenaline of running across the savannah chasing gazelles and impalas with spears, but from listening to the polyrhythmic swirls of the entomological soundscape. What we love most about insects are their sounds, and their ability to accomplish so much through the emergent intelligence of the swarm. Then of course we are in awe of their tenacity, our belief that they will survive our planet being hit by an asteroid or blown up in some senseless human nuclear holocaust or global warming tragedy. The bugs will go on, and with them their eternal songs.

I would prove my assertion not with statistics, but by allusion and awe. I would ask you to go out there and *listen,* taking in the beauty first by paying closer attention. I would not be the first by far to ask you to do so. Rachel Carson famously listened at night to a sound resembling a tiny bell, ringing over and over again. She named this creature "the fairy bell ringer" and marveled at a voice "so ethereal, so delicate, so otherworldly, that he should remain invisible, as he has through all the nights I have searched for him. It is exactly the sound that should come from a bell held in the hand of the tiniest elf, inexpressibly clear and silvery, so faint, so barely-to-be-heard that you hold your breath as you bend closer to the green glades from which the fairy chiming comes." Field recordist Lang Elliott surmises that this must be the song of the tinkling ground cricket, *Allonemobius tinnulus,* a luminous and familiar sound in the Eastern forests of early autumn, easy to hear but difficult to pinpoint. The challenge of attention lures you in. "The game is to listen. Not so much to the full orchestra as to the separate instruments, and to try to locate the players."

John Himmelman in his most excellent book *Cricket Radio* wonders if the scientist in Carson that wanted to flush out these tiny songsters might have been won over by the naturalist in her, who was content to describe the beautiful song that nature offers for us, as a background to our musings on the beautiful interconnectedness of all living things. He, too, can write poetically on the scientist's loving quandary:

> I've no doubt she knew those crickets were not actually calling for her pleasure. They were hard at work at the business of holding a place for their kind on this planet. . . . There was no joy in their song. There was no celebration; nor was there sadness or sorrow. Those players were throwing everything they had into propagating their species, and not by choice. They are hardwired to do so. Yes, Carson knew that, but she probably also knew that there is a kind of beauty in those cold, hard facts.

It's not only the information that touches us, but the love of sound around us *not* evolved for our pleasure. We love the complexity, the balance, the strange emphatic order, and the insistence of these mysterious sounds from creatures we can rarely ferret out. We get ideas from the world. But we also evolved our human nature and culture in the midst of this world. Not only from the necessary walk and the necessary scrape or possible danger in a threatening sound. We embrace possibilities, richness, beauty, complexity.

Rachel Carson, finding inspiration for the American environmental movement in the 1960s, did not feel the need to precisely identify which species of insect was making the sound she called "the fairy bell ringer." Why didn't this great biologist give us more detail about who she was hearing and describing so poetically? It's just too hard—our acoustic sense is much less developed to listen for detail than our visual sense. And one can hardly ever find these creatures that sing so boldly and delicately, especially at night.

As an insect-tainted musician I am myself divided about how much specific information we need to know in order to be musically attuned to and influenced by these six-legged singers. Himmelman spent close to eleven years learning the names and sounds of all the tiny singers he could find in his Connecticut neighborhood, and he decides that Carson is probably talking about Say's Trigs, *Anaxipha exigua*. Himmelman spent a decade listening to gain mastery of all these mysterious, dark-time sounds, so we know it can be done. The differences between these creatures can be quite subtle, so it's much harder than birdsong, and not as immediately inviting. But still, I think the great chorus of overlapping insect songs is most certainly complex, beautiful, and inviting, and that may have had the most direct influence on human musicality.

For our sense of music is only the latest such sense in the grand march of evolution. Insect songs also evolved from simple to complex, as Himmelman describes it: "The songs of those earliest sound-producing insects were fairly modest, likely composed of simple clicks and scrapes. As the wings developed more teeth for the files, and more efficient areas for sound amplification, those songs grew more complex. Female insects that could better locate calling males from a distance passed on their improved hearing traits. Males also benefited from being able to hear their competition. It pushed them to prove their worth with *the most strident song they could muster.*"

A reasonable explanation. Evolution offers the possibility for sexual selection to lead females to prefer certain male traits and behavior over others. Through generations of preference, these traits are refined, and sometimes seem extreme and beyond necessity. Peacocks tails, bowerbird bowers, many hour-long nightingale and humpback whale songs—if these are solutions to problems faced by the animals' survival, far easier solutions could have been preferred. But the females liked these, and such love for fashion shaped the course of animal aesthetics. Over millions of years of evolution, insect songs are selected out of many possibilities, most of which do not get selected. We didn't have to get the bug songs we do, but take a listen, try to know what has evolved, what songs we have ended up with. The ways insects make sounds have been fundamentally unchanged for 250 million years. Once I wrote that birdsongs are the oldest, most classical music we know. But insect rhythm is even older, these beats go back far toward the beginning of living time.

Himmelman and most scientists doubt that insects enjoy even their own sounds the same way we do. They need to sing, but they may not like to sing. They have no choice. They are little evolved machines for singing; little programmed brains with mechanical noisemaking apparatus. They are much more like the little computer programs that science sometimes seems to wish all living things could be, so it would be easier for us to understand them.

Richard Alexander wrote the first great summary of insect sound evolution in 1960. The more evolved the insect, the more rhythmic and complex its male calling songs. The males, says firm adaptationist Alexander, must locate the females from far away in dense habitat, while remaining hidden from predators. They need to keep singing for as much time as possible, with as much of a distinct sound as possible. For creatures who are generally able to produce only a few, simple mechanical sounds, it is no surprise that they evolved a system of repeating one sound after another in metrical precision to announce their presence, pulse, and stamina. Ergo, insect music is born. I say it's true music, since it communicates not as simple information, but as rhythmic flow and performance in a regular, aesthetically judged manner. The beat and the energy have to be just right for the females to care, and in some species, to respond with the appropriate sound of readiness. You could see it as a basic, programmed mating ritual that evolution has built toward, or you could see it as evolved music, with patterns of performed sound more significant than any meaning that can easily be translated or explained away.

That insects are evolved music machines was made clear to Alexander when he found he could get a katydid to alter his song upon hearing the triplet rhythms of his typewriter banging away at an entomological science paper. Your basic male true katydid, *Pterophylla camellifolia,* usually sings in the dark of night. But as Alexander was typing, he heard the katydid imitate his sounds whenever his old manual machine played triple rhythms close to the famous *katydid, katydidn't* that identify this species. Alexander slowed down his typing. The katydid slowed down. He speeded up. The katydid speeded up. They did not try to sing together with the typewriter in unison, but instead sang in the silences between the keystrokes, alternating, filling up the sonic space whenever there was room. Katydids sing only when there is enough room for their contribution to the overall song. If he typed continuously, says Alexander, the insect would have no place to join in. If not stimulated by the typewriter, the big green bug sang nothing at all.

So once you get inside their rhythms, one can musically interact with katydids. The famous insect sound science pioneer George
W. Pierce succeeded in getting a caged male true katydid to
change his number of pulses by playing him an artificial stimulus
with an old-fashioned electronic oscillator. *Katy did did did. Katy
did. Katy did did did did.* Pierce could get his caged prisoner up to
about five "*did*"s before the insect singer gave up. These creatures
will respond to us once we enter into the confines of their specific musical aesthetics.

Is this katydid music boring? Limited? That is not as interesting
a question as the realization that such music is sufficient; just enough
for the bugs to make their music work, fill the August night with
rhythmic, pulsing, space-filling sound, a three-part beat where the
discerning writer, if he's got an old manual typewriter, can find his
musical role.

Alexander hit upon a different generative music strategy than
the Strogatz sync algorithm that worked with the snowy tree and
other synchronizing crickets. The katydid does not sing continuously, but makes his *katydid* and then waits a few silent beats. He
sings again, with the space between. If he hears a rival, he sings just
a little sooner. If his rival adds a beat, *katydidnt*, then our katydid
also adds a beat. He challenges, but with grace, and a bit of distance.
It's not a fight, no crass attempt to overlap or jam the signals.
There are hundreds of these bugs doing this all at once, thus the
vast overlap. The night forest sounds alive with questions of what
Katy did or *didn't*. It's a pulsing, irregular, relentless music. Katydids
find mates, humans enjoy the groove of it all.

Plenty of other species of katydid don't make the signature
katydid sound, but the name is so good we use it for all of them.
The most common, continuous, underlying rhythmic thrum of an
August New England meadow is marked by the *swish swish swish* of
the Eastern sword-bearing conehead katydid (which I must say is

a magnificent name!). This katydid, when all alone, sings continuously and steadily, unless he is stimulated by another pulsed sound, a sound that has to be broadband, noisy, clearly pulsed, and containing ultrasound superhigh frequency sounds. Then our sword-bearer will cease singing, for about a second. Another simple rule is brilliantly illustrated in a paper on "acoustic startling" by Paul Faure and Ronald Hoy entitled "The Sounds of Silence" in 1999. Here they argue that if continuous singing is the default or null situation the male katydids find themselves in, then *not* making sound is a behavioral statement.

And from the human perspective, it is a musical statement. Starting and stopping also leads to the sense of a persistent, inexact, and living thrum that makes a night full of singing insects still sound musically alluring. The grand song of stops and starts makes for a more interesting music, a sign the coneheads are listening. *Swish swish swish. Swish. Swish swish swish.*

Such a conclusion to a paper might seem painfully obvious— so they're saying that if you play a loud katydid-like rhythm to these guys they'll stop? Sounds perfectly obvious, they're worried, cautious. Maybe. But it is signficant to detail the specific behavioral response that involves waiting a very specific amount of time, one second. Such sense of rhythm in a group of singers is what leads to the forming of a groove, an insect groove, not a human one—a mass rhythmic sound with its own decipherable rules.

Biologist Michael Ryan found a similar situation with large choruses of singing male Túngara frogs in Central America. Amphibians use rhythmic sound in a way most similar to crickets and katydids. It is well known that masses of chorusing frogs will cease their singing when they sense the approach of danger, say, a fringe-lipped bat ready to swoop down or an ecotourist hoping to record the mass peeper chorus on his smartphone. Ryan discovered that a group of Túngara frogs will stop singing also when they hear a neighboring group of frogs stop singing. Once again the perceived sound of silence becomes a signal.

They are listening to each other and know when they hear other singing creatures suddenly stop. Watch out . . . something must be up. Silence might be golden, but it might also be a sign of danger. The frogs and sword-bearers respond to the absence of sound and not only to the presence of sound. Sometimes the forest can be *too* quiet.

Here we have several species of insect and also amphibian who use rhythm or its absence for precise and practical ends. What does this have to do with music? Those of you who have followed my writing about improvisation, then birds, then whales, then evolution, know that I am rarely satisfied with a functional explanation for anything that happens in living nature—beauty entrances me too much, and I do not believe it is an illusion. For insects, simple rhythm and response is at the heart of their essence as musical creatures, as H. A. Allard surmised a century ago. And with these mathematical examples described above I am intrigued by the possibility that what humans hear in choruses of synchronizing crickets or hocketing katydids is not an enjoyment of the random, the unplanned, the chance caprices of nature, but glimmers of order in disorder that come as we listen to layers of tiny creatures playing by simple musical or mathematical rules.

Don't think that my hunt for musicality in the overlapping beats of katydids is some kind of musician's wishful thinking! In fact, musicality is spoken of in the heart of insect science's quest to figure out how these creatures are all connected through the bifurcating branches of evolution. A recent study by Chinese and American scientists demonstrated that even in the Jurassic age, far earlier than we had thought, katydids were making musical, thrumming tones, not just the scratchy noises we associate with more "primitive" organisms. How did Jun-Jie Gu, Fernando

Montealegre-Z, Daniel Robert, and their colleagues figure this out? Turns out you can figure out what kind of sound a katydid will make by studying its "stridulatory apparatus," the structure of its forewings.

Extremely well-preserved fossils of the 165-million-year-old species *Archaboilus musicus* reveal extremely symmetrical forewings with regularly spaced "file-teeth." These are clues that convinced these researchers that the 7 cm well-proportioned wings of this creature enabled it to produce a resonating, fairly pure tone of around 640 Hz, a note between D# and E an octave and a half above middle C. So far this is the earliest we have discovered an insect that has evolved to produce a pure tone. As to the function of such an adaptation, the multinational team hypothesized that this type of sound would be useful for the katydids to communicate across the uncluttered, spacious Jurassic forests of conifers and giant ferns. Given the pitch range, they imagine that dinosaurs and early mammals who might have fed on such insects would also have been able to hear the calls. Presto! An evolutionary vision of a reconstructed unhearable ancient music.

The scientists named this creature *musicus* because of its unique musicality, and prehistoric evolutionary quality that defines what is interesting about this species. This remarkable reconstruction of *katydiddying* shows pure tone musicality in bug song is much earlier than we previously thought. *And then the katydids lost it* over the millennia to devolve onward to scratchier, more primitive rhythmic sounds, which were already far more common among this line of singing. The *musicus* line went nowhere, and it took a long time for other species to evolve the wide range of sounds we have today. Of course, pure tone may not be more advanced than the frenzy of the beat. Both are independently interesting to us humans. We might have learned both musical attributes not only from our own movements and needs, but from *bugs*.

How does human rhythmatizing work? How do we synchronize to a beat? We have seen human inroads to understanding how crickets do it, but do we, too, follow simple mathematical rules as we listen? Science uses the word "entrainment" to explain how one oscillator synchronizes to another, feeling its way into a pulse that it hears using the basic rules at its disposal. It's another way to look at all that basic synchronization going on as the body and the universe adjust to the vast encompassing nested rhythms that all matter finds its place in the beating, repeating cyclical aspects of time. Martin Clayton, Rebecca Sager, and Udo Will wrote a massive article investigating whether this idea has any place in the domain of ethnomusicology, and this long rumination was published along with many thoughtful responses by thinkers from many different fields, making it one of the best kind of academic articles to read on the subject, one provocative argument with challenges from all over the intellectual map.

Coordinating rhythms synchronizing without external control is essential for cycles of nature, at the ecological level, and the maintaining of the body's balances at the level of the organism. They define the identity of the vast insect choruses that enable each individual insect singer to make his way into the total collective sound. They knit the seventeen years of the cicada waiting underground for the moment they know it is time to emerge. All are synchronized rhythms, each can be elucidated but their relationships remain elusive. Yet there is no one rhythm without all the necessary others. Is music an explicit revelation of this basic natural fact?

We pick up the speech rhythms of the people we talk to, we tap along to the beat without first figuring out what the beat is. We have a long-standing tendency to groove along with the beat, even if the beat is vastly polyrhythmic, full of overlapping confusion and no easy pulse. It is this kind of multifarious musical complexity that I believe humans first made sense of by finding that we were pleased by the chorusing sounds of insects. "One day, in a park close to my hometown, Leiden," writes Frank Koewenhoven of the Chime Foundation, "I was humming a tune when I noticed that clouds of midges in the air above my head started to 'dance' to my music. The insects moved in unison (in up- or downward direction) in response to the rhythmical sound signals they 'heard.'" As a scientist, he is wont to explain. "Presumably they reacted to air vibrations, but it was less obvious why or how all of them would respond to me—the external timekeeper."

All of human social interaction can be seen as a swirling journey through overlapping senses of rhythm. Cycles, oscillations, periods that beat simultaneously within and without us. All comes into synchrony, lined up or phased precisely in opposition to each other, filling in the spaces and silences. Entrainment is a conceptual model for all the ways rhythms can relate to one another through pulsing sense, guided by nothing more than the encounter of one musical rule with another, at all levels of biological, human, and social organization.

I know, it seems once again to be grand, vague, and cosmic. But at the same time it is maddeningly, minutely precise. In musicology the old way of thinking was to look for the roots of cultural difference in human motion, just like what Changizi tries to tell us is brand new. Musicologist and song collector Alan Lomax wrote back in the 1960s that "You can walk in a 1-1-1-1 meter, or in a 1-2-1-2 meter, or even in a 1-2-3-1-2-3. The upper body can simply go along with the legs or it can move to an independent meter or in an accompanying pattern . . . The combinations of the rhythmic patterns in the upper and lower body give rise to more complex meters. For example, Africans produce polyrhythms by moving arms and legs to different meters. One favorite Oriental rhythmic style consists of a steady four in the legs (and the percussion section) while the arms follow a free metered melody of a lead instrument." That kind of analyzing is sometimes seen by today's musicologists to be something akin to racial profiling, wildly out of fashion as more social and cultural explanations for musicking are preferred, staying clear of such resounding absolutes. I don't really buy it. I prefer the more beguiling appeal of the insect model for in-phase, out-of-phase rhythms.

It's what ethnomusicologists Steven Feld and Charles Keil write about in their quest to make sense of the *groove,* the mysterious sense of the best rhythmic music that quickly makes us all want to dance along. The Kaluli people Feld studied in New Guinea offered a whole musical explanation for the ecological balance they felt in their rainforest home, *dulugu ganalan,* or "lift-up-over-sounding," a wonderful idea that finds its way into all of my music books. But this time I'll add the more technical explanation for how these forest dwellers sense their relation to all the thrumming, beating, rhythmic overlaps of their Papuan home: relationships to their surroundings that are both "in synchrony and also out of phase."

Going along with the beat, but not quite on the beat. Don't mean a thing if it ain't got that swing. The perfect appeal of uneven evenness. Nature not Platonic but just slightly off. We find our way into reality by delving deep into the buzz, by charting the noise, mapping the chaos. Our world is not perfect, and was never meant to be. Once we recognize that, hear music in the fuzziness, only then are we halfway home.

Simha Aron writes of Central African music that its polyrhythms are full of quasiperiodicity, repeating patterns that never quite repeat the same way ever again. The difficulty of catching them, writing them down, or describing them is the key to the greatness of the groove. In hundreds of pages, he argues that the music he has painstakingly analyzed is as structurally complex and rich as the hundreds of years of Western classical tradition we have a far easier time taking seriously as deep expression. We have polyphony, layers of tones and harmony, while Africa has much more nuanced polyrhythmics, overlapping rhythms of great rule and complexity always more irregular and impossible to pin down than we would like. We don't take it seriously enough to easily join in and find the groove. I say, listen more seriously to the insects, and one more kind of human music will seem deeper and more historically resonant.

Do I insult thousands of years of human innovation here? Could we really learn such complexity in music, such overlapping, brilliant inexactness from insects? The Swedish researcher into the evolution of music, primate specialist Björn Merker, certainly thinks so. Merker notes that this kind of entrainment is, like the vocal learning that marked the uniqueness of songbirds, whales, and humans in my previous books, rare in the animal world. Bugs can synchronize, frogs can synchronize, even some species of crabs. But few other primates show much interest in dancing to a single beat. Might the rediscovery of rhythm, something way back in our evolutionary history, be one of those things that propelled humanity forward into the stratosphere of unique creativity and bliss?

He outlines yet another hypothesis for why humans care about synchronization, where other species might not. Go back to our relative who shares 99 percent of our genes. What makes them dance? Well, it happens very rarely. Sometimes a hungry group discovers a tree full of surprisingly ripe fruit. Maybe two groups who haven't seen each other in a while get all worked up in a fabulous reunion. On such festive occasions the apes launch into something called the carnival display: "The animals launch an excited bout of loud calling, stomping, bursts of running, slapping of tree buttresses, and other means of chaotic noise-making. . . . They may last for hours, even a whole night, and induce distant subgroups on the territory to approach and join the fray."

No synchronization to the groove with them, eh? So why do humans add to this wild rumpus the special fact of the steady, if elusive beat? Maybe we, too, need something of that thrumming, pulsing, party atmosphere of the great chorus of male crickets, katydids, or cicadas that leads female insects to their mates. The disco, the rave, the place of loud, synchronized music. That's what Merker wonders:

> Perhaps, then, the genus Homo descended from an ancestral subpopulation of the common ancestor of chimpanzees and humans that evolved the entrainment mechanism necessary to get hoots to superpose precisely in time by yoking them to a common tactus. Thus amplified the sound of the carnival display would reach migrating females to sway their choice of migratory target, giving the synchronizers a reproductive advantage driving a speciation event. If so, they would at the same time have taken the step to a fundamental structural device of music: the co-ordination of rhythmic behavior through mutual entrainment to an isochronous pulse.

Yes, we can latch onto the beat. Yes, something about us resists the urge to complete chaos in our noisemaking! Human music always seeks some kind of order or organization to our sound, even as we bring on the noise. We seek ever wilder attributes of thrum but we still need it to make sense. We don't want to be savage primates now, do we? We've got entrainment, we've got mathematics, we demand the groove! Indeed, Merker has even subjected humans to the kinds of tests Pierce and Alexander did with their captured katydids a few decades earlier—make your human subject hear a thump, then a thud, then try to clap along with it. With attractive pale-gray scatterplots they show that humans have two combined entrainment systems at work when we try to clap to a beat—a tendency to keep our own steady pulse, whatever we think it is, and to copy what we hear. These two vague ideas are the mechanisms that lead human beings to be able to make sense of rhythm, the rhythm of flashing fireflies, electronic dance beats, jungle drums, or the ripples of falling water. Once again we are among a small cadre of animals that cares about such patterns. Merker concludes this mysterious ability is not just a key in grasping the origins of music, but of human nature itself.

One of those parts of human nature that connects us this time not to whales and birds (those other creatures who love melody as much as we do), but to bugs and frogs, those who also love the beat. If you think such love is closer to language than to music, because messages are supposed to be more important than songs, then imagine that these repetitive sounds are like the simplest phrases transmitted by talking drums in Africa, where a series of drum patterns has been used for centuries, like a kind of ancient Morse code, to transmit words and phrases. John Carrington describes it thus: *ki ke ki ke ki ke ki ke,* allofyou allofyou allofyou allofyou, *ya . . . ku . . . ya . . . ku . . . ya . . . ku . . . ,* come . . . here . . . come . . . here . . . come . . . here . . . , and the choruses of creatures and humans gather and assemble.

The rest of West African drum languages, with their ingenious mirrorings of the tonal qualities of spoken languages, are much more akin to the working of modern information theory, a parallel which begins James Gleick's magisterial study of the history of information. Rhythms can almost talk, can express nearly everything spoken languages can express. But the endless repetition of the basic phrases does not do that, yet still needs to repeat, over and over again. It is a call to gather, a cry to dance. If we did not love the beat so much we would not want to hear the same sounds, over and over and over again.

But we do. One sound can be enough if it repeats enough enough enough enough times so the meaning becomes subservient to the sound. Our love for beating, pulsing music, runs way down deep to some of the most ancient and numerous species that populate this Earth. Do not be afraid of this connection, but use it to hear a surrounding world ever more purposeful, ever more beautiful.

FOUR

Listen Outside the Ear

I n the 1940s the Swedish entomologist Frej Ossiannilsson suspected that the world of insect sounds was wider than most
people thought. Noticing the curious up and down motions of
tiny leafhoppers, relatives of the cicadas, he decided to investigate.
He picked up the insects, most about the size of a grain of rice,
and put them at the end of a small glass tube, 1 cm in diameter
and 8 cm in length. Then he put the other end to his ear, and he
listened. The leafhoppers were making rhythmic sounds by thumping their tymbals. Ossiannilsson wrote down what he heard in
musical notation. Here is just one example of the many pages he
transcribed:

Sometimes the hopper was loud enough so that if he put it on a resonating surface, say a fiddle or violin, then the *tap-tap-tap*-ing was suitably amplified to be describable. Or, he used a variation of the old telephone game. Keep the bug in the tube, then wrap a fine wire tightly around the tube. Then extend the rest of the wire long and straight, and wrap it around another tube. Put said tube next to your ear. Sometimes notation was not enough; he had to resort to words:

I counted 26 notes. The last trilling note is more prolonged than the others and falls towards the end in intensity of sound, finally fading away altogether. A very imperfect endeavour to vocalize this song is the following:

"kr - kr - kr - krrr - kr - krrr - kr - kr - krrr - kr - kr - krrr - kr - kr - krrr -
- kr - kr - krrr-kr-kr-kr-krrr-kr-kr-kr-krrr-kr-kr-kr-krrr-kr-kr-
-kr-krrr-kr-kr-kr-krrrrrrrrrrrrrrrrrrrrrrr-greeo-greeo-greeo-greeo-greeo-greeo-
-greeo-greeo-greeo-greeo-greeo-greeo-greeo-greeo-greeo-greeo-greeo-greeo-
-greeo-greeo-greeo-greeo-greeeeeeeee".

When to use music notation and when to use words? Neither is enough for such alien and irregular code–like repeating sounds. It is remarkable that these sounds are so much more complex individually than the more familiar insect choruses of cicadas, crickets, and katydids. Of course these are nearly unknown because we need such specialized technology to hear them.

In earlier chapters I've shown how insect musical complexity comes from group dynamics—many simple sounds combined in a rule-based rhythmic way. But here we have tiny insects making sounds that are as intricate as the more basic birdsongs. It was truly a revelation to discover that such very small insects were producing signals of this level of structure. Ossiannilsson's hand-drawn catalog of the oscillograms looks like fragments of mysterious ciphers:

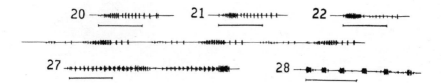

His groundbreaking 1949 book *Insect Drummers* describes the full sound range of ninety-six species of tiny plant hoppers and leafhoppers whose melodies he was the first to notice and describe in detail. Ossiannilsson called it all "insect drumming" because the tiny hoppers make the sound with a miniature version of the drum-like tymbal that their relatives the cicadas have, but we now know that they are not tapping on the membrane, but vibrating it with muscles that surround the round drumhead of an organ.

Bugs take in sound in through a variety of mysterious means. They feel the music with a precision nearly unattainable to human perception. So many insect rhythms are communicated through media we can barely recognize the existence of. By a range of sensory exotica, bugs can feel rumbles in the earth or the stalks they stand on that could more accurately be called vibrations, not quite sounds. But there is no boundary between the two for most insect species. They sense pulses and tones in ways that defy our dividing the senses of touch and hearing into two.

Many insects hear with hair follicles located in different parts of their bodies, most often the legs but also on their backs and heads. Many of the most acoustically oriented bugs have tympanal organs, like little eardrums, located sometimes on their heads but, in the case of crickets and their kin, right on the tibia part of their legs. The picture below shows the directional hearing range of each leg in a bush katydid:

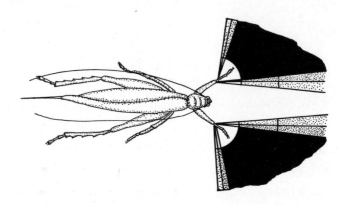

Some of these organs sense air displacement, others sense pressure. Some species are attuned to precise frequencies, others to more general vibrations. These listening methods are keyed to the various ways insects make sound.

Crickets and katydids make diverse rhythmic and tonal sounds by stridulation, where one part of the body is rubbed against another. Some rub legs against wings, wings against wings, and there is a water beetle that vibrates its own penis against his abdomen underwater to produce one of the loudest sounds made by any animal. Cicadas make the loudest airborne insect sounds with a tymbal in their abdomen that they vibrate to make an enormous noise. Here is a detailed diagram of their midsection:

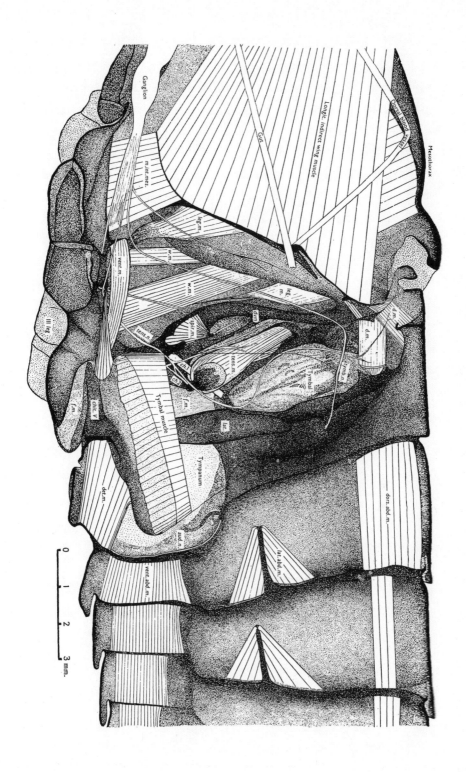

Ganglion

Longit. indirect wing muscle

Gut

Mesothorax

Dorsal blood vessel

m.int.mes.

leg.m.

w.m.

vent.m.

w.m.

leg. m.

d.m.

d.m.

tens.n.

cn.

cn.

d.m.

tens.n.

Tymbal

tymb.m.

III leg

cn.

f.m.

cn.

l.m.

cn.V

f.m.

lat.

Tymbal muscle

det.m.

Tympanum

vent.abd.m.

lat.abd.m.

abd.n.

dors.abd.m.

0

1

2

3 mm.

A similar organ is used by treehoppers to thrum vibrations down onto the plant stalks they inhabit. Bees and flies produce communicating sounds by beating their wings, and others create vibrations by shaking their bodies, or tapping their abdomens onto the substrate they stand on. Given the vast diversity of forms insects have evolved, if there is a way their bodies can be manipulated to create sound, some species have no doubt tried it.

When it comes to sonic communication, where does sound end and vibration begin? This can be a very difficult question to answer, says Peggy Hill in *Vibrational Communication in Animals*. For the ways insects pick up the vibrations are so different from the hearing we usually associate with sound—ears on the side of the head—that the difference between sound and feeling may be moot. Many species of flies and their relatives hear with the Johnston's organ that is at the base of their antennae. Here it is on one kind of mosquito:

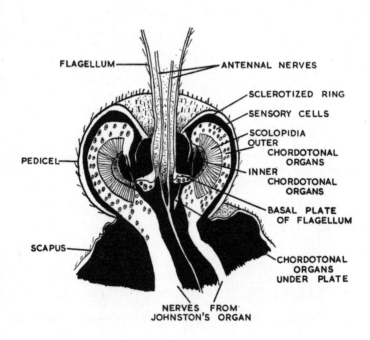

The Johnston's organ is endowed with a large array of nerve cells, which makes it supersensitive to sound, but in a manner totally different than a mammal's ear. This exotic body part can pick up vibration as well as sound, and Hill explains that it matters less whether the sound is heard or felt, but rather what the medium is through which it travels. It's a form of convergent evolution, where nature has evolved totally different specialized organs to achieve the same end in very different ways. Female plant hoppers can signal on rice plants and get responses from males nearly three feet away, perched on different branches of the plant. They only respond to that part of the signal that can be transmitted via the stalks, not anything that travels through the air. These sounds travel faster, farther, and more subtly, because sound actually moves more efficiently through solids than through air, since the molecules are more dense. The sounds of these tiny bugs all contain broadband pulses, which then can divide up as different frequencies travel through the solid stalk at different speeds. Differences in arrival time of the frequencies can help the receiver estimate the distance from the signaler.

Last summer I remember standing beneath one small fruit tree on Main Street as I marveled at the overlapping rhythmic complexity of the low canopy full of invisible snowy tree crickets, coming in and out of sync like a complex polyrhythmic band. The music was sublime. On the next page is one perched on a hole in a leaf.

Tree crickets have been found to choose specific tree species because of their specific resonant qualities. They want to be able to feel sound through the trees they alight upon and eat. On the other hand, a survey of fifteen species of lacewing and their associated song revealed no correlation between specific kinds of songs and specific habitat plants, suggesting that the preference for one kind of song rather than another is a result of the "arbitrary" kind of sexual selection where females just happen to

choose one kind of music over many generations just because they like it, for no practical reason at all.

However, actual evidence that females choose males on the basic of specific vibrations in bugs is rare. The ground weta of New Zealand, a giant cricket-like creature with a body up to 4 inches in length, only mates on large leaves upon which both males and females drum with the bottoms of their bellies. Each male sounds unique and different from all the others, and the female response sound also is distinctive between individuals. This is the kind of unique identifying behavior that we don't often find in insects, who we usually assume to be homogenous and swarm-like in their behavior.

Humans can also hear sound transmitted as vibrations. I think of Laurie Anderson's 1978 sculpture "The Handphone Table." Listeners at each end of a hollowed-out wooden table place their elbows on round indentations on each end of the table, and then place their hands on their ears. Loud sounds transmitted by speaker cones into the table are then transmitted through our own porous bones through our hands into our ears, giving us a glimmer of a sense of what crickets might feel being able to hear through their limbs.

In recent years we have developed better ways to record the taps and booms of vibrationally communicating insects. First phonograph cartridges, then later accelerometers, and most recently something called a laser vibrometer, which tracks Doppler shifts in reflected laser light, can be used to accurately track tiny bug vibratory signals and transpose them into sound. This is how Reginald Cocroft from the University of Missouri and his many students and collaborators have revealed to us some of the complex sounds of tropical treehoppers, sometimes of which there are hundreds on a single plant, producing a complex chorus like crickets or frogs.

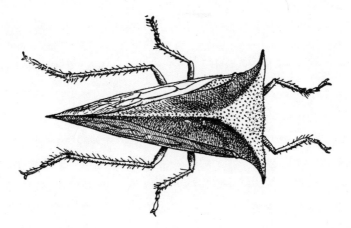

The remarkable thing about these sounds is how much more intricate they are than the simple chirps and scratches of crickets and katydids, and more structured and organized than the broad-band frequency thrums and whines of cicadas. How amazing that such intricacies in animal communication can be detected, at the very limits of human perception, by using sound-extending devices originally designed for very different purposes. The Cocroft lab not only advances our understanding of animal communication, but our aesthetic enjoyment of insect musical possibility. First off, it is absolutely astonishing that on a single plant, several male three-humped treehoppers can face off with each other by alternating, possibly competitive, calls. This is a sonogram of nine seconds of their encounter:

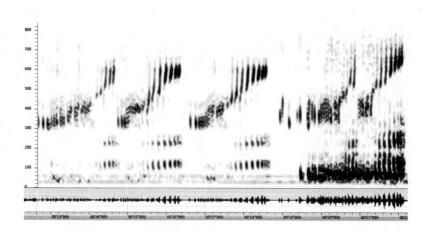

Like all sonograms in this book, this one maps frequency (pitch) on the vertical axis against time on the horizontal. The more vertical a line appears, the more the sound is a form of noise; the more horizontal, the closer it is to a clear pitched tone. The more separate structural elements you see in the picture, the more complex and structured the song is. And this is one of the most complicated songs made by any insect, and this one is vibrating his body on the tree, not making any kind of vocal sound at all. What he communicates through vibration is surprisingly more complicated than just about any insect song in the world.

Few audible, sung insect sounds approach this kind of complexity, and if you listen to it, the alternation between one male and another in Cocroft's famous recording is absolutely astonishing. This song battle is akin to what many bird species do, but these are far more complex organisms than the tiny rice-grain-sized hopping bugs. Who would imagine these most minute creatures could have a method of communication so involved?

Stunned with surprise when first hearing that treehoppers made sounds like this, I was inspired to create a piece of music out of loops of this particular insect's sound, noticing that as it repeats it leads to an unprecedented rhythmic and phrase structure that is like nothing I had ever thought of before. I intensified the musicality of the thing by slowing it down, resonating it, repeating it, adding more instances to emulate the idea of a single plant full of hundreds of such signaling bugs. This then becomes the background for a sonic landscape upon which I combine a clarinet part, organized by the completely alien plant-borne aesthetic vibrational world. You can hear it on the *Bug Music* CD. When I played this sound for entomologist E. O. Wilson at a conference once, he had no idea what could be making such a sound, and when I told him it was a treehopper he just smiled.

Ever on the lookout for parallels between music and science, I was happy to see that Cocroft is investigating just how the acoustic filtering of such sounds needs to be studied to figure out how much of this broadband sound is actually transmitted through the stalks of plants, and how much dissipates into the air. His diagram of what to look out for looks just like the kind of musical effects electronic musicians are always applying to sound:

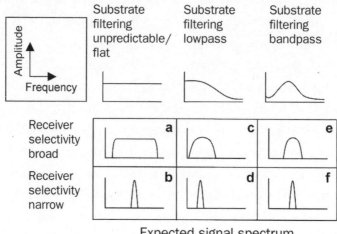

Expected signal spectrum

What this picture shows is the different ways of transmitting the sound through substrate (i.e., what the bug is standing on) can change its tonal qualities. When musicians think about such things they are going for which interests them. When the tree does it, it is a fact of nature, which the listening treehoppers just might innately pick up on. Move a treehopper to a different tree—not one of its natural hosts—and the signaling frequencies do not work correctly. They know something is wrong, and do not call as frequently as when on the correct plants. Cocroft and Rafael Rodriguez hypothesized that this is how new species of treehoppers develop: When an insect colonizes a new plant, he must evolve a new frequency for his signal, as indicated on this diagram that distinguishes between two related species. "Whine length" is a key factor. The females know what the correct sound is, and respond much more enthusiastically to the right whine, in pitch and in duration. This suggests that sexual selection, and the important factor of female choice, an aesthetic preference, has really made a difference in the evolution of these species. Cocroft notes that there are at least 200,000 species of insects that use vibrational communication to attract mates and defend their spot on the branch. Only a paltry few have been studied thus far. It is entirely possible that we will discover insect sounds of untold complexity, in vibrational ranges we can barely detect, in the future.

I am not the only one to find great musical possibility in such strange sounds. One of Cocroft's students, Peter Marting, has been working on treehopper communication. By placing an accelerometer inconspicuously on stalks of the Desmodium plant, he has been able to decipher very particular aspects of the song of *Tylopelta gibbera,* a tiny treehopper, like many, with no common name, native to the southern United States. In this species, Marting has been able to identify that the males and females sing a specific duet, like certain species of birds do. The male begins with an advertisement signal, which includes a few sharp pulses and then a whine. The female hopper responds with a soft moan. Depending on how he senses the female's response call, the male either walks toward the female or does an about-face, now ready to head in a new direction on the stalk.

If there are two males on the stalk, the situation changes. The female is going to mate with the first male who finds her. The males begin with the advertisement signal, then the female moans in response. But there's another male click and whine—*what!?* The first male now adds a second sound, which Marting calls the masking signal, a soft, continuous tone. Not loud, but just enough to cover up the pulsing clicks of the other male. He's trying to confuse the passing of the message, so the female can't tell which sound comes from whom. If the masking tone is produced exactly at the same time as the rival male's pulses begin, the female is most likely to get confused. The battle rages on. May the best and least-masked male singer win the challenge and get the girl.

It is absolutely remarkable that these treehoppers use sound in such a specific and sophisticated way, nearly akin to the observations

German birdsong scientists have made in Berlin on the jamming of rival signals by male nightingales. It is a precise and exact communication system, with each sound having a precise role in the signaling game. This schematic sonogram drawn by Marting highlights the different tonal qualities of each sound in this species's repertoire, and his research shows that the masking sound is most effective when it covers up the pulsing part of the male's love call:

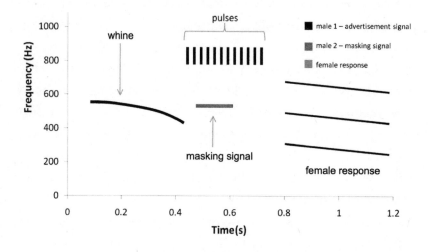

The sounds bugs make always make sense, even if it can be hard for us to decipher them. Call and response. Call, mask, and diminished response. Call again. Eventually the right response, and mating happens. Then the song begins again.

Marting is also a musician who has found plenty of use for the sounds of his research in his art. His alternative rock trio, Ptarmigan, released an album in 2011 called *The Forest Darling* with all sorts of resonances with his treehopper research. In the midst of various songs little blips and creaks appear, some of which are the sounds of insects never before recorded or heard by any humans. On some tracks he runs the vocals through the very devices used to run playback experiments with the treehoppers, to create a unique nature-based sound effect no one has ever used before:

> To talk to the insects in our lab we use a playback device called an "actuator" that attaches to the branch and vibrates like a treehopper to trick the insects into responding. Usually, we play the synthesized insect sounds through the actuator while we record it all using the accelerometer. For the album, we took the vocal track from "We, the Forest," played it through the actuator, and recorded it with the accelerometer. Thus, the vocal track was sent as a vibrational signal from the actuator through the living plant and picked up by the accelerometer about 20 cm away. *Treeverb.*

The effect is muffled, distant, ever more mysterious once you know how it is made. On another track, "Sentient," there is an electronic solo played by a random melody generator, a piece of software usually used by Marting to confuse insects in their on-stalk travels.

I wouldn't say Ptarmigan's music is immediately noticeable as being inspired by the insect world of vibrational communication, but it's a solid band nonetheless with a good story behind it. We usually prefer our popular music being only a little different than what we expect, that's what still keeps it listenable, popular, fitting into what our society wants. It is this paradox that all musicians bewitched by new and strange sounds must deal with—how to retain an audience, how to lead an audience on, from the familiar to the unknown or the insane. That's what philosopher Theodor Adorno famously said was wrong with pop music; by its very nature it can only pretend to be new and different because people, like humpback whales, don't really want songs that are completely new and different, only a little bit different, familiar enough to be danced and tapped to, new enough to excite us, but fundamentally always the same. That's why it's popular.

Most lovers of popular music, and there are a lot of us because the music *is* popular, don't take much stock in Adorno's views on something he cared little about, but he may have a point; think how most people react when they hear a kind of music that is genuinely, totally, utterly strange and new. We don't know what to make of it. Experimental musician, sound artist, composer, and musical philosopher David Dunn had produced such music for years, with varying reactions from the public, until he finally found out what his music was best for: disrupting the mating cycle of tiny pine bark beetles and making them tear each other to shreds.

Dunn was already performing out in the wilderness back in the 1980s. He played loud sirens to mockingbirds in the desert. He tossed a hydrophone into a local pond and heard an astonishing melee of underwater insect communication. But as a musician, he still first of all wants people to listen: "If I am doing a concert, I sometimes ask the audience to suspend their expectations of what music is—listen to this as if you would to a swamp or to a forest." Hear the alien communication between other animals as a moment of music, not language, where each syllable is not the same message called over and over again, "I'm here I'm here I'm here I'm here," but instead a tiny phrase so beguiling that the other sex who hears it is filled with such joy that they have no choice but to approach.

Since the year 2000, nearly seventy thousand acres of forest, an area equal to the size of the whole of Washington State, has died, because of the destructive actions of tiny bark beetles no bigger than a grain of rice. The beetles have in the past tended to attack immature, weaker trees, and the effect of their actions is tempered by the general balance of ecology. But this time, because of global shifts in the climate, things are truly getting out of hand. Some reports say that if you count all the species of forest-killing beetles, especially the spruce eaters in Alaska and the Yukon, more than 800,000 acres were destroyed in 2003 alone! All across the Rocky Mountains, huge swaths of once-green forest now lie brown and dessicated. Millions of tiny, tree-munching beetles are to blame.

In many people's minds all insects should be considered pests, threats, enemies to humanity, anything but objects of admiration and affection. Until now I have been blithely extolling their virtues, urging you to enjoy their sounds, making great claims as to their value not environmentally but culturally, claiming that they even teach us to dance. Yet we have of course evolved to fear insects. They are the absolute *other* among life-forms. Each one is tiny, simple, machine-like, predictable, everything that mammals with individual minds are not. Insects individually do a few things precisely and well, with no need to think about anything else. Together they move mountains, form vast societies, follow mathematical rules of music, and when times are tough and the world is out of balance, they kill. Oh, yes, do they kill. By 2020 between sixty and eighty percent of all the harvestable forests of British Columbia, once the richest forestry area in the world, are expected to be devastated by bark beetles. No single group of animal species has wrought this much destruction upon the natural environment since the Pleistocene.

And why has this never happened before? We don't really know, but it is likely that warming temperatures has upset the natural boom and bust cycle of such infestations, as now the beetles are reproducing more times in a single year. The winters aren't strong enough to kill them off. It's a great ecological tragedy that humans have so far been powerless to stop (though our poor forestry habits may share some of the blame for the crisis).

David Dunn saw the merciless work of the pinyon engraver beetle, *Ips confusus,* right outside his house in Santa Fe. One by one, all the pinyon pines were being killed. No one had any idea what to do about it. So what could a musician do, especially one who had spent years seeking out the far corners of perceptible natural sound? First he had to figure out how to listen. Just as Ossiannilsson decades before had turned long glass tubes into bug-amplifying devices, and Cocroft and Marting used vibrometers and accelerometers to turn inaudible vibrations into new musical sound to decode the mating rituals of plant hoppers, Dunn developed his own tools. After using homemade hydrophones to listen underwater to the incredibly complex gamelan-like peregrinations of submerged insects in ordinary backyard ponds, he wondered what sounds might be happening inside these dying trees.

He was tipped off by a chance remark by a Native Pueblo elder, who said that "the beetles come when our trees are crying." What sounds happen inside a tree? Could we find a way to listen deep in there? Dunn makes the most out of inexpensive tools easily available. His beetle listening device—we could call it an "arborophone"—was made out of a ten-dollar meat thermometer, with a tiny piezo bender disc from a Hallmark greeting card (the little device that makes the card sing when you open it up) as the sensor. He stuck it inside the phloem layer of a pinyon tree and began to hear astonishing, multipart sounds of the beetles not only munching, but communicating to each other, in ways no one had ever heard before.

"I had no other way of approaching it," says Dunn, "other than to imagine what their world was like, by trying to place myself inside their world." The meat thermometer functioned as a wave guide, to direct the source of the insect-made vibrations inside the tree. For several years he recorded hundreds of hours of the wide range of sounds made by the pinyon engravers, and composed out of this material a single hour-long piece called *The Sound of Light in Trees,* which was released by EarthEar Records in 2006. Dunn made this record as a true environmental soundscape composition, trying to organize the full range of sounds he heard inside these pinyon pines into a full aesthetic whole:

> There is a kind of *acoustical signature* to a small tree. But on a large tree, each branch has its own sound. When you move the transducer to a different location you find an entirely different sound world, with sub-communities and distinct behaviors and things that will reveal that you wouldn't find. This was my compositional strategy: If I had a really large single tree and I could put hundreds of these transducers and could record all simultaneously, I tried to convey the sum total of such a sound.

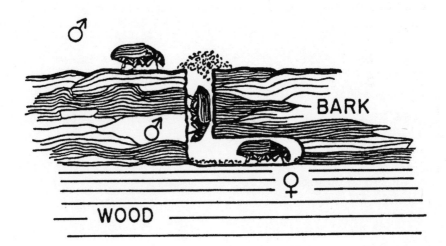

When I hear this recording, I confront a vast and strange sonic landscape, layers of unfamiliar sounds that I can't place in the least.

There are strange, muffled birdlike chirps, faint treehopperesque moans, then rocking stridulations that sound like alien crickets. If someone told me this was fossilized recordings of dinosaurs I would probably believe them. But when Dunn listens, he hears each sound exactly in its place. He has become a connoisseur of the alien sonic world, which he was the first to discover a way to listen to.

How do these beetles hear? As with many insects, the question does not have a simple answer. They have a tympanal organ that resembles an ear. But they also have tiny hair follicles that pick up all manner of sound and vibration. These bugs are so, so tiny and they make so many different kinds of sound that Dunn wonders if it might not be more accurate to say that "the entire beetle is the ear." That their whole bodies might be wrapped up in the matter of sounding, and of hearing, intertwined with their microenvironment inside the tree in an acoustic ecology that we might actually be able to hear and decipher while taking in Dunn's soundscape compositions made out of his field recordings. He knows this is a wholly wild idea:

> My working hypothesis for this project reads more like science fiction than science fact. I am theorizing that a much more complex microecology exists between bark beetles, various fungi, and their host trees. Sound probably has a much more profound role in regulating the dynamics of these relationships than previously suspected.

These are the kind of engravings the beetles make beneath the bark of the trees they destroy:

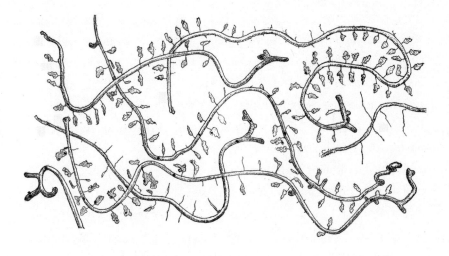

Dunn knows his approach cannot count as science before years of rigorous testing. And when he released the record he had no intention of doing that. "I readily admit just how fanciful my flights of hypothetical imagination might be, not to mention my lack of scientific credentials, but I also happen to think that this is one of the most important roles for artists in forging a new collaborative relation with science: science fiction that might lead to science fact." Artists can dare to dream where scientists cannot, or are at least discouraged to do so, since ideas like Dunn's prove very difficult to test. But they immediately inspire.

Of all soundscape composers, David Dunn is among the most possessed by speculative wonder. His compositions are each assembled precisely from hours of unique nature recordings of phenomena few others have deemed interesting, or even possible to record. Once the music is conserved, Dunn specifically wants you to listen carefully, not so much critically in the sense of deciding whether you like it or not, but meticulously, so you may be able to hear the senses of order that he believes can be explicitly heard. The beetles are not planning a grand acoustic raid on their host trees or our senses. They communicate for the usual specific male–female reasons. Their signaling does blend in beautifully with the innate sounds of their trees. Then in concert, their environment is destroyed. The forests are decimated, the nibbling, stridulating song goes on, and until now, no one has been able to hear it or even has suspected that sound could be so important a part of the beetles' epidemic lives.

The emergent soundscape inside these trees is chaotic, destructive, but that does not mean it is unlistenable. Dunn has aspirations for a theory of musical order emerging out of chaos, which he has worked on together with the theoretical physicist and chaotic systems modeler James Crutchfield. For the bark beetles this is manifest as a complex acoustic world where sounds are made far beyond what seems to be easily understood. Is the similarity in sound between beetle and tree pure coincidence, or might the beetles be able to pick up on acoustic cues to identify drought-stricken, vulnerable pines that make good candidates for attack? Maybe we cannot hear, as the Pueblos wanted us to, when the trees are crying, but perhaps the beetles get these cries right away. Their signaling is supposed to be about these necessary behaviors: host selection, coordination of tree attack, courtship, territorial competition, and excavation of the nuptial chambers where mating will take place. But after all this has happened, the beetles keep making all sorts of sounds for weeks—stridulating, chirping, clicking—long after the hard work is done. Dunn and Crutchfield hypothesize that they may have a far more complex social organization, something akin to an ant colony, where sonic communication is necessary to maintain social cohesion and group activity.

Dunn was crafting his wild compositions, influenced as much as possible by bark beetle aesthetics. With Crutchfield he was trying to turn his hunches into science. Meanwhile, the beetles were destroying huge swaths of great Western forest. This work could become much more than a curious experiment; perhaps it could help stop the voracious beasts! Reagan McGuire, a Flagstaff area writer, heard of Dunn's recording and remembered tales of how the U.S. military had used musical warfare from helicopters in Vietnam, and in Panama blasted Manuel Noriega out of his asylum in the local Vatican embassy by blaring rock music at him twenty-four hours a day. These methods were long known to be successful on humans, so if beetles care so much about sound, why not fight them with exactly the sounds which they like the least?

Together with Northern Arizona University beetle researcher Richard Hofstetter, McGuire and Dunn took some bark beetles into the lab and began to bombard them with sound. They tried all the most assaulting examples they could think of: Metallica, Guns N' Roses, even the screeds of Rush Limbaugh: "I wanted an authoritative, agitating, and repeatable voice I could play back again and again. I also wanted to stress the hell out of the beetles, and I thought that hate radio would do it. . . . It was not a political statement."

It also didn't work. The beetles had no interest in these scary human sounds. Then Hofstetter suggested the perfectly reasonable assumption of using beetle-like sounds. They piped in a louder-than-actual male advertisement sound and the females immediately tried to move toward the source of the sound.

Dunn suggested the following next experiment. Western pine beetles and southern pine beetles attack the same kind of tree, but you never find both species in a single tree. Why? They played the sound of a southern pine beetle to a colony of western beetles, and they saw a male mate with a female several times and then afterward chew her to pieces. "You know, you don't see that in nature," said McGuire. "It's just not natural." The wrong sound was enough to incite such deviance.

David Dunn is, as usual, going farther. He is finding that the most maddening sounds to a beetle are those that are least linear and most chaotic, ironically just like the music he has gotten most interested in making as a composer! Take that you passive contemporary audience . . . this music is so unpredictable and powerful that it can actually *kill*.

I asked him what he really means by chaotic music. "How chaotic are each of your circuits that you make?"

"They are mathematically defined as being chaotic. You sort of actively have to turn one knob. This pushes them through these bifurcation states. So they are doing these phase transitions within the phase space, and as they bifurcate they go from a single tone into noise. As it bifurcates it moves from a periodic circle of simple harmonic motion into these double scroll attractors. Currently in the system there are eight such oscillators and everything is in dyads so they are built up from groups of two into four, and then four. The only thing that connects them is the resistance network. Which means that if you change one factor, it changes everything, of course it is in totally unpredictable way."

"What does it sound like?" I asked.

"At times you are hearing just simple wave forms, other times you are hearing dense noise bands, and you just have to imagine everything in between where some of them are being noise bands, some of them are being simple oscillations and they are shifting and influencing so the transitions could be extraordinarily abrupt. Our familiarity with electronic oscillators is linear and limited, and they don't easily explain those sounds. These things are really fast transitions that explode, like the beetle sounds inside the trees. These complex behaviors emerge out of very simple elements;

you don't need very much guidance behind them at all. You get these semiperiodic kind of things that drift and you've got clicks, you got these incredible noise bands. It is the transitions I find really compelling. The bark beetle stridulations can go from these simple little clicks, to these fast dance noise bands, and they can do that so quickly. So that is very much what these oscillators do, too."

I put on Dunn's "beetle-stimulus" music and examine what effect it has on me. It is uneasy, strange, grumbling, violent, impure. If I knew nothing of its provenance I would have no idea what I'm hearing, except that it sounds like something is chewing mercilessly at the side of my ear through the headphones. *Let me out! Let me go! Can you explain?* Dunn plays such sounds back to the beetles and they tear each other to shreds. What more convincing reaction to one's music could one hope for than that? He knows his sounds matter, because it drives his insect audience to turn on themselves with unprecedented violence.

Despite the provocative nature of this research, there have really been absolutely *no* official scientific publications of bark beetle acoustic research. Jayne Yack's lab at Carleton University is working on the problem, but so far no refereed, officially sanctioned scientific publications have appeared. I did catch two poster presentations at the Invertebrate Sound and Vibration Meeting at the University of Missouri in June 2011, and there S. Sivalinghem delivered this report on the acoustic activity of *Ips pini,* the pine engraver bark beetle:

Females produced low-intensity (69 dB SPL; at 1 cm) chirps through a vertex-pronotum stridulatory mechanism. Signals consisted of multiple tooth-strikes with peak frequencies between 12–25 kHz. Distress chirps had significantly higher peak frequency (24 kHz) and tooth-strike rate than did pre-mating chirps (13 kHz), implying possible differences in signal function. Only signaling females entered male nuptial chambers, and chirp rates significantly decreased after entrance, suggesting that these signals function for species recognition. Also, chirps produced four minutes after entrance had significantly slower tooth-strike rates, indicating that pre-mating signals may serve different functions depending on the stage of the encounter.

Interesting—four minutes after entering the mating chamber the female sounds changed. And what of male sounds? Sivalinghem didn't record anything.

But his colleague Amanda Lindeman did a more broad survey of all the kinds of sounds the male beetles produce. She described "sounds produced by males in three different behavioral contexts: distress, male-female interactions and male-male aggressive interactions. Acoustic signals varied in their temporal and spectral properties depending on the behavioral context. For example, male distress signals were 'simple' chirps, characterized as a series of uninterrupted toothstrikes (mean: 28), and an average duration of 43ms. These chirps were broadband (13 to 27 kHz at −10 dB) with distinct peaks at around 9, 28, 56, and 75 kHz and an average dominant frequency at 8.91 kHz. Conversely, male chirps during male-female interactions were complex, with 3 to 5 distinct components. These chirps were twice as long as distress chirps, and had most dominant energy below 5 kHz. Other recorded signals were simple and complex male-male aggressive chirps, simple female chirps, and clicks during male-female encounters." Neither of these more mainstream scientific investigations of bark beetle sounds has yet been published. In fact the last refereed journal paper on the acoustics of these critters was published in 1988! Why nothing since then while the devastation wrought by the beetles has been so immense? Until David Dunn, no one thought the sounds were of great importance.

When I asked Sivalinghem what he thought of David Dunn's work in this area, he said that Dunn's conclusions were not so robust scientifically, but without his daring to listen inside the trees, no one would have thought this research was possible at all. So just as Dunn wished, his "science fiction" has begat a whole new branch on entomological acoustics, whose more rigorously quantified research results will soon be reaching us. Art comes more easily from nature than science, and that is as it should be. And the science of the sound will be deeper if it accepts the aesthetic attitude that keeps Dunn going: What is the sense of mind and order that the chaotic music of miniscule insects presents to us? Before calculating anything, we still must carefully listen.

And with all these vibration studies, listening outside the ear has revealed unknown realms of the Earth's imperceptible animal music. The farther we listen, the more we learn of the incredible lengths insects can go in their use and abuse of sound. For another astonishing example, listen to what insects do underwater. Two decades ago David Dunn revealed the richness of the entomological aquatic soundscape with his piece "Chaos and the Emergent Mind of the Pond," and only now have scientists made some headway with the submerged stridulations of waterborne beetles. It turns out that one of these tiny creatures makes the loudest sound compared to body weight of any animal on or beneath the Earth! *Micronecta scholtzi,* the lesser water boatman, is a European pond insect only a few millimeters in length. By rubbing a ridge on its miniscule 50 micrometer penis against its abdomen, it can make a sound 99 decibels in volume, louder than a jackhammer 50 feet away, a freight train whizzing by, or a symphony orchestra from the front row.

How can such a noise be possible? The boatman makes it by rubbing its own penis against its body. Readers, please don't try this at home, even above water. You cannot do better than this little-known water bug, more often heard than seen. When Scottish researcher James Windmill and his French collaborator Jérôme Sueur first dunked their hydrophone in the pond and heard this sound, they couldn't believe it, and were sure something was wrong with their instruments.

We usually assume it takes a big animal to make a tremendous racket, and on such a scale the lesser water boatman is a true outlier. True, a blue whale's subsonic tones can reach 188 decibels, but that whale is millions times bigger than this tiny bug. Why does this guy need to make such a massive sound to attract its mate? Actually no one knows. Surely the females aren't coming from *so* far away. The authors of the study, a physicist and a biologist together, suggest that this might be sexual selection run amok, an extreme like the nightingale's song or the peacock's tail, the kind of story I celebrated in *Survival of the Beautiful,* extremes of nature that evolution produces not because they are necessary, but because they are possible, and sometimes preferred by the aesthetics residing in females of the species, who somehow get away with it, showing that evolution can produce extremes of volume, complexity, and beauty, because the mechanism for runaway selection is always there, lurking beneath our wishful thinking for practicality and survival of the fittest.

Here is our penis-whacking outlier himself:

His massive penile noise might exist just because female water boatmen (boatwomen?) like it, and in nature, that may be just as good a reason as any. More practically minded biologists are usually not pleased with explanations like this. Nature is full of pragmatics waiting for us to uncover. Ought there not be a good reason for everything in acoustic ecology's perfect balance? It really depends on what you want to know.

The tremendous water boatman sound is so anomalous, so far from what we expect a little bug to be capable of, that we may not be able to explain it on rational, practical grounds. But who said nature is practical? It is a lifeworld of extremes—look what those tiny bark beetles are capable of! Look how complex the vibrations of treehoppers can be! Listen to how sound in the minute insect world does things we would never expect it to be able to achieve.

So I present the amazing water boatman to you, a story that, no surprise, has been widely reported in media all over the world. Usually the headlines announce "LOUDEST ANIMAL IN THE WORLD

IS A TINY BEETLE WHACKING OFF 100 DB WITH ITS PENIS" or something like that. Now it's not quite the loudest per se, but by far the loudest when compared to body weight. Is it fair for the media to exaggerate so? We want our stories to be extreme so that they catch us off guard and make us pay attention. I want you to be convinced that insect sounds are much more interesting than you thought before picking up this book. This story ought to help—most of the boatman's fabulous noise is only transmitted underwater, but some of it can reach our ears on land. So listen closely next time you walk past a late spring pond, teeming with life, singing bugs careening through the shallows and the deeps. You won't hear much, but if those boatmen are at work, a faint buzz may cut through.

If you drop a hydrophone down, though, it might be another story. For a sample of that, there is no better recording than Tom Lawrence's *Water Beetles of Pollardstown Fen,* released by the field recording label Gruenrekorder in 2011, certainly the finest series of underwater beetle recordings ever made, and one of the best field recordings ever made at that, easily rivaling the genre's best seller, *Songs of the Humpback Whale.* The range of sounds made by aquatic insects goes far beyond anything loudest or biggest. It is also most strange, most surprising, and most beautiful. You may imagine motorboats, birdsongs, or old-school electronic oscillators, but if you get your ears in that take-it-all-in state that David Dunn recommends, you will hear something totally beautiful. Suspend your disbelief after starting to take in all this stridulation, and you will experience an insect chorus at least as complex as what we hear on land. Sound behaves differently in water, such that it is very hard to tell where any particular sound comes from, since there is very little sense of audio directionality when submerged. This may be one reason the bugs need such a wide range of sounds to make themselves heard. The diversity of tones and rhythms is astonishing, and it does resemble a composition with a structure we can barely tap into. It's been going on for millions of years before humans appeared on this Earth. "This," suggests Tom Lawrence, "is the origin of music," among creatures who have not yet evolved the need to crawl up on land and begin to take stock of things.

Lawrence uses the field recordist's standard composition technique of compressing what he heard in hundreds of hours of field recordings into the most interesting playlist of fabulous sounds. But I suspect his working method is much more than that; each of his underwater bug pieces are true compositions, musical works made out of amazing source material. Not only a daring sound seeker, Lawrence is a fine electroacoustic composer as well. His longest track is a thirteen-minute performance of one water scorpion singing a very defensive sound, just 1 inch from the hydrophone. Though all these sounds have specific practical acoustic purposes in the lives of these insects, I do not think it is wrong for humans to call them beautiful and hear it all as music. As extreme aesthetic evolutions, these sounds may be appreciated for their collective beauty by us just as their individual beauty is appreciated by the female insects the sounds are directed toward. It's the least we can do for our insect relatives. We're all connected through the vast music of life.

Indeed, the presence of sounds even inside the body of insects has been proposed by some scientists as a very indicator of life itself. Going down to the nano level, far beyond what conventional microphones could hope to pick up, scientists at Clarkson University have recorded tones of vibrating, living molecules inside the bodies of mosquitoes and flies. Through a technique called atomic force microscopy, Igor Sokolov and his colleagues have been able to record tiny surface vibrations going on at the molecular level in immobilized insects, including flies, mosquitoes, and ladybugs.

In a comparison of live and dead bugs, the molecular motion is quite different.

Amplify the result into sound and one can listen to the very tone of life itself, far beneath and beyond the needs for communication, structure, or music. Why listen to such faint, foundational sounds at the very tiniest pulse of life? First of all, for the sake of curiosity, the old scientific goal that suggests that no frontier should be left unturned. Secondly, the distant implications could be tremendous. One day we might develop templates for exactly how our own living organs should sound, and develop the equivalent of atomic force stethoscopes to analyze the perfect thrumming sound of healthy human bodies, listening down at the tiniest molecular level. A doctor with a sophisticated nanomolecular listening device would be able to gauge your body's health by the detailed analysis by sound alone, a nano-stethoscope of the future.

I suppose all these edge-of-perception soundscapes we have considered in this chapter might be appreciated that way. Does an ideal, healthy, underwater bug soundscape have no human motors in the distance? Certainly an ideal pinyon pine soundscape has not a trace of beetle stridulation at all, unless you admit that some beetle infestation is a necessary part of forest ecology. And treehoppers, well, we have no idea what the healthy on-stalk vibrational soundscape ought to sound like. It is all beautiful, once you dare to listen. In the end such investigations suggest practical as well as artistic possibilities. The range of noise becomes musical material no one could have dreamed up in the ages before we could extend our senses to hear the very limits of movement and vibration at the tiniest reaches of the living world.

FIVE

From *El Grillo* to Das Techno

When I say that insect sound has influenced human music, people either fix me with a blank stare, or shake their heads and say, "Rothenberg, you've really taken this animal music obsession too far this time." Or they might hum Nikolai Rimsky-Korsakov's "Flight of the Bumblebee." I smile back and say you can't laugh at that piece, it's one of the most famous compositions of the nineteenth century and a litmus test for virtuosity on so many different instruments. Why? Because it's based on the sound of a bug. It's a song of the incompatibility of man and insect, and a struggle for a human instrumentalist to become what she is not.

It's hard to blend the discrete melodies and harmonies of our classical music with the weaving, buzzing, continuously sliding bee pitches. With all that chromatic warbling, melodic motion around and around, up and down, wavering and undecided, we see just how hard it is for our tempered instruments to sound much like an insect. In this famous minute-long showcase of dexterity, it's almost as if Rimsky wants to turn the orchestra into a warbling electronic oscillator, an instrument more comfortable with the sliding pitches and buzzing tone of the insect world. Plenty of musicians give up and never learn to play this piece, because they cannot play fast enough or because they do not really want to turn into a bee. And yet it's a great miniature, a piece that has stood that test of time so everyone knows it. Not just because it's funny, but because it shows that humans can use music to learn something about the natural world.

The first few measures:

Other well-known examples of insects in human music are few and far between, but extremes do make good examples. There's one piece of Renaissance music by Josquin Desprez that appears in many music textbooks, mostly because it's a brief, lucid piece called *El Grillo* (*The Cricket*), and it was composed around 1475, in the era of parallel harmonies long before that Baroque world of smooth counterpoint. The first thing cricket-like about it are the words:

El griiiiillllo
El Grillo è buon cantore
Che tiene longo veheheherrrrso
Dalle beve, grillo, canta!

zzhh zhh zhh zhhh; zzhh zhh zhh zhhh
Dalle dalle beve, grillo grillo canta
El griiiiillllo
El grillo è buon cantore.
Ma non fa come gli altri uccelli;
Come li han cantato un poco,
Van' de fatto in altro loco:
Sempre el grillo sta pur saldo,
Alhor canta sol per amore.

Translation: the cricket is a damn good singer, who can keep going a real long time. Sing well O cricket, sing sing sing, good times, cricket, chirp chirp singing, *zzh zzh zzh zzh,* he is a damn good singer. He don't skip town like those other birds, after they've sung their song, they fly off somewhere else. The cricket just stays put. On the hottest, stickiest days, he sings just for love.

OK, Desprez must know the cricket is no bird, but he does pick up on one interesting bit of observed ecology. Those crickets sing and sing and sing and don't need to move. Their prey can't find them, so we can only hope their lovers can.

And what's so good about the cricket's boring song? Plenty. It's rhythmic, pleasing. He even imitates its repetitiveness and even its noisiness. The tenacity of the cricket is most admirable. He loves music. He needs music. He cannot stop. Desprez wants some of that certainty, and finding crickets for inspiration, he gets it. This is one of his most beloved songs; we have been performing it for hundreds of years.

More than just inspiration, he dares to imitate the sound of insects in the music themselves—the repetition, the space, the same notes:

Dal-le   Be-ve   Gril-lo   can-ta   dal-le dal-le be-ve be-ve gril-lo gril-lo can-ta,   El   gril — - so.

In some performances of the piece the singers even make cricket-like *zzhhs* right in the middle of the piece. Even in the fifteenth century, musicians tried to imitate nature and knew nature would always remain a little bit beyond us. Even the simple, plaintive repeats of the cricket remain musically beyond us, because we can't quite be satisfied with such simplicity in our music.

We know such music is exactly enough for the insects who make it, but we humans demand much more. Too much more. We will never be satisfied with the music we have, and have to keep changing it, endlessly repeating ourselves while imagining we are doing something new. Crickets and all other singing species are far more satisfied with their basic, primal, grounded, necessary music than we will ever be. That is enough for them to demand our utmost respect, never mind how much nature needs their services and their art.

Human musicians have well realized this, and applied our rather inadequate classical notation to try to capture the nuances of *Gryllus* sounds for as long as we've had notation. For some reason the Hungarians were very diligent at the application of musical notation to natural sounds, and even adapted notation a bit in "A Zene Hangjegyekben—*Notae stridorus*" ("The Chirp Notation") by Gyula Pungur in 1891. Pungur gives a fine summary of the basic, simple chirps of the most common Eastern European cricket species. Here are a few of them:

I believe these transcriptions and sounds specifically influenced
Béla Bartók in his solo piano piece "The Night's Music," movement 4 of the 1926 suite *Out of Doors*. This was one of the composer's most popular pieces of this period, and the presence of
cricket-like repetitive dissonant irregularities is very audible right
from the beginning of the piece. Bartók loved bugs, and was a
devoted entomologist, with a vast collection of beetles and flies.
He likened the collection of insects to the collection of folk melodies, which he felt was not only a hobby, but more a responsibility
for the contemporary composer. We have to know what traditions
we are coming from, and remember the rich and unusual creativity held by diverse cultures, which the homogeneity of European
modernism had a tendency to eradicate.

László Somfai, a musicological expert on Bartók who wrote
a fifty-five page essay on just those piano pieces Bartók composed
in the year 1926, says we should not quibble with what sounds
represent what species when looking at how Bartók made use of
nature. He was no exact speciesist like French composer Olivier
Messiaen, who took pains to tell us exactly what phrase came

from what bird in his many ornithologically inspired works. No, says Somfai, our man Béla sought to identify "found sound objects" in nature and paint a musical picture of the actual natural world. "This stylization of the sounds of nature in Bartók's works . . . simplifies them into musical motives that assume their appointed places in a musical structure that is highly consciously designed." But we do hear the simple, even cricket chirps moving their way into clusters of noisy Hungarian Unka frog, *Bombina bombina,* with dissonant piano tone clusters musically mirroring the rough frequencies of nature's noises:

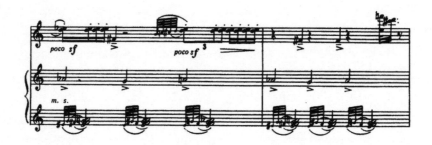

All I want to show you with this excerpt is how putting insects in human music can encourage the use of new dissonances that express the great distance between classical music's pure tones and the complexity of entomological sounds. Bartók heard the same irregularities in folk music, and that's why he heard so much in his country's venerable traditions that the contemporary composer could learn from—unusual harmonic movements, strange rhythms, all organic and understood by the population, not brand-new avant-gardisms that were hard for people to take. No, this dissonance was deep in the tradition, as dissonance in nature is deep in our ancestral biological heritage.

So maybe those musical notation examples of insect music are not the best ways to represent such textural and unpitched sounds.

A mid-twentieth century European insect field guide by Heiko Bellmann also thought about this, and tried to represent insect song patterns by abstract rhythmic glyphs:

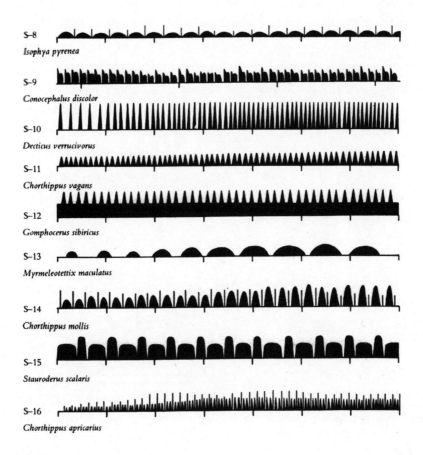

This is supposed to help us identify the insects if we run across them in the meadows, but it also represents a kind of experimental musical notation for unfamiliar noises, similar to what composers of electronic music and other compositions where the sounds included could not be represented on a usual score were doing from the 1950s onward. The appeal is immediately clear—we've got a graphic way that reveals the rhythms, shapes, and distinguishing qualities of each creature, that doesn't depend on inadequate ideas of note, scale, and pitch. In a way these experimental tools for composers came out of our attempts to understand insect and bird sounds, which right from the beginning elude traditional tools for writing down sound. Blend all these distinct creature sounds together and you have the beginnings of a new notion of combining sounds into a whole, with composition as swarm, a thrum of layers of rhythmic noise.

György Ligeti, another Hungarian, composed celebrated dissonant washes of orchestral strangeness in pieces like "Atmospheres" and "Ramifications." Listening back from today's perspective, they really do sound like layers of shimmering, screaming cicadas. His earlier piece, "Artikulation," was given a graphic score after the fact by Rainer Wehinger:

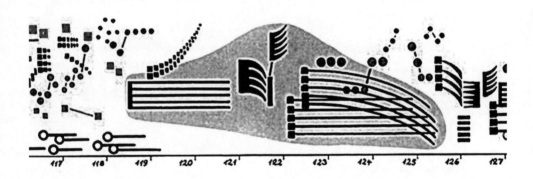

I wasn't surprised to hear from his son Lukas Ligeti, who told me that his father was haunted for years by a dream of a swarm of biting insects chasing him in a black cloud through the field, and this image drew him onward to seek to reveal this profound vision in sound.

Yet the traditions of Western classical music are by and large far away from the noisy wash demanded by those intent on dealing with insect music. I've plucked out a few anomalous examples, but to find music steeped in the world of bug sounds, we have to look beyond our own traditions to tribal musics thousands of years old. Pay a visit to the Ituri forest in West Africa and listen to the music that the Bayaka (sometimes they are called Ba-benzele, sometimes Mbuti) pygmies are making there. Here is a people whose traditional life is richly defined by a music that weaves humanity into nature, not carving our songs out of the surrounding fabric and separating ourselves from the surrounding world. In daily pygmy life there is song that gradually emerges out of rainforest sounds, most noted the shrieks and calls of birds, but underneath it the rhythmic pulse and thrum of thousands of insects and frogs, the defining ground of the soundscape but, as usual, something about which little has been said.

So much has been written about central African pygmies, from Colin Turnbull to Jerome Lewis, but I had to hunt hard to find anything specific about the rich ground of insect sounds that colors their music. We are fortunate to have hundreds of hours of fabulous recordings made by the American Louis Sarno, who left New Jersey to live with the pygmies in 1985 and has mostly been there ever since. I was fortunate to meet him in New York last year on one of his rare visits to the country he was born in. He says:

> Above all, it's to the sounds of the forest that I tune, not merely my ears, but my entire being. There are many levels of sound. The most basic, the electronic pulse which never ceases, is composed of legions of tireless insects—the crickets, katydids, and their kin. Special mention must be made of the awesome white noise of the cicadas. These sleek insects are notorious noisemakers. . . . More than once I've been in the midst of a delicate recording, some long sought-after sound such as the rising song of the red-chested cuckoo

sung by several birds at the same time, . . . when a single cicada has suddenly decided to advertise itself to the opposite sex and blasted its burst of white noise directly into my microphones, sending the recording level into overload.

More than once, too, I've abandoned my microphones to pursue the guilty cicada, chasing it from tree trunk to tree trunk, full of rage and grimly determined to destroy the insect with my projectiles of sticks and baseball-sized fruits. Yet in fact, no sound is more evocative of the forest, and when the Bayaka hear the voice of the cicada, which they call *élélé,* they say it makes their hearts glad.

On the track "Women Off to Gather Payu" on the book/CD set *Bayaka,* published by Ellipsis in 1996, we can really hear the way long, overlapping human choruses cut through the rhythmic, beating animal choruses. Gathering food is work, but with music it becomes art.

Mushroom gathering lends itself especially well to lyrical accompaniment, for it is not in the least bit strenuous and often takes place in beautiful and spacious primary forest. . . . Yodels—calls or cries in which there is a transition between chest and throat voice—are the most natural and effective way to use the voice in this environment, because the voice resonates through the trees; both high and low notes hang in the air at the same time.

Listen to it from thousands of miles and decades away and we hear an image of how our species might live and sing more closely to the world around us. Not only lilting female voices trance the pygmies into the swirl of their local forest sounds. We can also add the human kind of regular beat to the insects' more swirling, hypnotic one. In the nighttime *boyobi* ceremony, fast drumming is added to the insect and human chorus, and as we mark the time, the forest music clearly has its place, the waves of overlapping crickets and cicadas, a high wash of frequencies whose musical purpose comes through. Bugs are above it all.

Here's a sonogram of part of the puya gathering ceremony, showing how the overlapping multispecies' rhythms appear:

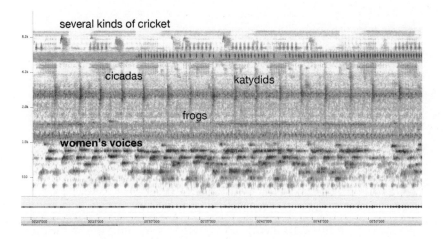

The point I want to make with this picture is that it looks clearly *organized,* with different sounds specifically appearing at clear frequency ranges over time. The natural rainforest soundscape is no random melee of cacophonous sounds, but some kind of natural, total composition that nature has evolved itself. Human hocketing song is at the bottom, and higher up the fuzzy frequencies of bugs, frogs, occasional birds with a clear rhythmic crack. It's a very organized continuous soundscape, a clear image of acoustic niches filling the screen, a sonic Mbuti design that science puts into a picture. You could almost draw it as you listen. Every creature has its place amid the sonic frequencies, and seems to stay out of each other's way. It's the clearest image of Bernie Krause's niche hypothesis that I've ever seen, because each kind of creature uses a specific sound frequency to fill the forest with its sound, in an easily audible and visible way.

Krause, one of the best-known nature sound recordists, has traveled the globe collecting the most beautiful and rarest natural sounds, which he has chronicled in books and recordings with titles like *Into a Wild Sanctuary* and *The Great Animal Orchestra*. Over the years he has developed a semi-scientific hypothesis that creatures in nature divide up the acoustic spectra as a result of natural selection and make their sounds in an acoustic niche, akin to an ecological niche, so their noises will be heard and they don't get in each other's way. I say "semi-scientific" because Krause has not felt it necessary to test his hypothesis before writing about it and presenting it, something scientists tend not to do. But as a musician and campaigner for a quieter, more sonically natural world, he is perfectly free to do so.

In recent years he has begun to work together with scientists to rigorously collect data on the niche hypothesis, and in the past year he has published some work together with Italian bird sound ecologists Almo Farina and Rachele Malavasi, which does support the conclusion that once birds have returned from their winter migrations, at first their songs seem to be a complete jumble, as they constantly get in each other's sonic ways, but after a few weeks, they settle in and use their relative acoustic niches much more successfully. So this intriguing hypothesis is starting to get some empirical support.

It is remarkable how little work of this kind has been done until now—we don't really know why birds sing at dawn, for example. Or why bugs sing at night. But clearly the pygmies have known for a long time what science would like to prove . . . that each species must find its own sonic place to fit into the soundscape, and the landscape, in a meaningful way, and this remarkable plot of sonic frequency against time bears it out, looking just like a musical score.

So much like a musical score that there is even some debate as to how accurate the image and recording are! This recording, one of the most successful commercial releases of pygmy music heard in its natural context, was made from raw tapes of Louis Sarno together with the studio alchemy of Bernie Krause. Now on *some* of the tracks on this 1997 Ellipsis Arts release, Krause specifically added some high frequency insect noises to mask the noise of the analog cassette tape Sarno used. But Krause told me, "not on this track, this is pure Bayaka singing in their pure forest."

Sarno, however, cautions me against using this recording as my visual example. "I've lived in that forest for years, and I hear some morning bugs here, while the recording is supposed to be happening in the late afternoon." How much does purity matter here? Not at all if we are making an artistic statement, and if Krause composed the final version using the sonogram as a guide, all kudos to him for making use of a new kind of musical score. But if we are making a statement about finding beautiful organization in the natural way some humans have integrated themselves into their rainforest home, *then* we might want to know for sure whether manipulation has been going on. I've got some of Sarno's raw field recordings, and they reveal nearly this same level of pure beauty. I don't need to judge the situation, but I do feel compelled to report the controversy.

Just listen to the *boyobi* ceremony recording—the bugs have their acoustic niche in the mix. After the humans stop, you may wonder, are the insects more synchronized than before? There is plenty of reason to assume they might be. Insects are known to respond to regularity in rhythm. They know well how to synchronize to a beat. We began by showing how you don't need much mathematics for that. Yet the sense of overlapping rhythm is more clear when you listen to it combined with the human music of the Ituri forest pygmies. Their music makes one of the best examples of a collective sound that fits into the natural world in which it has been produced.

The sonogram is remarkably similar to a schematic analysis Hewitt Pantaleoni made of a musical performance by a choir and percussion ensemble in Ghana:

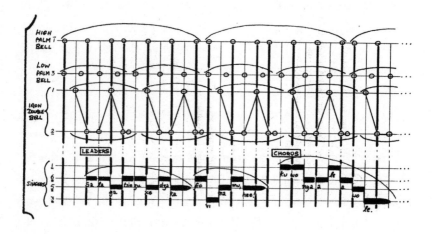

Perhaps you see some similarity between this schematic diagram and the sonogram. Or perhaps not. What I see is repeating simple patterns, overlapping, each at distinct places in the sonic sphere, independent, but fitting together in a way that makes the whole greater than some of its parts, the key property of any polyrhythmic, emergent musical order. The bell patterns always occupy higher frequencies than the singing voices, but the lower, singing voices offer the greatest variety of pitch and sound, just like the pygmies singing along with the way-up-there cycling beats of the bugs, birds, and frogs.

Just how old are the songs of the Bayaka pygmies? When Colin Turnbull asked his hosts to sing the oldest music they knew in 1961, they surprised him by singing "Clementine." Yet ancient Egyptian accounts describe musicians in the lower Nile adapting pygmy tunes even before the pyramids were up. This music has clearly been heard as something special for thousands of years. And music always gets around.

Even bug music. Start to hone in on the complexities of timbre that these critters resound, their incessant rhythms, and their trance-inducing overlapping patterns and we start to hear a musical tendency that traverses the globe. No surprise that in Bali, where traditional society is built upon layers of social and calendrical cycles to mark the repetition of time and the complexities of kinship, there is music based on superimposed alternating rhythms of echo and natural delay, from the clang of fast gamelan orchestras to the array of hundreds of chanting human voices in the famous *kecak* monkey chant, where each voice makes a cricket-like *cha* sound, all hocketing back and forth in an exciting fast beat, regular and irregular at once—*CHA! cha cha CHA cha cha cha CHA cha cha cha cha cha cha cha cha CHA cha cha cha CHA cha cha cha cha cha* . . . —while above, a drawn-out droning voice chants tales from the *Ramayana,* one after another for many hours of ritual intensity.

Loop a piece of that background human thrum and you have something that would blend right in with the warm rainforest night surrounding the ceremony. Indeed, American sound artist and composer Richard Lerman has recorded the sounds of Indonesian insects immediately after a gamelan performance. He found them synchronized with remarkable order, much more so than before the concert. That is the kind of news I want to hear—that insects might be able to listen to us, to grab a sense of order from us, and have a use for the human beat in sync with their own. Would there be anything remarkable about that? In Indonesia there is a kind of jaw harp called the *genggong* that is often played in ensembles that sound like a group of calling frogs or bugs.

I hunt for the clues that enable insect music to become human music, or people music to slip quietly into bug music. Our ears are fluid, and can hear what we will to hear. Plenty of people I've described this project to have found the whine of cicadas to be as annoying as Louis Sarno found them, messing up his delicate recordings, but at the same time part of us always loves these sounds because they are emblematic of something extreme and powerful in nature. I want to learn why it is that sometimes we value noise, love it for its pure power of sound, and at other times we shun it and scream as it disturbs us. This is not always a matter of personal choice, sometimes it is woven into the very fabric of our culture.

During her fieldwork years among the Temiar people of the Malaysian rainforest, anthropologist Marina Roseman was surprised that her informants had little interest in the beautiful, compex birdsong melodies she heard all around her in their environment. Instead, they preferred pulsing, beating, repetitive, noisy birds that were emulated in their own drumming on long bamboo tubes. "Barbet and cicada calls—pulsing like the heart, hidden in the dense jungle foliage, persistent yet unobtainable . . . set the cosmos in motion and affect the transformation of Temiar trance, a momentary intermingling of self and other." One of their spirit songs is even called "The Way of Old Woman Cicada," and the words go something like this:

Dancing in a slow step
the green tinge of sunset and
the late hour cicada sound

laaw laaw *marks the time*
of dizziness, whirling, and change.

When the Temiar walk into the forest during fruit season, they caution each other to listen to cicada sounds only with a "strong heart," lest they be drawn off into the forest and distracted doom. The proper beat of their own music is precisely calculated to "intensify longings of the heart," and, as you listen to their songs, it is no surprise that the bugs in the background sometimes seem to be beating in time. Human life is synchronized with the thrum of the rainforest world, where the right rhythm matters more than the contours of any song.

Their cosmology is exact and rigorous, matched to the powerful sounds of their rainforest home. This music is wrapped up in ceremonies of healing and meaning for these forest people, and they are one important example of a culture that values as music sounds many of us first would consider noise. That cicada sound is ultimately alluring, so be careful around something that can so quickly lead you into a trance.

Trance, says Gilbert Rouget in *Music and Trance,* means movement, noise, company, crisis, sensory overstimulation, which he distinguishes famously from ecstasy: immobility, silence, solitude, and sensory deprivation. Of course not all of us will agree. Through the thrum and enveloping of timbre, tone, and beat, music has long led us on into ecstasy. Rouget is one of few authors who tries to grapple with the mystery of how strange sounds envelop our consciousness, leading us to places dangerous and deep alike. The lives of traditional people who live mostly in rich, noisy forests are usually full of ritual dance, and trance that extends human lives into the soul of the forest. Still, some insects are comforting; others are entrancing, perhaps dangerous. Cricket vs. cicada. They are always there, singing behind everything else in the forest. Are they then the background to human life, grounding our music, or have they a clear part in our music? When we hear them synchronize with our shaman beats, we want to smile, because we believe we belong.

Composers who make music directly out of insect sounds today have two aesthetic choices: They can either work on the sound as an entity separate from human music, something pure and natural, to be taken on its own terms. Or they can join the entomological with the human, either constructed in the studio, or live in the world. I am immediately more impressed when people dare to make music live with animals, because it is so risky and leads to less expected music. On the other hand, as our musical tools today enable us to turn any sound into something far from its origin, totally unrecognizable, such prejudices might make little sense in the sonic world we now inhabit. Many electronic music composer/ performers have been especially impressed with the strangeness of insect sounds and the unusual directions they send us. Each may begin with similar timbres, but they understand the meanings and roles of their sounds in radically different ways.

Why make music directly out of the sounds of insects? The sound artist and former professor of ecology Francisco López says, don't do it to make some ecological point about the overlapping layers of nature, or to document a vanishing acoustic world. The reason for a composer to choose any sound is because he wants to make music out of that sound. Too much music made out of natural sounds, López claims, is marred by the ideology of longing for a romanticized natural world where humans are excluded. Too many bug-saturated recordings of the rainforest waste our time identifying every species, claiming to teach us, like a zoologist, of what creatures sing here and which ones sing there. Too many lovers of nature sound music implore us to consider all sound as music, announcing that the world as we naturally confront it is a vast musical composition, ours for the hearing.

For López all these clichés are wrong. A composer does not accept the spontaneous and accidental in the world of sound; no, the opposite should be the case. He is an expert in listening and assembling, and must make precise decisions as to the destiny of each sound he uses. Whether writing instructions on paper for people to make music from, or combining and recombining actual sounds onstage or in the studio, he is the boss, and he must encourage us to take sound more seriously, not for what it is supposed to signify, but for what it is. If the composition doesn't interest us because of the wonder of its sonic construction, then no explanation or story should be resorted to to buttress the work up.

López releases CDs with no information on the disc or the package; they are often printed all in black. He asks his audiences to wear blindfolds so they think of nothing but the sound as the music rolls on. On his 1997 release *La Selva* he tells you nothing about the Costa Rican rainforest where he has recorded all the sounds out of which he composed the continuously streaming multilayered piece. Bugs? Frogs? Birds? Which is which? Such a question matters not—what's at stake here is a musical composition, not a nature lesson. The rich, complex sonorities of thick forest noise are not what uninitiated listeners will immediately call musical, but López's work is designed to convince you that these sounds have become musical through his structured transformation of them. This is not an improvisation, it is no sudden encounter between a musician and a new environment. It is a carefully constructed sonic journey. Look at nothing while you hear it, devote all your attention to immediate sounds, think of nothing separate from the information and feelings that you hear.

What he does not want you to do is to hear this beautiful trance-inducing music and think, "Oh, how beautiful these bugs and birds do sing! Amazing how nature can offer such beauty." The beauty must be purely in the sound, with no ecological nature-saving story needed to justify it. López is a purist, and he will only ask for musical reasons to explain any joy we find in music.

Thus he wants to appear much more rigorous than John Cage, the famous pioneer of open listening and experimental music who urged us to take all sounds seriously because they came from places we did not expect. Cage was playful, philosophical, Zenlike, paradoxical, sometimes preferring wry stories to specific instruction when it came to composition—some of his pieces involve the performer sitting onstage, breaking sticks, or following obscure rituals. The works are full of elements far removed from the refinement of sound.

For López such an approach is chronically unserious. A composer must not shirk his role in choosing sounds that are beautiful, total, and important. The composer who uses sounds as timbrally complex as those coming from insects will have to explain why such sounds are musically interesting in the first place. Rather than following John Cage, as so many lovers of natural sounds like myself are wont to do, he instead calls himself a disciple of Pierre Schaeffer, the French composer and theorist who some say invented the whole discourse of sound art through the practice of *musique concrète,* which basically means making music out of the sounds of the everyday world, not the *abstrait* sounds of traditional musical instruments.

This does not mean simply accepting the sounds of real life as musical, which is what López says Cage is doing. Instead it meant building a vast theoretical edifice to try to explain how these ordinary sounds can be categorized, understood, and musically appraised, all without reference to the hundreds of years of Western musical tradition based on rhythm, melody, and harmony. Schaeffer was after that difficult to describe quality called timbre, the sense of color and density that distinguishes one musical instrument's sound quality from another, or one cicada's *whoom* or one cricket's *chhh* from another species's. His vast *Treatise on Musical Objects,* for decades available only in French, has been summarized and edited in his student Michel Chion's *Guide to Sound Objects,* finally in English in 2009. And in these dense pages appear a few lines that might help us explain why and how we musically enjoy the dense inharmonic sounds of insects.

The book is a long and technical collection of new categories out of which to comprehend sound, far from the usual musical categories of note, rhythm, tone color, volume, and articulation, and here are the two out of hundreds that might most help us make sense of the unique qualities held by insect sound. Number 78, the *weft:* a sound of prolonged duration, created by superimposing "sheaves," fusions of slowly evolving sounds . . . "macro-objects," slowly evolving structures. This is a category that values layers of sweeping, changing sounds, such as a tree full of hundreds of swelling cicadas.

Then a few pages later we have another intriguing sound object, Number 83, *accumulation:* the disorderly piling up of micro-sounds fused together by their similarity into a grand macro-object. Examples are a stream of pebbles ground together by a receding wave, a dawn chorus of twittering birds, or an orchestral string section plucking hundreds of shimmering pizzicatos. Many tiny blips blurred into one, as opposed to overlapping, textural swells.

These two processes are aesthetic principles that can by applied to the granular synthesis invented by Curtis Roads, as described in chapter three. And they may serve to explain what is interesting about a large class of insect sounds, though these might not be the primary sounds they were designed to explain. The two principles do help to explain what is going on in certain kinds of electronic musical effects that can help turn any sound into a mass of showering insect noises, something like GRM Tools "Pitch Ac-cumulator," a sound effect plug-in for making digital music on a computer, which was, not coincidentally, developed by Pierre Schaeffer's Groupe de Recherches Musicales in Paris.

Francisco López introduces his work *Hyper-Rainforest* to a blindfolded audience in Troy, New York: "What you are about to hear," he says, "is the culmination, somehow, of thirty years of recording in the rainforest. . . . I believe sound is a way to dis-cover something spiritual about yourself, and I hope you discover something about yourself today. What I hope to show you is that recording machines, and machines in general, are not neutral. They do things we cannot do, as we do things they cannot do. It is time we worked with machines to produce something more than reality."

Ah . . . more than reality. Never just the sounds of the world, which we know to be sounds of the world, but music, an art made of sound. So John Cage tells us there is no such thing as silence? Fuggedaboutit. There sure is such a thing as silence. Music makes it possible, when the sound stops. It takes music to make the ab-sence of sound serve a real function. Or does it? Remember those frogs and katydids that use silence as a communicative act. In a wash, a lek, of thousands of singing males desperate for the atten-tions of wanting females, sometimes the *ceasing* of the signal is what it takes for the signal to have its desired effect.

López is a most careful composer with accumulating walls and wefts—he works with layers of nature's noises while reminding us to forget where the noises come from. He is a true master of this form, taking the listener on unique journeys where not all of us are prepared to go. Close your eyes, wrap on the blindfold, take the risk. You will listen to what the composer wants you to hear.

López contributed beautiful tracks to my *Book of Music and Nature* CD and the more recent *Whale Music Remixed*. In both cases he presented long, intense pieces that I was forced to cut down to a manageable length, and each time this proved extremely difficult, because López is most precise as a composer, and he shapes complex layers of sound according to reason and plan so that he does succeed in convincing us to hear music in natural noises through the power of these sounds alone. He contrasts very long, slow fades with sudden drops or surges in volume, pulling you in to a whole new vocabulary of sound. I do think it is important to know its tones come from nature, but if the composer literally blindfolds you to mask your most obvious senses, then we must trust him that he truly wants you to hear sound not as found music, but as composed music. Decisions have been made. The listener must abide by them.

López would probably not be so interested in my question, "What can human music learn from insect sounds?" He might prefer the larger question: What does music learn from sounds? If the sounds you work with come from insects, fine. But only use them if they are interesting sounds. It matters not what they are, only what you can accomplish with them.

Contrast this with the more programmatic description of a piece that, upon first listening, might sound similar to López's *La Selva*. Robert Curgenven composed *Silent Landscapes No. 2* with a particular geographic journey in mind:

> Nightfall by a riverside camp near Wollumbin (Mt Warning), walking in dry grass, the sharp call of a single insect emerges. Above the nearby road, power lines catch the breeze—an echo finding resonance over 3000 kilometres west at Karlu Karlu (Devil's Marbles) in Central Australia, where the wind strikes a parallel rhythm some years before. Further north, other winds blow in grevilleas lining the Buchanan Highway, en route to the Tanami Desert. Along a river, 20 metres

deep in a flood that isolates a town, crickets pulse agitatedly on the Tropics' edge. Two thousand kilometres east, aeolian currents bring the Musical Fence in Central Queensland to a slow crescendo. Finally, 2000 kilometres south east again, returning through the grass to camp, the cycle is, for now, complete.

Curgenven, an Australian field recordist with thousands of soundscape recordings in his collection, assembles several distinct sonic environments together precisely because of their overlapping mash-up similarities. He wants you to know his piece is a specific sonic journey from eastern Australia way over to the middle, down somewhere else, then back to the first site, unified not just by the composer's travels, but also by virtue of amenable, related sounds swelling gently from one place to another, like familiar landmarks glimpsed or songlines voiced into being.

In contrast to López, this composer wants to tell a story that links a sound structure to a specific map of places experienced, in the actual world. He wants the listener to know that. The music must here represent precise, real places the recordist has been. It sounds like nature, it follows a journey. The structure is clear, the purpose for each location evident: Hearing one sound immediately reminds the composer of somewhere else suddenly far away, but possessing a relevant sound . . . suddenly we are there, like a view out a train window cascading into déjà vu. So you still think listening is forgetting the name of the thing one hears? Not if you want to remember the story when the piece is done.

Insects always sound like insects, right? Not in the world of today, when any sound just cries out for transformation into something absolutely remote. When I first heard British composer Mira Calix's astonishing work *Nunu,* I imagined that it, too, was a sound experience created in the studio out of choruses of insects.

I was amazed how she was able to turn the noisy, scractchy timbres of the bugs into pure, luminous tones. Hmm . . . I wondered, what kind of filters was she using, what kind of resonators? The piece proceeds with hypnotic, repeating tones, not exactly minimalist, but an evolving, ever-changing drone. I am drawn in by the beautiful sonorities, it is hard not to fall sway to such entomological charms. I'm trying to listen blind, I want to enjoy sound as sound, but then I learn how the piece was actually made.

Nunu was commissioned by the London Sinfonietta, and performed live onstage by the orchestra together with live insects sampled in real time by Calix and mixed into the fray. She manages to transform cyclical, looping chirps of crickets and whines of cicadas into hauntingly beautiful tones, using familiar but still astonishing effects. Cicadas, cockroaches, crickets, and beetles were all in one terrarium, but contact microphones were arranged so each bug could be sampled and manipulated separately. The situation sounds quite spontaneous, but the recorded result is remarkably structured and harmonic in a more traditional, rhythmically hypnotic manner than the López and Curgenven pieces.

By now you might think we are on a trajectory into the appreciation of a very obscure branch of music . . . insect-assembled electronica. So far Calix's is the most sonically accessible because of its repeating, lilting drone of minor chords. It is instantly emotional. How does the piece differ when we learn the insects are resonating live on stage?

First off, it makes me immediately want to try this myself. Especially when we hear, just after ten minutes into the thirteen-minute piece, the unmistakable *phaaaroooaah* of a seventeen-year cicada. Where did she get one of those in London? Wait a minute . . . do other cicadas make such a tone? Seems like Marina Roseman's recording from Malaysia also has such a sound . . . I must look into this. How is the *Magicicada* exactly in tune with the minor wash . . . did she prepare for this or is the recorded edition of the piece a studio creation? López would tell me that all these questions are distracting from the musical experience, but as a musician and writer awash in bug music and nothing but bug music during the time of the composition of this text, I am constantly asking questions. I am constantly hearing things—hums, buzzes, whirrs, whines, scratches, scrapes, washes, tones—all reverberating in my ears during this year of insect thinking.

Calix uses one clever approach that makes electronic music palatable to many more people: the repeating, harmonious, drone-like minimal phrase. This is why Philip Glass, Terry Riley, Gavin Bryars, and Steve Reich have gotten popular—they took the incessant repetition from world music and pop music and brought it to the more elite concert stage. With the world of music made by machines the tendency to endlessly repeat comes naturally—machines do not get tired of doing the same thing over and over again. Is this something people have always actually wanted from music but have been afraid to ask human musicians to provide? I think so. People after a while can come to prefer drum machines to real drummers, because they keep more rigorous time than any imperfect living mammal. They produce something close to the Platonic perfection of a beat, not always perfectly regular, but with irregularities that can be exactly programmed. Complete control of the beat, turning human variation into insect purity, fuzz, clack, and *chhhh*.

In electronic music today emotional clarity comes through with the klanging harmonies of musicians like Scanner, who succeeds so well by always adding a slight minor wash behind his far-out experimentations and samples of secret conversations and mumblings. In his duet with percussionist Pete Lockett, a piece called "Plush Insect," there are shaker-like bug beats, crickets morphed into telephones, a warm ringing coming out of the tabla into a long tone, and under it all a steady groove. If the beat is steady, do we now have a music more people will like?

This is an old debate for anyone who has been experimenting with making unusual sounds into music. If you just add a steady rhythm, will people consider it popular music? So much of the world's human music is based on a consistent groove, overlapping interesting sounds, and very little change in harmony. That is what inspired world music pioneer Ben Mandelson aka Hijaz Mustapha to once say "four fifths of the world cannot be wrong." And yet in the world of elite or supposedly classical music, certainly in the West, when you add an endlessly repeating beat to the mix, you downgrade your work to pop status. Clearly people like regular beats, but do we like them somehow too much to take seriously? The story is complicated in our time because of the rhythmic possibilities of the machine, first drum machines, then computers, which never tire of repeating the same thing over and over again. In fact, that might be a simple description of what such machines are best at doing. After the technology comes the deluge—of a new aesthetic, where people start to prefer hyperregular drum machines to untrustworthy real drummers. We come to love the precisely mechanical, endlessly repeating rhythms of the electronic world.

So what does this have to do with insects? *They are our original teachers of rhythm.* Their sound world offers of scads of regular beats, sometimes exactly in sync, sometimes slightly off—irregular, over-lapping, forming complex polyrhythms, sometimes by accident, at other times by evolved design. Those of us who believe in using natural sound in music have faith that there is something richly rewarding about using such sounds, something more organic and real, deeper than sounds we might artificially conjure with elec-tronic source material at the start. We sample the sonic world of nature to soften the precision of the artificial sound world, to bring the irregular rightness of nature into the human dream of absolute control. The whole enterprise is fraught with paradox—we know natural sound has its million-years' purpose and is beyond the questing uncertainty of human test and experiment, and it is perfect as is, so why mess with it? Humans mess with everything; we love music, the regular beat takes us in, and we endlessly want to enrich it while constantly keeping it the same.

Birds and whales, even rushing water, all my previous topics, are much more invitingly musical than insects, with their buzz, whine, and general distance from the human way of being an animal. But in their very distance, bugs invite attention and wonder, and as our music welcomes ever more noise into its palette, these original purveyors of the regular beat fly into our consciousness with ever more thrum and scrape.

Graeme Revell founded the industrial noise band SPK in Australia in the 1980s, inspired by the strange rhythms he heard in the nonsense voices of mental patients in the hospital where he was working as an orderly. This band is famous for some pretty harsh, noisy releases, and right from the beginning Revell notes how inspired he also was by the parallels between insect sounds and the whirr of industrial machinery that so marks our modern age. He later became one of the most successful film composers in Hollywood, writing music for films that sound like a background in noise aesthetics might really help one get the sound right: *Sin City*, *Red Planet*, *Bride of Chucky*, *The Crow*, *Collateral Damage,* and *Shark Night 3D*, just to name a few. But for us he is important because he released a cult recording called *The Insect Musicians* in 1986, which made use of the then–cutting edge Fairlight CMI sampler, the first electronic instrument able to sample real world sound with high fidelity.

Not only are the pieces on the album composed entirely out of a wide variety of insect noises, but Revell's liner notes are probably the best example of any musician writing about the aesthetic conundrum of sampling itself. Now that he has finally gotten his hands on an instrument capable of fluidly turning any sound into raw, acoustic material that can be transformed into any other sound, this master of noise realizes that this is a very dangerous capability indeed:

> An unforeseen difficulty presented itself during the composi-
> tion of *The Insect Musicians* as a result of this degree of control.
> Once we can divide a sound into minute segments and then
> redraw (using a light pen) each of those segments, the result-
> ing modified waveform may bear absolutely *no* relation to the
> source at all. To the audience with no prior comprehension of
> digital analysis, the process must then seem either invisible or
> a sheer fakery. The musician could indeed tinker indefinitely
> to create the perfect replica of whatever instrument, if that
> was his aim, but all that would prove was that Fourier was
> correct when he hypothesised that any sound could be re-
> created by the right combination of sine waves.

Revell very rigorously analyzes what he is trying to accomplish with the taking of insect sound as musical material: each crea-ture's sound sampled to precision and then played on a keyboard as timbral material, worked out into scales and melodies back when the sampler was a sudden new possibility, not an assumed tool of electronic musical production.

It was a whole new world back then, and already Revell knew there was a problem with all this flexibility. The only solution would be to keep the technology fluid and inspiring, something akin to poetry:

> A poetic technology must satisfy somewhat greater condi-
> tions than simple technical capacity. Like any poetry it must

open up a space of multiple meanings. . . . For what is shown is that an unlimited array of instruments and music can be created from the sounds of nature, including those of human activity. . . . In the microscopic analysis of the sounds and their organization (Rhythm) we find suggested new structures of musical syntax and semantics. Though it is notable that from the first listening one will notice a few greater affinity [sic] between certain ethnic ("primitive") musics and natural sonorities. *The Insect Musicians* is therefore both very new and, at the same time, very old. It is nature and hypernature in a sort of indivisible whole.

The Insect Musicians is a tour de force of 1980s sampling wizardry. The technology was new then, and the music, still strange and revolutionary, sounds dated in a way technology-driven music sometimes does. Each sampled note has the same volume, inflection, or velocity. The curiosity of the insect-based tones does start to get at the listener, in a way older, or more recent, pieces do not. My favorite from the disc is the one with the most steady beat, "Invaders of the Heart," created from the sound of distressed honeybees, wood-boring beetles, European cicadas, and the death's-head hawk moth, not all the most musical of species, but when sampled, they all become timbres to use in a grand MIDI arrangement of tones and beats. From synthetic-sounding gunshots and a few marimba-like tests, soon a regular machine beat arrives and the bees' choir above it.

An electronic witches' dance! An early video game soundtrack for the arrival of the villains from outer space! It does not really sound *alive,* but contrived in the way old electronic music often does. There is something demented and extreme about it, a nod toward madness, those babbling Australian mental patients. Or is it a foreshadowing of the scary movie soundtracks Revell will later have so much success writing? He's definitely got a knack for grand, evocative orchestration of weird synthetic bug-based sounds.

The more I listen to it, the more I like it. The tools of sampling were limited back then compared to what any notebook computer can achieve today, but electronic music has such a deep yearning for retromania, trying to capture the past when the future seemed so much wilder than it turned out to be.

One specific quality makes sampled music sound dated: the sameness of timbre of each sampled note, whatever pitch is played with it, and the lack of realism because each note played on the keyboard has the same volume. The technology was available for Revell to move beyond this, it came with the first velocity-sensitive electronic keyboard, the Yamaha DX7 in the mid 1980s, but Revell's use of insect timbres does have this stunted quality, possibly by design, possibly by expediency. It all sounds more controlled and mechanical than it needs to be. And yet . . . he probably just likes that aspect of it, influenced as he is by the pounding of machines. By controlling the insects he lets us hear the insects. Since sampling was so new at the time, maybe he didn't want to confuse the listener by making his new bug instruments sound too much like new, unidentifiable instruments. He wanted to be sure we heard exactly what he was up to.

Note that there are plenty of musicians who think the very idea of sampling tones and putting them on keyboards for others to play is just a bad idea. I heard an interview with singer/songwriter Ben Folds on the radio the other day where he explained why he doesn't like playing electronic pianos, no matter how masterfully they have been sampled, since these days of sampled electronic instrument can use hundreds, if not thousands of separate samples to emulate the fluid qualities of a real instrument. Tone, said Folds, is a very personal thing. Whoever played all those separate piano notes, on whatever fancy instrument, was probably sitting, bored, in a studio. The player wasn't really playing anything. Folds hears boredom in every sample; like many acoustic musicians, he sticks to the real acoustic instrument whenever possible.

When it comes to acoustic instruments, Ben Folds is probably right. Sampling a tone is far away from playing the tone. I can never accept a sampled facsimile of a clarinet, since I know what it means to play a clarinet. I am happy to use samples for percussion, rhythms, bass tones, even strings in the background like a looming pad, but I try to make them sound different from the real thing. And for washes of background sounds I tend to prefer sounds from nature, and here insects work especially well. I would sample their whole chorus, with all its richness and confusion, and let them all sing, and on top of it try to find a human part over and above their intact music. Because Revell is right, if your sample from nature becomes just a single note, what matters is how you play those notes, and too often electronic instruments emphasize their artificiality, and the life is sucked out of those sounds.

So this may be why there are not too many examples where insect sounds are sampled as literally as Revell has done with *The Insect Musicians*. For that reason alone all would-be bug musicians should listen to it, and consider it. It's nearly two decades old. Have we advanced our appreciation for entomological sounds since then? The rare opportunities offered by the Fairlight to those few who could afford its $20,000 price tag are now accessible to anyone with a laptop or tablet. Sound can be endlessly refined on the most commonplace tools. Have we learned how to listen any better? Critics today decry people's reliance on cheap headphones and low-resolution compressed MP3 sound files, but I'm talking aesthetics. Do we appreciate bug noise as something sublime? There are newer examples of human-made bug music out there. And some make a reference to looking forward, rather than back, announcing that we are better prepared, more savvy, ready to take on a new world of sound.

The British experimental sound duo The Black Dog put out a recent album called *Music for Real Airports,* a kind of critical answer to Brian Eno's 1978 *Music for Airports* record, which was at the time considered a brilliant alternative to the muzak airports used to endlessly stream. The Black Dog says Eno's record is too limiting, "largely elegiac," still a form of calming anesthetic muzak even if it was trying to offer an alternative. Airports are too exciting, "important and revealing. They are dystopian microcosms of a possible future society. . . . Airports promise travel, exploration and excitement but endlessly break that promise with their stale, tedious pressure. They are intense and overwhelming environments." Out of the murmurings of human voices echoing off the formica floors and aluminum walls, a steady techno beat emerges, certainly a machine that makes you want to dance. But then after a few minutes, washes of sound rise up that sound solidly like insect choruses. Are they? Does it matter? Why do I want them to be insects?

I have assembled my playlist of the best insect-related sound pieces I could find. You'll find it at the end of this book. My top twenty come culled from an initial list of nearly a hundred, all pieces in different genres where the sound of insects or an entomological quality adds to the experience. As I play the stuff for people, some point out to me that the sounds I call insectible might not really be coming from bugs. Some of these Black Dog tones are clearly from airplanes, motors, and beneath it all a steady, open, computer drumbeat.

How do I know bugs are in the mix if I don't ask the musicians or they don't tell me? My answer is that it doesn't completely matter whether or not the sounds I imagine coming from bugs are actual bugs or not. Listening closer to "Future Delay Thinking," my favorite track from The Black Dog's *Airport* project, it does seem likely the sounds are produced by synthesizers, or at least samples from machines. But they have that complex tone, wash-like intensity, and frequency-filling noisishness that is insect sound at its essence. With electronics, bug music becomes our music.

There is one sense in which sampling an insect sound and massaging it into human music might not be the best way to enter the entomological aesthetic. Electronic synthesizers might offer an advantage over the sampler when it comes to emulating insectable noises. A sampler captures a piece of a real world sound, then just transposes it as we play different instances of it from different notes. A synthesizer, an earlier technology, works differently. An electronic oscillator creates a simple tone, perhaps a sine, square, or sawtooth pure wave, and then it is modulated by different carrier frequencies. Sounds like engineering, I know. But this is exactly how actual insects create sounds. Or at least how scientists model their tiny insect brains creating sounds.

Read insect sound science papers and they sound a lot like electronic music science papers; all this talk of oscillators, with carrier frequencies, and control frequencies, the simple wave forms and filters that are the building blocks of electronic music. Where a sampler offers you a piece of a real world sound, ready to be cut, pasted, and massaged up and down a virtual keyboard, a synthesizer, whether an actual hardware one or a software emulation of it, is imitating the way a bug itself makes music. Each key you press triggers different parameters, so the way it plays up and down the keyboard can be most unpredictable, and unintentionally mirroring the real world of insects making sound. So an electronic piece can sound entomological even if real insect sounds are not there.

In the beginning most musicians wanted their electronic instruments to imitate real, acoustic sounds, but over time the special hard-hitting strange sounds of electronica took hold of us, and we started to look for sounds that were as different as possible from acoustic instruments, but musical in a new, previously uncategorizable way. These may be the very kinds of sounds Schaeffer tried to explain with his dreams of *weft* and *accumulation,* but maybe we should have named them *cricket, katydid, beetle,* or *cicada.* Or simply *insect chorus* or *rainforest* or *August Nights* to truly grasp the enormity of the kinds of sounds we might go for. Let's create a Bug Night to end all Bug Nights, a grand steamy late summer midnight humid experience!

People did not invent synthesizers to imitate insects, but it turns out they are very good at doing this. So once you have bug music in your ears you will soon be able to hear it everywhere. What used to be a tangled morass of wires coming out of silver-box machines now can appear virtually on your computer. Let me give an example of just two of these sound-making programs that excel at emulating insect sounds. Take the freeware synth Automat, developed by Stefan Kirch. Software synthesizers emulate old analog equipment by mirroring the electrical processes that used to happen with voltages, hums, and solid analog oscillators by emulating them in the digital world. Automat is popular because, first of all, it is free, and secondly, it is immensely and immediately strange, producing right from the get-go sounds that one does not expect. It has two easy functions for generating new sounds: a randomize button, which suddenly readjusts all parameters to surprise you with something unexpected. And, more unusually, it has an EVOLVE button that gradually changes the sound program into something else, producing subtle, not total variation.

Programming electronic sounds is an addictive habit—once you start messing with the sounds you'll want to mess some more. Many electronic musicians agree they spend more time tweaking their sound presets than making music with them. This is in marked difference from practicing acoustic instruments, where you have to play them for years to develop your own unique sound. Electronic music instantly gives you hundreds of options; the trick is to develop appreciation for these tones and to know how to move from one to the next, and to know how to choose. The choices exponentially increase with each new generation of technology, but our powers of perception and discrimination do not rise so rapidly to the occasion. We always need to listen more, to listen better, and more carefully. That's why I'm asking you to think of these synthesizer programs in a new way . . . as tools to investigate the insect aesthetic, the bug sound value . . . that rich blend of noise, texture, and rhythm that we hear as uniquely alive and wonderful, evoking long, warm summer nights or lonely, autumn moist-leaf afternoons just before frost as the final crickets strive to survive.

My Automat patch "Bug Nite" is based on a simple waveform of white noise, modulated by various sine waves and delays. I made it by many repeats of the randomize function, hundreds really, stopping when I suddenly realized I'd got a sound that retained some of that pulsing, noisy, yet organized quality of a midnight garden full of *chh-chh*-ing katydids and bush crickets. I didn't have so much use for this virtual device, but now that I've been listening for entomology in so much music, the value of Automat has become clearer. Playing this synth I begin to learn what I want in an electronic sound: something from a machine, but sounding alive. But it has to grab me. I want to hear rhythm, a groove, but an inexact groove. I want rich texture, depth, but not something exactly predictable.

Samples of real bugs can have a predictable quality as one plays them up and down the keyboard. Synthesized sounds are eminently more artificial, but when modulated and moved around, they can behave in strange ways. When any computer program surprises us, we say there are glitches and bugs. When music has this quality, we say it is organic, alive, tapping into the forces of life itself, that place we dream our machines may someday go.

Surprise, affability, rhythm, the unpredictable, glimpses of the great world bug—those are some of the qualities Automat offers. It may be best to use when you have no idea what sound you want, or when very controlled, comprehensible sounds seem clearly boring. Of course, most composers have very exact opinions about what kind of sounds they like, even when it comes to the search for the perfect insect tone. My favorite tool is a program by Urs Heckmann, a synth plug-in by the name of Zebra, a very comprehensive sound design tool that is especially clear and well conceived, combining many kinds of electronic music modules. But my approach has always been to learn as little as possible about how such things are put together in the virtual, emulated digital world, but to just start playing them to see if I am pleasantly surprised.

Where Automat says surprise, though, Zebra says control. Everything can be subtlely and exactly adjusted to massage the sound, and since I like the idea of working live and in performance, rather than planning everything out, like the actual choruses of insects on a warm singing night, this is the feature where I spend most of my playing time. Zebra has a Performance window with four XY pads, which have been mapped, by the best sound programmers, to those parameters most likely to affect the sound in the most interesting ways. As I play, I can precisely tweak the entomological aspects of the tone, to directly understand what it is that makes a chorus of insects an actually musical sound.

It is not only the sense of rhythm blended with surprise that does it. We choose a synth out of all possible synths first and foremost because it sounds wonderful, often claiming something like warmth, suggesting a retromaniacal warp back to the days of analog synthesizers which, though large and unwieldy, made their sounds with real voltages and real wires of electricity, not digital, parsed and partial imitations of the continuous out of the digital all broken up into 1s and 0s. Everything about the precise digital world sometimes seems far too exact, and we often look back to a world of inadvertent mystery and rough, round sounds.

I felt I needed to travel all the way to Germany to see Heckmann at work in his u-he studios to find out exactly how he could have created a piece of software with such elegance and possibility. When I went to visit Heckmann in his secret laboratory somewhere in Berlin, he told me that a whole new generation of listeners and music-makers have emerged who prefer the edgy grit and grating enharmonic 1-upon-0 noise of the digital world. They no longer care for this supposed warmth. The era of glitch and scratch is a direct challenge to this.

What I found did surprise me: an immaculate office with one museum-like room full of classic old music equipment, including a few items shipped directly from famous Hollywood film composer Hans Zimmer who used Zebra extensively in his scores for the films *Inception* and *Angels and Demons*, which required the specific sound of the bell at the Vatican that is only struck when the Pope passes on as no accurate sample of the sound exists. The exact tone was easily re-created with the precision tools of Zebra.

I want to take the emotional beauty of the many kinds of tones and timbres made by insects and find tools to make music out of them. Zebra works well for this because you have precise control as you play of many musical parameters. There are so many parameters to be tweaked, one has no idea where to begin, no sense of what to do with such fabulous potential for sound. The biggest hurdle for all computer music is the controller problem, how to interface man and machine so you can really play your laptop as an instrument, not sitting content to get lost in its possibilities. But do I want to play the insect chorus, or learn from the insect chorus to humanize it, or electrify it?

Certainly our classical composers who wrote music by writing instructions to produce music, rather than directly shaping the sound, knew that you could at the time only learn from insect sound by finding qualities inside it that suggested new directions for stretching human musical units and structures. With direct composition out of natural sounds the tendency is to simply take a beautiful insect chorus, listen to it, maybe make a loop out of it that intensifies the local rhythm of one section to get that ultimate repetitiveness that it turns out people actually *like* in music, maybe transpose it, tune it a bit so it sounds more like pure notes and less like original noise. Many beautiful musical phrases can come from such a method, but with Zebra there is an immediate way to play with the rhythmic qualities that hold an insect chorus together. I've made an "Insect Chorus" patch that has not a single sample of a bug, just a serious of independent oscillators, like models of bugs, and each one can be spontaneously changed in rhythm and buzz by messing with the XY pads. A well-programmed Zebra sound has the four pads already assigned so the musician can immediately start playing the sound without thinking about it too much.

What I like about these insect-like sounds is that adjusting those pads changes the frequency of the independent insect beats and filters their high frequencies in an intuitive way, so the music evolves as the sound is changed. It is as if I conduct the artificial bug sound chorus as my fingers do the walking. I feel my way through the overlapping scratch beats and modulated oscillators, feeling that this is what it must be like to conduct insect choruses, knowing full well the irony that in real insect choruses no one is in charge. Whatever music appears only emerges because of the independent creatures each doing their own thing, the only beat they know and the one they're meant to do.

Every synthesizer program is like a graphic philosophy of sound, presenting a structure and an interface to the same problem: the creation of endless possibilities of sound and a playable interface to turn these strange offerings into music. Programming these XY pads is not so easy, since one has to make sure that tweaking them as you play is going to make musical sense, and not sheer randomness or too much glitch. But so many of Zebra's preset sounds can be insectified if you push the XY parameters to their limits. And I have always favored a playalong, test out, rather than a plain approach to making music with the natural world. You must understand me when I say that the same approach can work when playing electronic virtual machines. First get insect sounds on your brain, decide you like them and want to make music with them. Pretty soon you will hear them everywhere and want to find your way into their inharmonic, chorusing, and rhythmic beauty.

So what do I like about these sounds anyway? Is this just a test, to decide how much music you can get out of bugs? In a way, yes. I've spent a few years delving into a kind of sound that previously I, too, would brush off as being little more than a beguiling noise. But listen more closely, and you will start to love it. Tweak those pads and you start to have an instant control of what really is a mathematical model of how insects make sound and combine their rhythms upon each other. The electronic world of insects made with Zebra may not always sound just like the real insects, but they are put together in an analogical way. As science models complex ecological struggles and happenings in nature, the software synthesizer models a world of many oscillating insects. Delve into the sound, and muckrake with the sound. Twist and turn it into different forms and decide which ones you like and which ones you dislike.

Wait a minute, isn't that what my hero John Cage urged us never to do? That's right, this great twentieth-century composer and philosopher of music had this advice for all would-be artists in the new world: "You must free yourselves from your likes and dislikes." That's how he was led to recommend the use of chance in how to move from one musical state to the next. I watched him at work, and he definitely brought a precise, aesthetic sense to his compositions. He may have used randomness to generate them, but he was quite particular about what ideas of music he chose to accept, when putting his name to a work. You can always tell that a Cage is a Cage. In the 1930s he presciently said that one day composers would be making music directly out of electronic sounds—I'm not sure it was a world full of thumping techno that he had in mind, but I like to think he would approve of the question I put to the inanimate synthesizer, "How and why can you sound so much like a meadow full of insects?"

I aim for complex thrumming textural sounds, and slow changes, changes I have some control upon. Is each oscillator a single bug, or does each sound stand for a whole species of bug? This is not a theoretical or actually very intellectual music that I am making here, it is a live experiment in finding a warm, alluring kind of sound. I invite you to listen—if this music grabs only me, I am not succeeding here; hopefully you will care about this music not only because my enthusiasm for the whole story is infecting you, but there is something surprising, inviting, and attractive about this bug aesthetic in music. The machine is not making it on its own, it is *not* just modeling the way insects think. A musician must interact with the structure that enables him to play his way through the way insects think.

I prefer my electronic music to be live, most certainly to be played, not programmed, so that a human has demonstrated something musical can be performed with a sense of insectability behind each musical act. The Zebra synth enables a performer to explore his inner (or is it more accurately his outer?) insect. The thrums should consistently evolve, not always the same way.

It works! I'm listening. I want to hear and create more. It places me in an artificial midnight summer meadow. All of a sudden I'm there. Now I want to shut down the machines, get out in the real world, and bring some real musicians to perform live with the thrums of bugs that have become newly musical to my human ears by playing too long with machines.

SIX

Throat-Singing with the Katydids of Glynwood

What human sounds can most easily join in with a vast nighttime meadow of singing insects? I take my friend, the most excellent overtone singer Timothy Hill, and we head out to the nearby Glynwood Farm during the humid time of August right in the middle of the night. Tim is a fabulous musician, both a singer/songwriter and a carefully trained overtone singer, who has spent years in the company of David Hykes and his Harmonic Choir, who have pioneered Central Asian throat-singing as an American art, where a single singer can produce a whole series of harmonic overtones, the miracle of one person producing a chord with his or her voice. Though this technique originates with Tibetan ritual-singing among Buddhist monks who sing in subharmonic, booming, super-low tones, in Mongolia and Tuva the same technique is used for a melodic, higher-ringing, more secular effect.

Hykes made the whole thing calmer, more evocative in a

spiritual sense back in the 1970s. I have long admired this music for the way it makes music out of overlapping textures produced by shifting the human voice into a sound-making realm it does not normally inhabit. With my newfound focus on bug music, I suddenly realize there is something in common between a human harmonic singer and a cicada—each makes a long, rising, rich, intense, and complete harmonic sound, with one singer showing he is capable of a damn enormous sound.

In Tibet, harmonic singing is booming and ominous; transforming ordinary, high-speaking voices into whale-like, impossibly deep bass rumbling thrums. In Mongolia, a higher resonance is used to evolve melodies that emerge out of the cavities of a singer's head, letting one person keep a grounding drone behind changing high pitches. These techniques are not natural for humans to do and take a lot of careful training, or perhaps un-learning of how one is supposed to sing. Such exercises are not good for your voice in the normal sense, and it is remarkable that someone like Timothy Hill can sing his own songs so well and clearly, and also lapse right into this superhuman kind of tone. I know it can sound spiritual, or cool in the way a buzzy, catchy hook grabs the listener in so many kinds of world music, but I really wanted to hear what such human luminous sounds could do when coming out of a field of singing insects, so many that no single sound source of them could be identified or caught. How would the pure *oohs* and *oms* of an overtone singer add a human touch to the world of insect music?

The Glynwood Farm is one large, open hillside that rises up like a giant bear's back, somewhere in the lower Hudson Valley. Once a private estate belonging to diplomat George Perkins Jr., it's now an institute that promotes sustainable local agriculture. From the point of view of insects, on this August night it sure seems pretty healthy. The crickets are relentless, chirping without a pause.

Their singing never exhausts them. Even the sex it leads to does not exhaust them, something all cricket handlers know well. The most vicious crickets need to mate right before a fight, it primes them up. This is not supposed to work for human athletes—remember your coach's advice before the big game!

Never mind. Do the crickets need to hear an overtone singer in a dark meadow intruding upon their mating grounds? They are not indifferent—depending on the notes Tim sings the crickets seem to change the speed of their chirping. *One two three four* digga digga *six seven eight nine.* It comes in and out of phase, hard to hold down into our simple beating rhythms. In the distance the bugs themselves seem to explore ambiguous overtones, a luminous living meadow texture streams into position. At one point the human overtone voice gets so strong the crickets seem to pause to listen, then as soon as it fades their chorus starts up again, filling up the silence. Back in the studio I slow the whole thing down and it all gets even more within human reach. Lower the pitch and the individual creatures sound more clearly accessible to us, each chirping a simple rhythm, but never too simple.

Overtone singing seems the perfect human way to enter their world, because it, too, is a kind of music with no necessary beginning or end, but it is an ever-present possibility we can choose to tap into, or tune out of. The harmonic series, the way Pythagoras's mathematical ratios define the resonance of the octave, the same and yet not the same, and the basic intervals of fifth, fourth, and that wolf-tone bluesy triad in between major and minor, a single voice can cast all of that out if you train the air cavities in your head to resonate each tone. It is a rigorous and out-of-the-box kind of training that most voice lessons do not prepare you for, but Tim has been doing it for thirty years. Harmonic singing taps into the basic resonances of nature that humans have evolved to hear in harmonically related ways, and these overtones carry on to the insect world as well. Overtone singing fits into the insect chorus in a primal, ancient way. The recording envelops me, I want to hear it over and over again, and it offers a kind of clue for how human music might grow closer to insect music, with a live encounter.

We are overwhelmed by the pulsing night soundscape, but the human resonating song does have a place in this puzzle of organic noise. I walk toward a big old apple tree full of katydids, they add a pulse to the noise-shimmer of the bush crickets, and the chirping of the tree crickets. The overtone human voice is quite different from the insects, and immensely strange right from the get-go. Perhaps because of this strangeness it immediately fits into the soundscape, and as I walk through the dark fields, barely able to see where I step, I compose as a listener, intensified with microphone and pumped-up headphones, tuning the landscape as I go, not looking for a documentation of the experience but a full-fledged revelation of its texture.

It seems a privilege to be in the midst of such a grand orchestra, resonating wildly at so many frequencies. How can it sound so much like it makes sense even though no one is in charge? Either the attuned slow listener lowers his expectations, or the structure of this music emerges out of all these disparate processes doing their part, and responding like tiny codes to the one special sound that means something to them. Everyone listens in the midst of the fray for something that matters—we are told these little crickets sing only to find a mate, but as with birds and whales, the singing may also be part of the very essence of their species, and thus be a defining part of their lives not to be explained away in the categorizing as only function.

All this texture is music, as sound and as image, beautiful to listen to, strange to inhabit. So little is written on the power of texture and timbre in the history and theory of music. Clearly the buzz and scrape of resonance, the dirtiness of distortion, has been an essential part of human music-making for centuries, and no one has bothered to explain why. Timbre is never described clearly in music textbooks, which understandably devote much more time to melody, rhythm, harmony, and form, all aspects of music that are much easier to talk about and analyze. But tone is the most personal of musical things, and it is the most salient quality that distinguishes one instrument or one virtuoso from another. It may be that greatness of tone and texture is what most separates an extraordinary from an ordinary musician, so it may be important that such aspects of music are hard to quantify or describe, but we know they matter and we seek complexity and roughness in texture as much as we value purity in tone.

I cannot be sure that the crickets and katydids are listening to Tim's droning, complex wave-like tones, but I suspect they do. I believe insects listen to everything, that they respond to sound like little machines following rules that they have evolved to follow for millions of years. The complexity of their timbre swarm is far away from the rhetoric describing human music, so we approach the encounter with very little expectation, very little to say. I listen to what he is doing with my headphones turned way up, so any move I make intensifies the sound.

I direct him: "OK Tim, step back twenty paces, turn toward that katydid tree, away from the horse. Sing again." It is like our friend Mr. Fung wandering for years across the Orient looking for the perfect atmosphere of singing *Ensifera.* All of us are searching for that enveloping soundscape that takes us beyond to indescribable realms of beauty, what the Persian philosophers once called the *sharawadji effect,* the greatest of all sonic illusions. Illusions? Sound appears and then it disappears, so its claim to make real transformations to us is a kind of illusion. But bug sounds don't stop. They go on and on. There are always many more of them than we can ever latch onto.

Don't ignore the airplane overhead . . . *use* the airplane, imagine it to be a giant bug. Test your texture against nature's texture, nature's texture vs. machine texture. How can you tell one from the other? Are nature's textures always more soothing than the thrum of a machine? When I lived next to the Brooklyn–Queens Expressway in Brooklyn Heights, after a time I came to find the incessant swish of the traffic soothing, like a meadow of thrumming insects. But when I left the city to visit an autumn meadow night, the beauty of the cricket sounds in the still full-leaved trees made my cry. That's when I knew it was time to move out of the city. Bringing Tim out to sing in the midst of such a meadow brings that fifteen-year memory to the fore. My time has come full circle with the incessant cycles of cricket time.

Later I bring Tim into the studio where I can exert total control of an artificial orchestra of booming cicadas and repeating cricket loops from all over the world. Here I find myself in the midst of a complete creative analysis of the confluence of human and insect music, where tones are balanced against noise. Does the creative world opened up by the bugs need the human? The pure pitches and their overtones voiced by Tim do add something to the wash of white noise and its antidotes. Since I am constructing the chorus in the studio, I play with what pitch is best for Tim's voice. Though he did record it live listening to my handmade chorus of bugs, culled from all over the world, my favorite rhythmic and textual recordings, further effected on the computer into larger, longer washes of sound, I tune him down, down, down to enter those frequencies no unadorned bug can touch. Meanwhile I pitch them down a bit, through transposing and grain-splitting delays, because let's face it, we humans prefer pitches lower than the follicles on the legs of crickets can hear. In the studio I tune the textures to make bug music an idea, not a documentation. I seek the kind of timbres the insect world encourages me to enjoy.

Still, transpose a human *ommmm*-ing voice and it is a series of overlapping, pure resonances. A cicada is still a beautiful wash of white/pink/hard-to-pick-the-color noise. The sonograms of such noise are far more beautiful than the simple documentations of clear pitches. Remember, this picture shows only *one* instance of Tim's voice. If we see it we are helped to hear it:

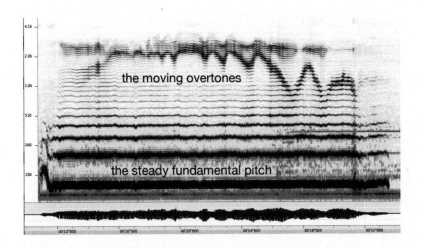

The horizontal, parallel lines in the sonogram show the steady pitch that grounds the single-sung note, but the curve above shows he is able to manipulate the higher partials to create the sense of a single voice singing in harmony with itself. Magnificent!

Next is one single late-summer cicada, offering up a single tone of rich enharmonic complexity, where glimmers of a clear pitch appear, but mostly a very complex variety of purely specific noise:

the sound of the hieroglyphic cicada

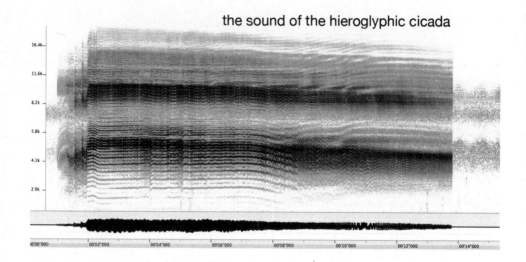

The harmonic content of a noisy sound is more confusing, more abstract, but also has parallel overtones curving into each other. Here noise turns out to be surprisingly beautiful and enigmatic when it is turned into frequencies analyzed against the seconds as they go by.

I could stare at these parallel sonograms for a long time and get lost in their different but related kinds of visual complexity, images that pull direct sense right out of what first seems a wash of strange noise. There are overtones inside all complex sounds, made by humans or by insects, glimmers of pure pitch struggling to get out amid vast, sonic confusion. We need to go deeper into these edge-musics we can barely explain, that will waft over us and mark the power of each season to remind us who and where we are.

Finally, here is a sonogram of Tim singing along with crickets live in the wild night meadow:

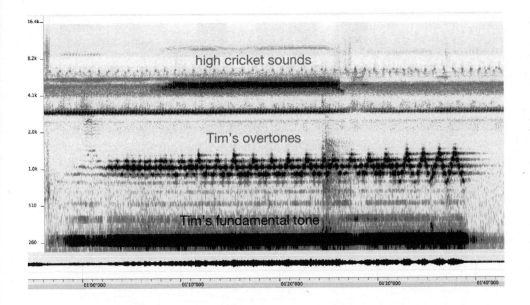

You may wonder as you look at this score/documentation of the moment whether or not Tim's wafting overtones make the high, noisy crickets sing, or is the confluence of sounds merely the result of chance? Compare this to the earlier human/pygmy soundscape—once again we have each kind of animal inhabiting their own sonic range, but this overtone song in meadow image seems understandably more unusual, less balanced, and expected. The soundscape, with or without a human musical intervention, is never merely random or an accident of unrelated noise.

These slightly related diagrams of parallel continuous sounds, one remarkably human and the other noisily cicadian, make me think of the visual art of the pygmies, steeped as they are in a world of overlapping insect and other forest sounds. Look at this pattern from the fabulous book *Mbuti Design* by Georges Meurant. This lavish, illustrated volume collects patterns used by Central African forest dwellers, either designs painted on their bodies for ritual performances, or patterns printed or painted onto cloth. As soon as I saw these images I saw a metaphorical score for the insect music of the rainforest, regular patterns layered upon one another, rhythmic but not quite exact, fitting together in this mystically thrumming way we can hear but not easily describe. Just look at these overlapping scratches of rhythm, from the simple to the complicated. This picture could show layers of graded thrum, with each sound in its proper place, with parallels and influence from one simultaneous line to the other:

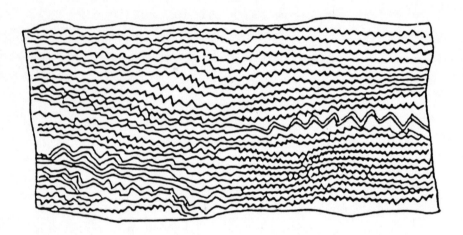

This tapestry visually reflects an aesthetic that developed in the midst of a consistently noisy environment, where human music cuts through to the chase. The pygmy songs and drumming give a regular ground and pulse to the sonic environment, but they do not take away from the integrity of the natural music. What is remarkable about this pygmy music is that it fits so well into the outdoor world in which it is made, and the fine recordings made by Louis Sarno have a certain genius because they make sure to include the bug music along with the people music. If our music is truly appropriate to the scene and place, then the overall sound-scape is improved by our presence, not polluted. Sarno says the

Bayaka women's kind of singing uniquely cuts through the forest sound. Indeed, it may succeed most because it turns noise into music: It takes sound that might bother or annoy us and reveals it as something with order, pattern, and form that can be enjoyed directly to make the natural world a more valuable and worshipful place.

Timothy Hill's overtone singing at the Glynwood Farm at night aspires to a similar integration of human and animal sounds.

In addition to beautiful texture, a new music emerges when we hear the crickets' many layers as hundreds of overlapping cycling beats, repeating instances, and glimmers of rhythm. *Analytical Studies in World Music,* by Michael Tenzer, suggests that music emerges out of raw sound when it is periodic, where the sound appears somewhere in the midst of repeating lengths of time, be it beats, phrases, choruses, strophes, movements, or times of the day. Something has to repeat according to a regular rhythm. The animal world can take this to far extremes. A fin whale can emit one subsonic pulse exactly every two minutes and hear the whole thing as a precise beat, transmittable across entire oceans in less than an hour. A whole population of *Magicicada* can emerge on cue, every seventeen years, making their entire life cycle a huge multiyear pulsing rhythm, the longest gestation cycle in the animal world, one of the longest "beats" any organism can know. Their whole lives could be thus conceived as music.

With repeating periods here we don't just mean regular pulses or beats, stuff you can dance to. Any sound fragment, when looped, can start to suggest a rhythm. Layer many of these on top of one another in irregular lengths and you begin to suggest the complexity of a real insect orchestra. The unevenness of it all may at first seem jarring or confusing, but with time the fragments of beat and pulse can grab our musical attentions. That's one way to make our own human Bug Music, and it's a strategy I employ extensively to reveal incipient insect musicality on the CD released in tandem with this book. Experimenting with the unevenness characteristic of the insect soundscape allows the human musician to understand, through practice, just what makes a chorus of insects have musical value. Hundreds of independent, irregular rhythms, perhaps listening to each other, perhaps following their own internal drummers, all but part of a giant rhythmic surge where females in the midst must find their eventual mates—a familiar image and a familiar situation.

Yet maybe the musicality is not so simple. Perhaps the texture itself is worth performing through. We've heard enough above about the limitations of natural sound and making strange, bug whine notes to be played on a regular keyboard, like the pioneering but somewhat dated sound in Graeme Revell's *The Insect Musicians*. Today we have heard so much of sampling, little rhythmic fragments that give a new dance piece some instant pure funk from another era, or strange bits of tone that produce instant exotica. No wonder some musicians have been tempted to bend the rules, to find ways of delving deeper into the periodic possibilities of repeating structures.

The musicality of the cicada may be in the precision of its noise, easy to see in the sonogram and possible to hear once we take the time to learn to listen. Is this textural music far-off and extreme? Actually these techniques are used in musics designed first and foremost to be danceable and popular. The German electronic musician Robert Henke, also known as Monolake, is one of the developers of the popular electronic music program Ableton Live, used by DJs and devotees of techno music to make repetitive, danceable beats. But above all else, Henke says that in music he is most interested in complex textures.

Henke's musical sensibility comes out of 1990s Berlin, but the software he inspired, Ableton Live, can do almost anything on-stage live. In contrast to most computer software programs, this one is designed to be used by musicians performing onstage, tweaking their laptops on the fly, using the machine to instantaneously make music, rather than just play prerecorded parts. You can play any sound file on your computer, transform it, play with it in the moment, and if you want, synchronize everything automatically so it all follows a steady beat of your choosing. Or, you can turn off all that synchronization and listen to the in-and-out phasing of overlapping irregular loops, like the melee of many insect species all singing through a dark, summer night at once.

The musician-friendly aspect of this software has given rise to a whole new kind of electronic music-making, where the computer becomes a much more friendly device for the live transforming of sound. Although I mostly use this software, and its ability to host and manage all manner of electronic effects to transform the live sound of my clarinets, in these years I'm spending influenced by insect sounds, I continue to learn how to "insectify" all the sounds I've got. Henke has created a tool called Granulator, that excels in constructing bug-like sounds, because it is designed for making textures. Henke is deeply interested in textural sounds, which he likes to overlay on top of signature, regular, mechanical-sounding beats. "I like slowly evolving sounds . . . and I like sharing my ideas," he announces in a video explaining the tool. It plays back a stream of loops of very tiny fragments. "I can randomize the position where the sample starts playing . . . it produces a swarm of possibilities." It builds on the theories of Curtis Roads to divide the sound you start with into microscopic, tiny instances of tone or noise. These can then be recombined in layers of complexity and irregularity. It literally produces a swarm of sound, so no surprise it is perfect for insect emulation and learning from entomological tunes. Inside Granulator, we are all arthropods, and a tiny blip of our sounds can be made infinitely large.

Who *likes* sounds of this nature? Ambiguous, cloud-like, swirling, and transforming textures are quite appealing, especially if the ground of your music is a regular, addictive machine-like dance beat and you don't want to be tied to the limitations of tonality or harmony. Clouds of sound become music if they just allude to chords and progressions. Rough noises can be softened, pure tones can be roughened, but the results are unpredictable. Some of the techniques programmed into Granulator are simply wrong according to electronic music theory: You can modulate the sound with a wave of pure noise, rather than anything with discipline. "In music," says Henke, "what is totally wrong can sometimes be right." If the sound begs you to listen further to it, explore its enveloping possibilities. I saw Henke perform a concert alone in a black-box room with two hundred and fifty speakers; he was also projecting videos on all six surfaces of the space. He stood behind his computer, smiling when his machine produced a powerful sound blending together with others producing results he did not expect. You had to be there. You are supposed to be there. It will never happen exactly like that way again.

In 2012 Henke released an album as Monolake called *Ghosts*. The record was made entirely in the studio, but comes with liner notes of a story that brings in insects and death from an imaginary rainforest scientific expedition. It's clear Henke knows there is something beautifully entomological about his project. Here's the story he tells about it:

How I hate those dirty little flies. Impossible to sleep, it is too hot, no wind, just motionless humid air. Five weeks with no change and the gods are laughing at us. Every part of my body hurts, and I cannot think straight. Last Friday the solar panel cracked in the middle of the night, I have no idea why and I almost don't care anymore, they will not find anything here anyway. Am I awake now?

They set up tons of equipment and the results so far: The strange noises during the nights got louder and louder. Some kind of monotonous moans that seem to come from no-where. The scientists run around and pretend that they know what goes on but they have no clue. And they are frightened, I can see it. How they look around, how they stop chatting when they get closer. How they avoid talking with me about their work: Ah yeah, we make some progress, it takes time to initialize the system, we have some preliminary data but things need to be calibrated first . . . The fact that Jonathan died in the cave whilst connecting the data lines does not help much to improve the situation. He was not afraid. I am also not afraid. I am just here to write things down. They tell me what they say is important for the world and I write it down. I had more demanding jobs. Apart from the flies.

I asked Robert whether he ever takes his laptop into the wil-derness into situations like the tale he weaves above. "Well," he told me, "once I was barefoot at an outdoor rave in Australia, and I felt a searing pain in my toe that immediately went right up to my head, and I suddenly blacked out. 'Crikey,' said my hosts, 'you must've been bitten by a bull ant, mate.' After that I decided it was safer to stay home in Berlin and imagine such journeys."

Since so much of what comes out of Granulator sounds like it is made by insects, I decided to put some of my own insect sounds into it and see what it feels like to play them in this expanded in-strument that is so much more than a basic sampler. I load in a piece of Jean Roché's fabulous recording of some night bugs in Cam-eroon. Isolating a particularly rhythmically interesting fragment,

I start messing with it, adding some frequency modulation harmonic richness to get a solid, thrumming beat. But wait—do I really want a thrumming beat? It does sound like the slowed-down experience of being inside an insect's head, reminiscent of that remarkable molecular mosquito recording. But what does it have to do with my original source of night-thrumming bugs? At first, it seems hardly anything. But then I listen back, and some sense of the organic richness of the source sound does remain. What is most interesting about the process still is that the musical ways of transforming the sound are so convoluted and unfamiliar.

My whole motivation in making my own music comes from incessant boredom. I have always questioned my abilities as a teacher of music because I'm really not interested in sounding quite like anyone else, and if I'm teaching, I always ask students to create their own unique musical identities, rather than telling them how to do the job, how to make the sounds required from them that someone might ask them to make. I'm always looking for something I've never heard before, a movement of sound that will surprise me but still remain perceptible as something musical. That's why I like music tools that do not explain themselves too readily.

Creating spontaneously, with improvisation, doesn't mean aimless tweaking and buzzing around. The key is to make something meaningful out of all these strange noises and unfamiliar textures. The early pioneers of turning all noises into music, like Luigi Russolo, John Cage, and Edgard Varèse, all dreamed of a world where the full arena of sounds could be available directly to composers, without the difficulty of finding musicians to realize the sounds they were hearing in their imaginations.

Now we have that world where any sound is fair game for musical transformation, but we still have not advanced in a clear sense of aesthetic on how to make sense of it all. Pierre Schaeffer tried to explain the meanings of all these sounds in the aforementioned *Treatise on Musical Objects,* but his theorizing did not penetrate the general musical aesthetic. What did happen is that all this sonic experimentation made its way more easily into popular music than classical music, probably because pop music always wants to sound a little bit new without sounding too new; it must be familiar enough for people to like it, catchy enough to hook you in with something only slightly different from all you've ever heard before. That's what critics of the whole thing like Theodor Adorno hated about it, and that's what the rest of us like. It's got the same catchy beat, but a slightly different sound, a new sort of buzz, a bit of a weird texture that still lures us in.

The very machine-like limitations of the electronic beat seemed at first too perfect, then a whole genre of music emerged to love it. The crisp strangeness of digital sound at first seemed cold compared to the warm, body-touching hum of analog electronics, but then a new audience grew to love the glitch and skip and crisp sound of the computer error, where all sounds run together like that digital soundmaking toy when its batteries run low. Like so many great human innovations, what began as a mistake ends up as innovation. We start to like what at first annoys, later lures us in for reasons we don't understand, and then we can't get enough of it.

If people dance to it, even the weirdest of sounds can cross the line into popular music. Robert Henke's music is usually based on a 4/4 machine-made rhythm, because that is the axiom upon which his whole musical journey is based. I start by thinking it is boring, that we tend to restrict ourselves and dance to beats too simple and predictable, but after a while I start to like it, too. Within the greatest constraints we reach the greatest heights, or so Stravinsky is supposed to have said. As long as the crowd is dancing they are happy to take in strange swirling sounds that cannot be grounded in their experience. We hear things that sound like no instrument anyone could singularly play. What's that you say? It is the munching noise of hundreds of tiny beetles boring their way through distraught evergreen forests? Wow! But the sound does not give its origins away, it only swirls and delights in directions that move us. This is where nature becomes music, where the field of recordings turns into art.

So when does texture need a beat? When it makes the listener too uneasy all on its own. With the pulse behind it, we can accept any manner of strangeness. Insects with their irregular rhythms provide a fair contrast to our love of regular rhythms. The sounds swirl and amass, grains piling upon grains, tiny moments of noise straining for big ideas.

If Monolake seems far afield from the music of bugs, then consider the work of Irene Moon of the Begonia Society, a performance artist who began her work as part of the Athens, Georgia, music scene in the 1990s, playing in between sets of the college town's famous alternative rock bands. An entomologist by day, Moon has created a unique form of performance art which turns Powerpoint, the conventional tool of scientist and marketer alike, into a demented tool for musical philosophizing. She tells tales out of the scientific literature of social insects, mixed with collage and strange song, reading academic texts in a slightly satirical manner to uncover the deep absurdity beneath them to produce an art form totally unique. No musician I have ever heard knows more about entomology through firsthand experience—Moon has worked in entomological laboratories from Florida to Tennessee and has a PhD in the field. She wouldn't have minded that Australian barefoot rave at all. "The sting of the bull ant," she tells me, "is supposed to be good for you." A true love of bugs informs her works, and her live shows are full of wild bug costumes, strange ditties, and the sounds of chewing ants and pulsing crickets. No one would doubt her qualifications and no Irene Moon performance is much like anything else at all.

As the above slide appears behind her on the screen Moon, perhaps wearing diaphanous giant wings, proceeds with the text:

Only male crickets chirp, or stridulate. It is thought that they produce four distinct varieties of song depending on the situation. Very loud to keep out intruders, a soft one for the ladies, a mad streak of jealousy if another fellow comes near, and the "Barry White": a post love-making trill.

Funny thing, if one was to need a snicker or giggle in a difficult social situation—Tell this little tidbit and seem more intelligent than you appear. Crickets are, of course, being insects, cold-blooded. I am not referring to "a killer" as they most often eat vegetative matter, No. Since they are cold-blooded their body processes are affected by the environmental temperature and they, unlike us, must rely on external heating elements to keep warm. This could be the sun or your heating vent, a cricket cares little. Anyway, the song of a cricket will actually speed up or slow down depending on temperature in a consistent and repeatable manner.

Fantastic!

This performance art is from a real entomologist, working today at the American Museum of Natural History on a worldwide project enumerating bugs to figure out how their populations have been affected by global warming. Days in the laboratory, late nights onstage.

Moon is not the only entomologist who dresses up as a giant bug and gesticulates across the stage. E. O. Wilson used to do that in his freshman biology class at Harvard in front of three hundred enthralled students. But Moon is not worried that her scientific credibility will be tainted if she turns entomology into art:

> Science is just really cool. Much of the creative process in art and in science is exactly the same—What would sound good? If I mix orange with blue what kind of color am I going to get? The schism between art and science is an artificial construct; perhaps it was made by people who don't walk in either world. The enthusiasm and obsessiveness of scientists who devote their whole lives to one tiny little question is very similar to an artist's passion which is needed to produce something great that is ever elusive, just a little bit out of reach. The epiphanies in each field are very much the same.

So I began with Béla Bartók and György Ligeti and now we've ended up in art galleries and dance floors in Berlin. What is this—all music remixed as one? Don't blame me, but swat at the insects. They've done this. They changed me. They've changed so many other musicians and composers as well. They've let me admit many more kinds of sounds as music. Bring on the buzz! Let in the flies!

A handful of big-time pop artists have made insects a part of their success. The first example that comes to mind is Michelle Shocked's first album, *Texas Campfire Tapes,* which was recorded at night at a campground at a folk festival in 1986, on a Sony Walkman. In addition to the freshness of the sound and the energy of the songs, the most noticeable thing about this record is the constant sound of rhythmic, synchronized crickets in the background. They were really there. The recording was made secretly by an English record producer and it was hailed as the discovery of a brand new homegrown talent, in the style of the earlier generation of Alan Lomax wandering the South looking for real roots blues singers. Shocked had no idea the performance was recorded, or even released in Britain to great commercial and critical success. She felt her works were stolen, ripped out of context, and released without her characteristic stories and commentary. Plus the Walkman was running on low batteries and recorded at a slightly higher speed. It didn't even sound like her, and for years nobody noticed. She adjusted the recording in 2003 and released it more properly.

Never mind the controversy, the performances sound truly authentic, and the rhythm of the guitar gels nicely with the beat of the crickets, who immediately make the whole performance sound right out of the true fabric of a summer night. The beat of the crickets proves that steady rhythm chimed on the Earth long before humans ever appeared. They give her a capella verses a steady ancient pulse. And then why do the crickets always seem in tune, chiming exactly the right note and the right beat to ground the guitar? They have no doubt about their rhythm and its place. It's a texture, not a pitch, and something about its resonance is always welcome. We harken back to this record today and hear it as an authentic, genuinely unplugged example of original folk music right from the woods. Insect rhythms can cycle clearly behind our rhythms; they always find a way to sound together in our ears.

In 2006 the British electro-pop star Imogen Heap was asked by the art presenters Artangel to be part of a commissioned project where many notable artists wrote songs inspired by the Book of Exodus, called *Plague Songs*. Her piece was called "Glittering Clouds," based on the plague of locusts. The regular dance beats all seem to be made out of samples of grating insects, and behind are occasional clouds of insect-like washes of noise. So far this is the most pop-like and smoothly produced of the bug songs we've considered. After a while it sounds like any synth-pop potential hits, and the bugs recede into the background behind the familiar elements of beat, bass, bells, and overlaid voices. This song convinces me there's a place for the bugs in even the slickest productions.

In the end, the language of popular music may make the finest use of insects when it returns to the source, back in the rainforest. For the last two decades a handful of popular musicians have emerged from the rainforest island of New Guinea, and with the help of Australian music producer David Bridie made several records with subtle but catchy electronic beats that have carried the fine music of this part of the world to a global audience who loves a groove. The most distinctive thing about these records is that sound of the forest, mostly a thrumming chorus of insects, heard not just in the background but sometimes in the foreground of the songs. The first artist Bridie worked with was George Telek, first when Bridie's band Not Drowning Waving traveled to West Papua to make the record *Tabaran* in 1990, and later on Telek's own album, *Serious Tam,* which was released all over the planet through Peter Gabriel's Real World label. I always liked this record because the sound of the place where the music came from was given center stage in the mix, in a similar way to Sarno and

Krause's forest pygmy recordings. The difference here is that a 4/4 beat is added, firmly placing the music into the electro/pop/world music category.

I know this music is no pure, traditional, primitive tribe release. By the twenty-first century few music cultures are isolated or innocent. The presence of the modern world has long penetrated the reaches of the world's most remote tribes. And might we have learned the regular beat from these original rainforest insects in the first place? Consider that thought for a moment. Get some rainforest bug sounds, ethnic vocals, add a grooving beat, and you've got a world music hit, right? Not so simple. All elements have to be combined with the greatest sensitivity and verve. Usually this doesn't happen. The results sound vulgar, or worse, just like everything else you've already heard.

The latest release by David Bridie and musicians of New Guinea is one of the best, because it shows not only the power of music to meld many cultures together, but also the power of music to realize the cries of insurgent politics. *Strange Birds in Paradise* is credited to David Bridie and Arnold Ap, the great Papuan musician, anthropologist, and cultural leader whose songs were banned by the Indonesian government, which has ruled West Papua since 1964. Only the eastern part of the vast island was allowed to become the independent state of Papua New Guinea, and the western half still remains under Indonesian control. It is valued for its mineral and forest resources and there is little sign its rulers want to give it up. But the native population remembers well that Ap was assassinated by the ruling regime in 1984, and the native musicians Hein Arumisore, Jacob Rumbiak, and Gillius Kogoya have collaborated with Bridie to bring these forbidden songs of Papuan identity back to global consciousness. The recording is the soundtrack to an Australian film of the same name that tells the story of how the anthems of Papuan freedom are still banned in a nation that the Indonesian army controls as an unruly wing of the vast Indonesian archipelago. When the word gets out about this project, these courageous, indigenous Papuan musicians will most likely be forbidden to return to their home nation, just because they dared to bring these outlawed songs to the attention of the world.

The pathos and purity of the Ap melodies are clear enough, even without this moving true story. The harmonies are in parallel, like all those Melanesian choir songs we sometimes hear, yearning back to the directness of all that pre–Baroque Gregorian smoothness. The insects chime beyond the limitations of any single pitch, as they often like to do. They start and stop, with their own rhythms, oblivious to what humans want to hear. But our human cries for freedom go so well with their eternal songs across million-year spans of time. They will go on through the high trees no matter what regime is in charge. Add a beat and people will get up and dance, for all over the world we know well the globalized beat of the beloved machine. Even in Papua the cry of the cricket might just as easily be the ring of a mobile phone. It is a happy thing to welcome the sounds of all creatures into the grooving, familiar music of the dance floor. It's old-fashioned and petty to worry about the global music machine corrupting the pure, beautiful music of threatened cultures. That's what world music critics and professors feared for years, at least until about five years ago. Now it's the global music *business* that has collapsed as the planetary proliferation of intermingled sounds only rises. Papuans should dance to whatever grooves they want. That's what freedom means, and I know one day they will taste it.

You who have heard about and perhaps listened to all these varying streams of human/insect music should at least have learned that people music has all sorts of uses for bug music. We can learn a sense of eco-sonic balance all the way from that extraordinary pygmy and rainforest arrangement with every sound in its proper place. That sonogram was as organized as a printout from a calculated mathematic dance track. We humans just have to know when to let go, when to leave space for the powerful audio rush of a wide frequency spread of insect insight.

The production through increasingly sophisticated technology of ever more careful swirling and complicated sound textures moves beyond notes, chords, tones, and easy rhythms into new kinds of musical sound that we will need new language to describe. The more we listen to these new textures in music the more we will figure out what to say about it. Sometimes we need a familiar beat to be coaxed in to the strangeness of a rainforest's natural older-than-human rhythms. Then at other times we need to turn off the regular beats we know so well, and listen for other reasons. The human dance can and will change. Millions of years before our music, and even bird and whale music, lie complex textures and ways of communicating that can still seem to sound as if they come from a far and distant future. They have gone on forever already and I hope they will never stop. After all this listening for insect sound in human music, at last I feel ready to try to join in with the real thing.

· · · · · · · · · ·

SEVEN

Sax and Cicadas

2011 was the big year for Brood XIX, the largest of the thirteen-year cicada populations, promising great sounds of loud bugs converging the forests of Illinois, Missouri, Tennessee, and more. I knew I had to get down there for this extraordinary wash of rhythm and noise, to hear this great din of insect emergence once again. This time I would be prepared, and would figure out how to make music with them, no matter how many diaphanous wings I'd have to swallow.

And yet, when I called my friends in St. Louis, they said, "Cicadas in June? What are you talking about? They usually come out in August."

"Oh, this year they will arrive in June. Lots of them. Thousands. *Millions* actually."

"Well, nothing like that is here yet," I heard in late May. "Nobody's said anything about it." And that went on for several weeks until one day I got an e-mail that said, "They're here," and once again the people's memories were jogged to take in the great noisy music that nearly all had forgotten.

To document this journey, I knew I needed a photographer. Charles Lindsay was certainly the man for the job. I knew I could trust him since one year before we had gone together to Montana to collect sounds and stories for a multimedia piece ostensibly based on the struggles for water in the American West, which ended up being entitled "The Electrosense of Paddlefish," referring to those great dinosaur-like creatures who communicate in the dark waters of the Missouri with ancient electric impulses few other organisms can use. As that trip involved visits to a bar famous for its adjacent tank full of mermaids, a creationist museum, and a toxic pit mine slowly filling up to one day poison the citizens of Butte, Montana, I figured Lindsay would understand why we should journey through swarms of millions of tymbaling creatures who could only be experienced less than once a decade.

"Yes, I'll do it," he barked on an iPhone as he stood by the Very Large Array of radio telescopes somewhere out in the Great Basin. "But it will have to be a fly-in, fly-out situation. June will be a very busy time for me." Lindsay was serving as the first-ever artist-in-residence at SETI, the Search for Extraterrestrial Intelligence, out in Silicon Valley, California. Charlie had convinced them that his unique, intense photo-based artworks, created by a carbon-based chemical process of his own invention, had enough to do with alien worlds to welcome him in to the space explorer fold. But they let him go to investigate these creatures closer to home.

"Forget that wild goose chase, Charlie, we got aliens right here in Missouri, the Show-Me state. I need you with me back on Earth."

"OK man, but just this once. I am preparing to go trout fishing in space."

. . .

Searching for outbreaks of cicadas has gotten a lot easier since the days of Riley and Marlatt's pinpoints making those hundred-year-old brood maps. Now there are websites full of professional and citizens' reports on where the bugs are. After picking up a car at the airport we're looking online for exactly which city parks are likely destinations for our time travelers, but when we approach the South Mason Road exit on Route 64 we hear a din so loud that it reaches us even with the windows closed. We roll down the glass and a huge swirl of sound surrounds us. "I see," muses Charlie. "This must be the place."

Our up-to-the-minute online report of where the bugs are suggests that Edgar M. Queeny County Park is the place to go, and our ears confirm what the Internet tells us. Roll down the windows, and just listen. Follow the sound to its loudest source. The park is teeming with cicadas, a whole wash of beautiful noise. *TshtkeTchtke-EHHHHH-ou! TshtkeTchtke-EHHHHH-ou!* We try to approach individuals near as we can, to get clean sounds out of them beyond the great swell.

"Wow!" I am amazed. "I may never work with birds again." The cicadas climb all over the headphones, and all over our heads. The best spots are the low hedges right near the parking lot. They are also high in the trees, but those are too far from us for the best sound. I pick a few up to adjust for greatest acoustic separation. They are curiously warm to the touch. For a second I feel I'm handling a warm-blooded beast.

Charlie laughs, "Soon they'll be crawling out of your mouth."

A few cicadas fly by the microphone with a loud *whoomph*. They are deep in the trance of the culmination of their lives. Joggers puff by, shaking their heads. One stops to marvel at the strange beasts with our parabolic microphones and wild headgear. I explain

the situation. "What?" a woman doesn't believe it. "You came all the way from New York to see this? Come to my backyard, you'll see layers of rotting cicada shells on the lawn."

"No thanks," I smile. "I prefer them alive and lost in song."

"You actually enjoy this racket?"

"It's a song of love, of course I like it. And to think that we can only hear it once every thirteen years."

"That's too often if you ask me."

"Put on these headphones, you can hear it all larger than life."

"No thanks," and she runs off, eager to get home to a lawn full of dead cicadas.

As the swells expand the *tsh tsh tsh*es become harder to hear. The whole mass begins to swell together, a synchronized chorus of noise waves, some enigmatic ocean of insects in love. Such sounds are so total, so evocative, that it is a bit surprising that few visual artists have been able to depict it. Probably the most well-known in America to have specifically tried to illustrate the great chorus of insects is the Buffalo-based painter and wallpaper designer, Charles Burchfield, whose 1917 painting *The Insect Chorus* reveals on the following page how just listening to singing bugs can lull the viewer from an ordinary suburban backyard into the beginnings of pure abstraction. Thus the path of the whole twentieth century in art begins by taking the noises of bugs most seriously.

Each abstract visual element in this image has been tagged to specific insect sounds by the artist and his many interpreters, from the angular antenna–like lines in the grass, supposedly field or bush crickets, to the angles in the leaves suggesting the tree crickets, on up to the swirls in the trees evoking the grand cicadas. A late summer chorus to be sure, but the image holds just as well for the late spring periodicial explosion. Cicada sounds make the green trees alive with brown, black, and orange noise. He paints it like he sees it. Close your eyes and you may see patterns just like these yourself as you listen, traces of light left on the retina as it hypothesizes meaning into all the sound.

As you all no doubt remember, only the *cassinis* synchronize, while the *decims* combine into a clear-toned forest frequency. Each presumably does it to intensify its presence, or perhaps the mood. Might they each fill a separate acoustic niche like all those sounds in the Bayaka forest? One might hope nature uses such logic, but by now you should know the view I prefer: that nature just evolves its own weirdnesses, if the weird gets through. Prime-year cycle cicadas are an anomaly, but a possible anomaly. And so they have appeared.

I do need a better answer, though, to those who hear no beauty in this relentless noise. First off I will ask them to put on the phones, and listen with the volume turned up. Then they will hear continuity swirl inside their heads, and the scratchy tones fill their whole process of thought. Either it grabs you as a trance, and you succumb, or you pull off the cans and shout, echoing Baudelaire, "Enough, take me anywhere, anywhere, *out* of this cicada world."

Then comes the whole story, the grand cycle of thirteen years, the vast majority of their lives silent underground, and the stark rarity of the emergence and the chance to hear this grand, gathering chorus of singing males. When you know what it stands for and how unusual it is, your curiosity may be piqued. We love the noise ever more when we know it is soon to stop, and what a privilege it is to be able to witness it.

Charlie and I are collecting sounds and pictures, sinking deeper into the thrum and the mood. We endeavour to climb as deep into this phenomenon as we can, finding the tools to most touch the sound. We follow our maps and our reports to hunt the densest concentration of the singing bugs, and to struggle to find a way to make live and immediate music with them.

The direction is north, toward Champaign, where we are set to perform live with cicadas and percussionist Jason Finkelman, two days hence. En route we will need to recruit some insect musicians to join our show.

Leaving north from the parks of St. Louis we enter open farmland and the great noise recedes. We are distracted by a spaceship-like metal structure next to the highway that I recognize as a Finnish FutureHome, just like the one my friend Martin Pedanik has in Estonia. That detour gets us lost in the adjacent giant antique shop, but soon we are back on our way.

Near the exit to Lake Springfield smack dab in the middle of Illinois we hear the greatest din that has caught us thus far. Even with the air conditioning cranked and the windows closed, we hear this wave of cicadas. So we leave the interstate to investigate. Driving past the lake the sound only gets louder, and it culminates at a single tree at the corner of East Lake Shore Drive and Vigal Road, one small round tree with a sign pointing to a KOA Campground down the pike. We look at each other and smile. We have found it. The great swarm. The world tree. Grand Cicada Central, the concatenation of all things *Magicidada*. This is the epicenter, this afternoon moment, the place of human cicada music that we have been waiting for.

Of course, scientists among you, reality is nothing as pointed as that. We simply found the right tree at the right time that was teeming with so many cicadas that it was impossible to think about anything else. Cicadas were our world, our total sound field. The tree was low, the insects were all so close to us. Time to go in.

First we unpack the recording devices. We've got so many cicadas all around us that at first it seems merely a total wash of white white noise. Charlie gives up on sound alone. "This is all too much, I'm going to get some visuals here," then he takes out his camera and is off on what he does best: collect fabulous macabre imagery in still photos and video.

Creeping right to the edge of the world tree, the epicenter, the tree of innumerable insect souls. Living, noisy cicadas drop from branches into our hair, all over our clothes, soon inside our clothes, just hanging there, singing. They start to tickle, I begin to laugh. I run for the open field, giggling. What else can I do, the scene seems so ridiculous.

It's about to get even more absurd. I have no choice in such situations except to pull out an instrument. More used to the delicate earthiness of the clarinet, with this great volume I have no choice. Must pull out the saxophone, to cut to the chase, or cut through the *swiiiisssssssssshhhhhhhssssssssssshhhhhhsssss* . . . I pull the straight golden horn out of its case and immediately cicadas are excited, they jump right onto the shine. I'm worried about starting to play because I don't want to crush any of them who might try to climb from the inside of the horn out one of the tone holes. They're all over my brown shirt, outside, stuck to the stripes, and inside, holding their ground. They're all over my scraggly hair, alighted on my ears, tymbaling up a storm. It is essential to wear sunglasses just to keep them from bounding and bouncing into the eyes.

As I finally get up the nerve to play I find I must hunch over to keep the swarm from overwhelming me. The noise is deafening, but the soprano is used to cutting through. A tentative, minor melody comes out. I reach out, and try. Up, down, a look around. Upon holding out a long tone I suddenly hear the cicadas swelling along with me. *Contact! Contact!* They're certainly crawling up my naked back under my shirt, but I'm more excited about possible contact in sound. They are all rising in volume in a great big *swish*. I imagine it is certain notes that I play that bring on the sync. Later, though, I read about the three concurrent thirteen-year species and I learn I'm in the midst of a swarm of *tredecassinis,* and the swell is just what they do, whether or not a sax is pontificating in their midst.

But who thinks of causality at a time like that? I am awash in a mist of tymbalic noise, the strangest orchestra I have ever tried to join. How could they possibly care about my sound, so different it is than their own, so fixated they are on the mantra of *fly! sing! mate! die!* And yet, fly at the sax they do, jump to the shine,

swell with sound all over my hair. I had read that in Zen temples
when a gong is struck, all the cicadas jump right at it. They love
sound, all sound, surprising sound, expected sounds. They need
not think much about it as they have been waiting for this moment for thirteen years.

Noise is a subjective thing. If it is supposed to be unwanted
sound, then why do we sometimes crave it? Why do we take pure,
clear sounds, and add a buzz, make them noisier, sticking those
rattles on the mbira thumb pianos, or plugging a guitar into a fuzz
box to dirty up the tone? I have been asking this question over
and over again and it turns out to be one of those aspects of the
world's music about which the least is often said. I think of the
African mbira thumb piano and its characteristic buzzing sound
what Ephat Mujuru called the rough, dizzy voice of the ancestors,
maybe those insect ancestors of us all. Musicologists keep telling

me Bruno Nettl said somewhere, though I can't find it, that the pure sound is the classical, the refined, the codified, while noise implies danger, roughness, the sound of the people, the sound of nature. We always need at least some of that to truly feel alive. Even this guitar stomp box exists, ready to buzz up your sound:

And yet this world tree of cicadas really is too much. It's just a total wash of sound, far away from the angularity of my horn, it's cut-to-the-chase pierciness that has pushed the popularity of the soprano sax, so hard to play in tune, but able to pierce through the white noise. If the female cicadas like it, it's good enough music, right? Am I getting any wing-flicks, girls? Who is that crawling down my pants? Enough! And I make a run for the car . . .

Why play one, clear, single human sound into such a panoply of noise? First, it's a humbling experience, being one of the thousand musicians, the rest of them desperately beating their tymbals for their very lives, caught up in the desperate unique propagation of their species through sound. Then, it is a strangely inspiring moment, you are taking your single pure tone and trying to find a way for it to have meaning in the midst of all this atonality. Arnold Schoenberg would have understood, he who wrote that we must learn the whole history of counterpoint and increasing harmonic complexity only to, at the end, cast it all away in the name of something new and pure. The cicadas would have floored him, and maybe they did, driving him west to spend his final decades teaching young composers to write angular music for cartoons.

The bugs outnumber us, bug music swallows humanity up in the end. Sure it is noise—simple, programmed, essential, necessary noise—that looms out of our past and streams over our future, outpacing us, outflanking us, outselling us far in the distance in the end. Spare me man's redundancy! What need has nature for all our uneasiness, testing, and pain! Can you count thirteen years underground and know exactly when to come up? Of course not, that's not how we live. We exist to wonder about all these matters and play games with the truth, testing our artistic dreams against the inscrutability of impractical cycles of time. How's that for a definition of music for you? Tossing out sounds along improbable cycles of time. Forget about it, just play. And shake all those bugs out of your shirt.

Lindsay snaps away, protecting his lenses from our subject matter. With his practiced eye he gets the best shots, still and video, evolving a story out of our encounter with the cicadas' great tree of origin, like the Norse Yggdrasil. The more we listen and try to join in, the closer we get to sensing their world.

But we have a concert to play and just a few hours to get there. "Hey," says Charlie, "we need to bring some of this sound to the show."

"OK," I agree. "Get out that jar. Pick a handful of the best singers, and let's get out of here."

So Charlie opens the plastic soup container and brushes a few dozen cicadas into the bottom with the plastic lid. There are so many bugs on the leaves that it's no trouble to shove them all in. We punch a few air holes in the top to make sure no bugs will be harmed in the process, and pack all our equipment back in the car. No matter how much I shake my hair there are still a few cicadas in it. And even after I shake out my shirt there are still a few stuck on me somewhere. Inside the car a few are buzzing around. We roll down the windows and help them escape.

As we drive the remaining hour from Springfield to Champaign, the cicadas in the jar seem to respond differently to different music. They seem to get into the Rolling Stones. They don't really like Keith Jarrett. They have a particular penchant for Ethiopian and Zimbabwean dance beats. I feel like we could learn a thing or two from them.

As we arrive at our hotel we hastily hide the creatures inside an equipment bag as we approach the check-in desk. The cicadas are chirping and clicking from inside the black bag.

"Don't mind that," I say casually. It is a gussied-up university building, turned into a somewhat hip hotel, maybe the hippest in all of Champaign. "Routine radiation detection. The sounds indicate everything is normal here."

"Oh, that's good to hear," says the desk clerk cheerily. "We wouldn't want you bringing up any pets to the room is all."

"Certainly not," I answer.

We change for the show and bring our charges back into the vehicle. We drive a few miles and are met by percussionist Jason Finkelman, who has set up the show in the basement of a downtown art gallery. The place is surprisingly packed. I had no idea anyone would know who we were, or what we were planning to do.

"Some interesting people are in the audience tonight," Jason smiles.

I look around and nod. I spy my friend Richard Powers, the greatest American novelist of my generation, and then a wizened, white-haired figure at the back.

"That," grins Jason, "is Bruno Nettl."

Can it be true? I don't believe it.

"It does look like him," I say. "Don't tell him, but I wasn't even sure he was still alive."

"Very much so," says Jason. "And he tries to go to every concert in town."

If the founder of American ethnomusicology is out there, a man I wouldn't hesitate to call a truly historical figure, who wrote his pioneering works fifty years ago, then I will have to change my introductory remarks to say something that might appeal to his gray eminence.

"We dedicate this concert," I begin shakily, "to this great emergence of cicada music that happens around here only once every thirteen years. We are all fortunate to be in the midst of it, and able to take the time to listen in to one of the rarest sonic happenings in the insect world."

I glance up at Nettl, who waits patiently. So I go on: "The sounds of insects are not usually associated with music, but most of the time we think of the annoying buzz of flies, the whine of mosquitoes about to bite us, or the nibbling of termites slowly eating our houses into dust." OK. "But this cicada sound is different. It is the accumulation of long calls of *phaaaaroooah* all at once into a continuous high tone, plus the surges and waves of two other species. It's easy to hear it all as a great wash of static, a white noise covering over all music.

"Yet noise is a part of all music. Pure tones are just shadows of music, machine creations, ideas abstracted from the mess and unevenness of the real world. We need noise to make music, we need uncertainty in order to survive. And with that in mind we have brought a few of these insect musicians along to join us. Charles . . . can you release the band?"

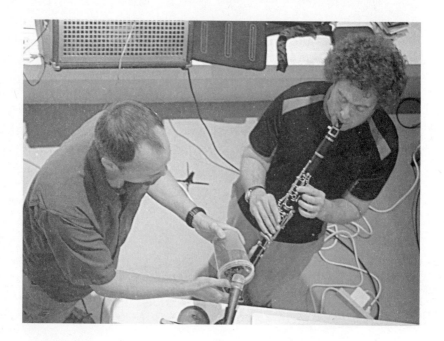

And Lindsay produces the plastic jar with the members of the *Magicicada* community. They are a bit sluggish after all this travel and confinement, but he places one directly on the microphone and the cicada begins to flex his tymbal. I produce some scratchy noises with my computer, and he starts to produce a strange ratchety sound. Listening to it months later, I realize it must be a *tredecula,* but at the time it just sounded like a strange insect noise. This *tredecula* was very well behaved, staying put on the microphone during the whole show, contributing much live noise to the show.

His compatriots flew sluggishy around the room, stopping on amplifiers or mike stands, taking in the sound.

What do I suppose they were taking in? Cicadas do not need to think too much to make important music. Do I really think their music is important? It is the longest nymph cycle in the animal world, and they are among the most perplexingly precise annual timekeepers. They are the only living prime number generators we know of. They are unique participants in a grand natural rhythm even the masters of irregular rhythmic cycles on Indonesian gamelan would be shocked to learn of. We can only hypothesize why it might have evolved, we can only invent mathematical models to explain it, but we cannot really know what it is like to experience such precise timekeeping with the brain of an animal so small and finely tuned.

These facts make me want to love their noise all the more. I compare this ultimate consuming sound to the more delicate chirps of crickets with which this book began, a cool nostalgic sound that makes us cringe with the sense of fatality. Death is always near, it will come to us all. The sound of the cricket in the late autumn leaves is a desperate cry to live on to the winter, a wish that will never be fulfilled. Bug music is the most ancient and the most primal music, the emergence of great rhythmic complexity from the minds of creatures who have no conception whatsoever what they are in the midst of. Dance, song, evolution, transformation—really, do you need to know any of it to grasp the power of the beat? Of course not.

Older than bird music, way farther back than whale music, the fact that simple individual insect brains produce vast endless song shows once again that music lived on in this world of life long before any creatures developed a kind of communication that could be called language. Rhythm is an original fact of the natural world, and the insects first beat and bow it into being. They celebrate the dance of the world.

It is a privilege and joy to be able to make music with them, to reveal, in this two-story downtown Champaign Gallery called Indi Go, that humans and cicadas can produce a strange sound-work together that those of at least two species may enjoy. No need for us to be alone on this planet when it comes time to break into song.

Bruno Nettl tries to leave quietly, but I stop him by the exit. "What did you think of this human-cicada music? Can you tell us what it means?"

"The desire to see in music something beyond itself has long been a significant strand of thought, especially in the last two hundred years," he once wrote in a book.

"So did you like it?" I asked.

"The music we like conforms to an ideal, often an ideal that is only the scholar's own." Spoken like a wise Zen master. "We are often interested in exotic virtuosos." The cicadas could certainly be heard as that. Or was he talking about us?

All of us were surprised by the show, an improvised surprise blending cicada song, clarinet, electronics, and drums. Even while playing we knew not what to expect. Audience and performers alike walked into the night with a new appreciation for the value of sound. And sound keeps us alive, singing long into the darkness, helping us remember how great it is to be able to hear music in the trees all around us and dream that we can join in.

The next day we return to the world tree and release our cicada musicians back to their home. Not even one was harmed.

They all tumble into the grass, sit tight for a moment, and then slowly walk away. Hearing the sound all around them they fly back into the trees. The whole mood is different today, it's early and the area is not yet in full sun. It's just not the same, there's only an average amount of cicada noise, nothing special, no great inspiring sound. The perfect moment was only yesterday.

We have no time to wait, but instead get ready to head west, on to Missouri and the great gathering of insect song scientists and ever more cicadas. We don't know it yet, but we will not find a single site as magnificent as this one. For us, the song of the cicadas has already begun to recede. Months later I think about it and I long to hear it again. When this book arrives on paper I'll once again be able to hear them outside my own house. And when they leave I will right away begin the long march of forgetting, the long sorrow wondering back on what I was doing seventeen years ago.

Sure, I can chase down their emergences every few years, always find some somewhere, but what is that all trying to prove? Seventeen years ago I wouldn't have dreamt of playing along with all this noise. I heard nothing musical in it, but it did prevent me from doing anything else at all for several weeks save writing that poem, which I quoted at the beginning of this book. Like the nymphs underground, it has taken me seventeen years to realize how important that moment was. Yet when it comes to cicadas, perfect moments will, rarely, return. We need to be ready for them.

Over the passing years I started listening to more and more animal sounds, began to care about their ancient, venerable right to endure here on Earth long before and after anything humans might do to the planet. I began to think if I could learn from this necessary and eternal depth I might make music more grounded, more essential than before. I played my clarinet in ever stranger places.

And then technology evolved. The computer became a friendlier place to transform the strangest of sounds in far more fluid directions. Rhythms were reborn in new repetitions of uneven, ovelapping lengths like the choruses of hundreds of katydids on sticky summer nights. The hissing of summer lawns could be transformed all over and upon itself magically inside a box. *Magicicada. Magikatydida. Magicriketopia.* Or why not the insect with the strangest of all singers' names, possibly the best for an incipient band: The Partially Musical Coneheads.

With easier possibilities for sonic manipulation strange sounds became ever more familiar. Auto-Tune no longer corrects only out-of-tune pop stars, but is now an electronic effect we come to expect. Distortion, degradation, fuzz, crackle, and pop are all new sounds we don't always want to eliminate, but often admire. The original musical sensations we humans might have first learned from bugs, hundreds of thousands of years ago, are now back in our most popular songs, and some of our most experimental songs.

If noise is still unwanted sound, then sometimes we crave the unwanted. The uneven, the unwashed, the unpalatable, the un-born. I long for the tones that can only be heard but once every seventeen years. Perhaps after reading this far you will long for them, too. If you get the book in time they may still be out there. Quick, set it down and go outside to the trees to listen. Or you may be intrigued enough to plot your journey in the coming years to find this sound as difficult to comprehend as it is rare.

Yet the easiest to find insect music may be even more beautiful. Perhaps before you heard crickets and katydids as random noise and now you know their music is the organized result of simple rules. These rhythms may calm you or scare you, and what you think doesn't matter as far as they're concerned. Long before humans ever arrived, and long after we're gone, the ancient rhythm and noise of the singing insect world will live on, proving that music is in the basis and the roots of continuing life. These sounds wax and wane with the temperature and the tides, and their steadfastness always reminds us that time keeps coming back upon itself, no matter how worried we are that all we love may be inadvertently destroyed. Sound or silence, which makes you happiest? Those who hear insect noise as music have truly found a place in nature's wild music.

The seasons go on, the snows approach, all bug music fades as this year is gone. All music that is made is destined to end. Do not despair, the songs will return. Just wait another seventeen years.

That is a long time, but not an impossible time. Ou-Yang Hsiu gets
the last word on the deep melancholy that always also includes hope:

> *Myriads of creatures—each after its own shape and kin*
> *Hold at their season ceaseless tournaments of song;*
> *Swiftly, swiftly, their days run out,*
> *time transmutes them, and then there is silence—*
>
> *Desert-silence where they sang.*

The Opposite of Terrorism

Winter comes and the annual call of crickets goes, and summer heats up and the June roar of the periodic cicadas fades away, not to return for another thirteen or seventeen years. It is a rare enough event that it is hard for us to remember the sound, not to mention the wonder at the awesome march of evolution that has led to such a strange adaptation.

The intrepid cicada hunter can usually find one brood or another, ready to emerge somewhere in the eastern United States. When you are ready to hear this bug music again, just check the records and take a trip. The astrologer O'Grady encourages me to go check it out. "These creatures are clearly very important to you . . . just notice how they appeared the very year you were born," he pulls out my frayed chart. "Now it is difficult to put cicadas into the astrological narrative, but the field is no stranger to evolution itself. Remember that we've had to reckon with the deplanetization of Pluto . . ."

"Come on Sean, how can you really believe that the stars are interested in our tiny lives here on Earth?"

"Of course it is a fiction," he smiles. "But fictions can be quite useful. Like your fiction that you can make music with cicadas."

"All right, listen to me do it. And remember that it was you who brought me out to listen to these swarms in the first place."

In 2012, Brood I was set to emerge in a very localized part of Virginia, starting just north of Lexington and extending down to Roanoke. This is the smallest of the nineteen broods and the most concentrated in a focused place. And it's only nine hours away from where I live.

John Cooley went down there in the beginning of May charting the precise strength and location of the emergence and comparing the results to what he observed here last time, just seventeen years ago. That was an eventful beat in the rhythm of his own life, not only the life of the *Magicicada,* since that is when he and David Marshall uncovered the details of the three male songs and the female wing-flick response, revealing the periodical cicadas' mating ritual as the most complex in the insect world.

This time the tools had improved. He was driving around with a computerized data-logging system, where his machine could automatically register the GPS coordinates of any spot he indicates where the cicadas are present. There were some anomalies . . . a mysterious emergence happened in Tennessee, hundreds of miles west of where the nearest Brood I cicadas were expected. One never knows just where and when an animal might turn up. Though we can with reasonable certainty predict where and when these clockwork creatures will appear. We always expect the seventeen-year cicada. But you have to be very patient if you plan to ally them with your memories of the last time they were here.

Making music with cicadas has never been one of Cooley's priorities. He's a straight-arrow scientist who sees these little critters as tiny machines, or little software routines, programmed to respond precisely to their own sounds and no others. Yet since I first met him one year before, he's gotten slightly intrigued by my musical aspirations, and he swears he'll teach me how to reliably interact with these cicadas.

"Amazing that you've actually shown up here, David," he seems genuinely excited. "Finally we can go out in the field together. I know you want interaction. I think I know how to incite it." He's got bags of female cicadas ensnared on branches, just itching for it. The males buzzing around them are all excited, and they can't get into the screen cages. He smiles, "They might even be ready to mate with you, if you provide just the right sounds."

The study site is in a secret location in the mountains just west of Lexington, Virginia, the epicenter of this most concentrated of cicada emergences, Brood I. Cooley has found an ideal study site at the edge of a recent clearcut in the forest, with a lot of open space and many small trees. The *Magicicada* like the tops of the trees, are usually hard to see if easy to hear. But here the trees are so tiny the bugs are singing all around us. And with all those unmated females trapped in screen bags, the males are especially excited.

All Cooley has to do is whistle the *septendecim*'s *pharoah* calling song and rival males start echoing him. I am impressed. When I manage to match the notes on my clarinet they also respond to me, but Cooley's whistle is still better.

"Oh, this is nothing," John smiles. "You have to learn the females' wing-flick. If you make this tiny snap with your finger at just the right interval after the *pharoah* ends, he will move on to his second song, which we call Court II. Timing is everything. You have to make the flicking sound about one third of a second after the male stops singing. A quarter second is too short, and a half second is too much."

Sure enough, Cooley is a master of insect timing and the male moves on to the second song, a more rapid *pharoah pharoah pharoah*. I try to copy him, but my beat is off. After a while I start to get it as well. But the male is confused. He doesn't move on to the next sound.

"Oh, he needs to see something that looks close enough to a female cicada to want to mate with it. Take this standard, brown, home lightswitch. It also makes a nice clicking sound. Watch when he hears this." Sure enough, the male cicada climbs onto the switch and tries to mate with it, making his third sound, the one he makes during mating, known as Court III, a kind of *te te te te te te te te* rapid laugh at exactly the right frequency as the *phaaaar* part of the main song.

"Why does he need to sing *while* mating?" I ask. "Hasn't he already gotten the girl? Is he just enjoying himself?"

"Oh, I doubt that," says Cooley. "I think it's probably something like this: These females are hearing the sounds of three closely related species all going on simultaneously. They need to be sure they are mating with a male of just the right species, their own. Even while mating they might not be sure, *unless* they are hearing the truly correct sound." With his music, he is reassuring her everything is all right.

With instruction from the master, in listening and responding, I feel better prepared to make bug music than ever before. This time when we find the perfect music-making site, a thin copse of trees with adjacent open space on both sides, somewhere up a lane called Unexpected Road, we can hear the chorus of three species of seventeen-year cicadas, each making not only one main characteristic sound, but two other secondary sounds as mating is encouraged and then is happening. That makes a nine-part orchestral piece of carefully composed insect music, the most complex courtship behavior of any bug.

At first listen it is just a wash of white noise, but as we pay closer attention to it, the deeper musicality of the noise comes out. All this listening and reading has made such alien music a little bit closer to human comprehension.

This time I've brought along my son Umru Rothenberg, age thirteen, and he has the fine idea to play the iPad along with the cicadas as I play my clarinet. The touchscreen tablet makes a large variety of strange electronic sounds, and some of them seem to blend surprisingly well with the noise of the cicadas. He's at the age where he has to be talked into coming on wild adventures like this, where he could easily slip away into a world he doesn't want his parents to understand. But I am so glad he finally agreed to come with me, so he can make kinds of music only his generation will feel intuitively and know.

He doesn't say much about the whole experience, but he grasps the task at hand immediately, no instructions needed—this may be the very music iPads were designed to play. Running software called Animoog, the iPad produces detuned swells of buzz-like swooshes that weave around the synchronized, noisy waves of the afternoon *cassinis,* not pitched but expanding and contracting in a clear beat. Whenever the sound fades all the males swirl into the sky before alighting upon a new leaf and starting their *hwaaaaaaaap* again.

This is some of the strangest music I've ever played (and I do seek out the strange), but after these several seasons of trying it some sense is starting to be made. You can hear it and more on the *Bug Music* CD, the soundtrack to this book. Available everywhere . . . if music is still being sold by the time this book comes out.

The second day I bring Tim Blunk to the same place to take in the noise. He spent thirteen years in prison before his own emergence. Same number of years as my son has been alive. Neither one of them has previously had the chance to make music along with such creatures and such sounds, but each quickly finds a way to find their place.

Tim is playing a small mbira from the collection he imports from Africa. Like the music of the cicadas, it has both a clear tone and a clear buzz. After one day of listening to Cooley, Tim has got all the specific sounds down. He is explaining the nuances of the various courting songs to the two film crews that are with us documenting the scene: one for Animal Planet and the other for my friend the independent director Richard Robinson, who immediately saw that an interesting story could be told blending the parallel adventures of the periodic cicada and the man imprisioned for many years for trying to blow up the Capitol.

"Sure it was the wrong thing to do," Tim explains to the cameras. "But when you're living underground, with a tight group of radicals, it's easy to lose your sense of what's right and wrong when the rage within you builds up, stronger and stronger with each year you're not allowed to show your face or tell the world what you're really up to."

"Like a cicada slowly growing and feeding underground for thirteen or seventeen years?" I ask.

"Probably not very much like that at all, David, but like me these insects have been doing time. I do share that, at least, with them."

Cooley cautions us once again not to take these metaphors and analogies seriously. "Remember, David, these insects are just like little machines." Little software programs. Little apps with not so many neurons for a brain.

"Sure, John, but then how can they do the amazing thing of counting the exact right number of years underground before it's time to come out? We have no idea how they do that and we can't figure it out." I counter.

"One day I hope we will. Science does advance you know."

"So does music. Think how far we've come to learn how to appreciate all this noise!" It's there of course in the earliest of human music, with our love for the song of the wind in the trees, for the thrum and the shake and the scratch of the uneven, the fuzz, the brush. The impossibility of silence that comes with seeking out the most ineffable of sounds.

There's really only one question I want to ask Tim Blunk out here. I knew it was important to me to bring him out to witness the release of the periodic cicadas and I knew he would find his own way to join in with the sound. I know why he did what he did back in the 1980s and I know he learned well enough that his anger was well justified while his actions were not. He has done his time, and emerged when that time was done without knowing anything along the way about when he would get out. In that sense his life's journey has been far more open-ended than that of the cicada, like the lives of all of us other humans much more fortunate than him for not having to endure such suffering and penance.

I suppose that's what it means to be a human who counts the beats of time, from rhythms in a song to the great species-defining rhythms of the emergence of life. We really don't know where exactly we are going or what it is we will remember from any of the events that happen to us. Other animals don't have to think about such things, they just proceed through life as if they always know precisely what to do. I'm not sure I would enjoy that kind of life, but I would like to understand it a bit better. I suppose that's why I think we should all spend some time making music with the natural world.

"So, Tim, what is the opposite of terrorism?"

"What . . . huh? Oh . . . hard to hear you with all this bug music swirling all around. It's amazing! But the opposite . . . of . . . ?"

"It's not meant to be a trick question."

"I guess it isn't the worst question. The opposite of terrorism? Maybe poetry."

"Does a small group of people commit poetry to affect the population at large?"

"I see what you mean."

"Terrorism is meant to incite fear. What is poetry supposed to do?"

"Make people feel love. Or courage. Or peace?"

"Poetry as a random act to induce love?" I suddenly remember, for some reason at this exact moment, that opera singer Pavarotti once admitted to being afraid of high notes. "Of course I am afraid," he said. "What sane man is not?" I wonder what he would have sung along with cicadas. We all fear noise until we learn what can be done with it. Learn the subtle kinds of noise that make up this great song and it becomes a noise of many colors, an enveloping music we are able to love.

The opposite act to the one that brings fear is the one that opens you up to the sheer beauty of the unknown that you first wanted to laugh at or ignore. Music might be the greatest form of poetry since words can never completely explain it. In its greatest mystery it may be accessible to all living things, even those we cannot talk to or control. With music we can deal with the brightest light and the dankest darkness of the things we have all been through. These melodies and rhythms really can reach from our species on out into the world of cicadas, a species very different from us in so many ways except that they, too, need to sing, mate, live, and die.

That's what I want to teach when I bring all of you, my friends and readers, out into the world to hear things it is so easy to forget, and so important to remember.

All depends on your ears.

For Further Reading

Until now there has never been a book arguing emphatically for the musicality of insects, but there have certainly been enough clues throughout the boom and buzz of literature. There is one classic book on cicadas that includes a bit of musical notation, John Myers, *Insect Singers* (Routledge, 1929), but it is mostly concerned with species found only in New Zealand. Gene Kritsky wrote the best recent historical overview of the story of thirteen- and seventeen-year cicadas in the United States, *Periodical Cicadas: The Plague and the Puzzle* (Indiana Academy of Science, 2004). The classic work on the topic by C. L. Marlatt, *The Periodical Cicada* (U.S. Dept. of Agriculture, 1907) is available for free online, http://archive.org/details/periodicalcicad00marlgoog.

There is a handful of classic humanistic works on the larger significance of insects in culture, from the many writings of naturalist Jean-Henri Fabre, most available for free download, such as

The Life of the Grasshopper [1891] (http://archive.org/details/lifeofthegrass00fabriala), and Vincent Dethier's *Crickets and Katydids, Concerts and Solos* (Harvard, 1992). There is the recent and magnificent *Insectopedia* by Hugh Raffles (Pantheon, 2010) and the more technical *Insect Media: An Archaeology of Animals and Technology* by Jussi Parikka (Minnesota, 2010). Still, there is no better source for literary references on singing insects in all the world's languages than the five self-published volumes in *Land of the Locusts* assembled by Keith Kevan in Montreal in the 1980s and 1990s. You can contact the Lyman Entomological Museum to get ahold of those.

On the synchronization of crickets you can get the widest perspective in Steven Strogatz, *Sync* (Hyperion, 2003), and the best technical summary can be found in Michael Greenfield, *Signalers and Receivers: Mechanisms and Evolution of Arthropod Communication* (Oxford, 2002). For the details of insect acoustic communication in general, check out H. Carl Gerhardt and Franz Huber, *Acoustic Communication in Insects and Anurans* (Chicago, 2002). See also Darryl T. Gwynne, *Katydids and Bush-Crickets* (Cornell, 2001) and Sakis Drosopoulos and Michael Claridge, eds., *Insect Sounds and Communication* (CRC, 2005). On communication in insects beyond the frequencies we call sound, see Peggy Hill, *Vibrational Communication in Animals* (Harvard, 2008) and of course Frej Ossiannilsson, *Insect Drummers* (Swedish Entomological Society, 1949), online at http://ag.udel.edu/delpha/6030.pdf.

The finest accessible book on the detailed sounds of crickets and katydids is John Himmelman's *Cricket Radio: Tuning In the Night-Singing Insects* (Harvard, 2011), which also includes great audio recordings, which are available free online (http://www.cricketradiobroadcast.com/Cricket_Radio_Songs.html). This is just a fantastic book, and all who want to pursue the topic further should read it. The best photo/sound guide to American crickets, katydids, and cicadas is Lang Elliott and Wil Hershberger, *The Songs of Insects* (Houghton Mifflin, 2007), which contains great sonograms, high-resolution recordings, and amazing photos of all our most musical insects. Elliott's Web page is also a great place to explore the music of nature in all its glory, www.musicofnature .com. Other stellar examples of recordings of insect music include Jean Roché, *Cigales et Grillons* (http://www.musicme.com/Jean -Roche/albums/Cigales-Et-Grillons-3307513003922.html), and Tom Lawrence, *Water Beetles of Pollardstown Fen* (http://www.gru enrekorder.de/?page id=5235). The sound quality on these two releases is truly extraordinary.

On the link between insect sounds and electronic music, I recommend Curtis Roads, *Microsound* (MIT, 2004), and the edited collection I put together with Marta Ulvaeus, *The Book of Music and Nature* (Wesleyan, 2001). Recent books that explore the connection between natural noise and human musical aesthetics include Salomé Voegelin, *Listening to Noise and Silence* (Continuum, 2010), Joseph Nechvatal, *Immersion into Noise* (Open Humanities, 2011), and Joanna Demers, *Listening Through the Noise: The Aesthetics of Experimental Electronic Music* (Oxford, 2010), which is the most successful in addressing the aesthetic value of what some call unwanted sound.

My previous books *Why Birds Sing* and *Thousand Mile Song* both have associated websites with all kinds of sounds and links, and the one for this book, www.bugmusicbook.com, will have the same additional content to enhance your entomo-musical experiences. Once again, I have the same suggestion, though this time finding your goal is much easier—just go outside on a warm, summer night and carefully listen. Listen long enough until you feel ready to somehow join in.

The Bug Songs Playlist

You might find it difficult to discover human music inspired by or composed out of insect sounds, but I combed the world looking for examples that touched me. The following are my twenty-six favorite examples:

Josquin Despréz, "El Grillo," Ensemble Les Cours Européennes, *Musique de la Renaissance au Temps de Botticelli*

Harry James, "Flight of the Bumblebee" (Nikolai Rimsky-Korsakov), *Rare War Time Recordings vol. 1*

Béla Bartók, "Out of Doors: The Night's Music," Jeno Jando, *Bártók: Out of Doors*

I Gusti Putu Putra, "Balinese Monkey Chant 2: Forest Scene," *Kecak from Bali*

Richard Lerman, "Insects After Gamelan," *Within Earreach*

BaBenzele Pygmies, "Women Off to Gather Payu," *Bayaka—The Extraordinary Music of the BaBenzele Pygmies*

György Ligeti, "Artikulation," *Forbidden Planets—Music from the Pioneers of Electronic Sound*

Francisco López, "La Selva (Excerpt)," *The Disc of Music and Nature*

Tom Lawrence, "Seven Springs," *Water Beetles of Pollardstown Fen*

David Dunn, "The Sound of Light in Trees," *The Sound of Light in Trees*

Mira Calix, "Nunu," *3 Commissions*

Douglas Quin, "Aria Locustae," *Oropendola*

Lars Fredriksson, "Invocation II: Three Harmonious Bells," *Ting Qiu: Mr. Fung's Ensemble of 108 Singing Crickets*

Jean Poinsignon, "Cigales cymbals," *Bestioles le temps s'étend . . .*

Boštjan Perovsek, *Touchings*

Ricardo Villalobos and Max Loderbauer, "Resvete," *Re: ECM*

Graeme Revell, "Invaders of the Heart," *The Insect Musicians*

Loga, "620," *An Anthology of Chinese Experimental Music*

Monolake, "Toku," *Ghosts*

The Black Dog, "Future Delay Thinking," *Music for Real Airports*

Mungolian Jet Set, "Glitches'n'Bugs," *We Gave It All Away . . . And Now We Are Taking It Back*

Michelle Shocked, "The Incomplete Image," *Texas Campfire Tapes*

Imogen Heap, "Glittering Clouds (Locusts)," *Plague Songs*

Telek, "Tolili," *Serious Tam*

David Bridie and Arnold Ap, "Apuse," *Strange Birds in Paradise: A West Papuan Soundtrack*

Hazmat Modine, "Cicada," *Cicada*

Deadmau5 (featuring Chris James), "The Veldt" [original mix], *The Veldt EP*

You will find most of these pieces in an iTunes playlist at https://c.itunes.apple.com/us/imix/bug-music/id545659782.

Bug Music: The CD

David Rothenberg: bass clarinet, clarinet, seljefløyte, soprano saxophone, electronics, bug sounds

Robert Jürjendal, guitar (2, 6, 9, 14)
Timothy Hill, overtone singing (8, 11)
Umru Rothenberg, iPad (1)
Charles Lindsay, cicada wrangler (7)

Produced by David Rothenberg
Recorded on location and at B Street Studios, Cold Spring
All titles published by Mysterious Mountain Music (BMI)
©℗ 2013

Thanks to Lang Elliot and Rex Cocroft for some of the insect sounds.

"Some hear bug music. Some hear people music. All depends on your ears," wrote Wâfu in 1866 in Kyoto. Maybe you get it, maybe you don't, but it's most likely that human music evolved out of the millions of years of listening to the sounds of bugs that filled the soundscape of our ancestors. How can you tell if what you're hearing is bug music? Some of what I've done here is jam live with insects, out in dark fields at night or amidst swarms of cicadas by day, swarms you'll only run across every thirteen or seventeen years. Other pieces take these insect noises and stretch or loop them in the studio, where one sound can be transformed into nearly any other sound. Yet I've tried to learn from the bugs, change the sense of what I like and what I play, to join in to the scratch and thrum of these ancient rhythms, falling in and out of sync, just as they have done for millennia before human beings arrived on the scene.

Scratch, Chirp. Buzz, Thwoom. Scrape. Snip. Insects make all kinds of noise that don't immediately seem like music, but people have always loved the way these sounds envelop our minds and send our bodies deep into a trance. Sometimes I have used purely electronic sounds that seem to outbug the real work of bugs, so close to the oscillators and filters of electronic music are the mechanisms of our ancient little friends. You won't always be able to tell what is entomological and what is technological. That matters not. As Aristotle taught us, technology finishes what nature has begun.

The three live tracks were recorded out in the field, with no overdubbing by real human musicians and real insects. The others were created in the studio, but all the music has been played, not programmed. *Phaaaroah!*

1. Magicicada Unexpected Road
Father and son on clarinet and iPad respectively confront the smallest of the periodic cicada broods in Lexington, Virginia, spring 2012. A live performance with no overdubbing.

2. Katydid Prehistory
Named in honor of *Archaboilus musicus,* the 165-million-year-old

prehistoric katydid, whose fossil remains reveal an ability to sing distinct pitches, an ability that its genus later devolved away into more scratchy noise.

3. Insect Drummers 1: Inside the Mosquito's Brain

The three pieces in the "Insect Drummers" suite, named in honor of Frej Ossiannilsson's important Swedish study, present interactions between clarinets and synthesized insect sounds played in Native Instruments Reaktor. Part 1 is inspired by Igor Sokolov's research into the sounds produced by molecules inside the mosquito's brain. Can we hear the difference between life and death at the nano level?

4. What Makes Them Dance?

Uhler's Katydid, mentioned nowhere in the text, is said to have the most complicated single insect sound. Here a wash of its songs is granulated into a moving cloud, mixed with an easy groove.

5. Treehop

Rex Cocroft's famous recording of several three-humped tree-hoppers tapping on a tree branch leads to a full range of vibrational possibilities. Do we follow their irregular beats, or try to tame them into human senses of measure?

6. Riddim Bugz

Here, for once, the beats of bugs are quantized into regularity. Featuring the red-headed meadow katydid, mole cricket, confused ground cricket, and the common virtuoso katydid, over the regular beat of Robinson's cicada.

7. Phaaaroah!

All the insect sounds here come from the Brood XIX cicadas Charles and I encountered in Missouri in June 2011. Special thanks to Lindsay's expert cicada handling abilities—he figured out how to get them to chirp on cue.

8. Glynwood Nights
Tim Hill and I climb the hills of Glynwood late one August night in 2011. The result is live and somewhat slowed down to reveal the subtleties of human/bug interaction.

9. Insect Drummers 2: The Water Boatman's Loudest Penis
Yes, it is true that one of the loudest sounds in the animal world comes from a tiny underwater beetle called the Lesser Water Boatman vibrating its penis under the surface of a pond. Do not try this at home.

10. Listen Outside the Ear.
The Norwegian overtone flute seljefløyte has no finger holes, and thus plays only the tones in the natural harmonic series, like harmonics played on a guitar. Here its open-ended sound is combined with a chorus of swordbearing katydids and partially musical coneheads.

11. Chirped to Death
Timothy Hill sings in the studio over a bed of snowy tree cricket rhythms. Compare this to the sound of overtone singing in the wild in track 8.

12. Kikitara
A granulated Cameroon cicada provides the thrumming backdrop here.

13. Insect Drummers 3: Your Sound Can Kill
Engraver beetles are decimating the forests of the American West, some gobbling up pines, others into spruce. David Dunn has used extreme electronic sounds to attempt to destroy them. This piece explores the possibility that sound can kill.

14. Final Creatures
Live from the tower of St. John's Church in Tartu, Estonia, concert which only fifty people were allowed to attend. Guitar and clarinet are mixed with the night sounds of a Borneo rainforest.

15. Magicicada Warm Springs
Back in Virginia, live with bass clarinet and the vocal *swish* to incite the cicadas.

16. The Year of Insect Thinking
The squeals of a pine sawyer beetle inside a wash of noise.

Terra Nova Music TN 1309

available wherever music is still sold in 2013

Acknowledgments

Insect sounds are all around us, but most of us do not listen to them too closely. Thanks to all who have helped me take this subject all the more seriously. Starting with the 1996 emergence of periodic cicadas in Cold Spring, John P. O'Grady and Amy Lee Knisley were there as the insect singers swirled all over our heads. I knew one day I would write a book about them.

I needed to get in touch with the scientists. Over the years, David Marshall and John Cooley have been dutiful correspondents. We finally met at the 2011 International Meeting on Invertebrate Sound and Vibration (http://isv2011.missouri.edu), thanks to the generosity and open-mindedness of Johannes Schul. Thanks to Lang Elliott for offering me his vast archive of insect sounds for my own experimentation, and to Rex Cocroft for letting me use his fabulous treehopper sound.

Thanks to Adam Rudolph and Bengt Berger for helping me find Lars Fredriksson, the Mr. Fung of the Ensemble of 108

Singing Crickets. Bridget Nicholls of www.Pestival.org has always been a fabulous resource for all creative evocations of the entomological universe. Her co-conspirator Mark Pilkington of Strange Attractor has always had a sense for what strange stone to turn over next.

Angela Impey and Ben Mandelson always knew what ethnomusicology might have to offer my quest. Thanks to Noel Lobley at the Pitt-Rivers Museum for introducing me to Louis Sarno, and to Bernie Krause for talking about his adventures with rainforest recordings and animal sound niches.

In Berlin thanks to Robert Henke, Jessica Ullrich, Lars Schmidt, Susanne Heiter, and Urs Heckmann for humoring my attempts to connect electronic music to insect thinking.

Thanks to Charles Lindsay for coming on the Midwestern cicada journey, and to Jason Finkelman for setting up the Champaign concert, and to Nelie Hodgman McNeal for taking us in in St. Louis. Thanks to Umru Rothenberg, Tim Blunk, Tim Lawrence, and Richard Robinson for heading down to Virginia to face Brood I. Thanks to Dave and Carolyn Llewellyn of Glynwood Farm for letting us record there. Thanks to all musicians involved in this project from long before it ever was a project: Douglas Quin, Irene Moon, John Wieczorek, Timothy Hill, David Dunn, Bjarne Kvinnsland, Billy Gomberg, Garth Stevenson, Jaron Lanier, Lukas Ligeti, Art Labriola, Ben Neill, Peter Marting, DJ Zemi 17, DJ Spooky, DJ Strangefruit and Knut Sævik of Mungolian Jetset, Scanner, Ebe Oke, Jan Bang, Petri Kuljuntausta, and especially Robert Jürjendal for all these years of transatlantic collaboration.

Thanks to Tanya Merrill for expert research assistance, and to my agent, Michele Rubin, for placing this book with Daniela Rapp at St. Martin's Press. Thanks to Johanne Landry and Anne Charpentier at the Insectarium in Montreal, and to Stéphanie

Boucher at the Lyman Entomological Museum at McGill University for getting me the fabulous Keith Kevan volumes.

Thanks to all at the New Jersey Institute of Technology for encouraging my research escapades, including Fadi Deek, Rob Friedman, Don Sebastian, Carol Johnson, Burt Kimmelman, Andrew Klobucar, and Chris Funkhouser.

Other helpful readers and confidantes include Hugh Raffles, Rachel Mundy, Ofer Tchernichovski, Michael Deal, V.J. Manzo, Michael Greenfield, Rachele Malavasi, Jussi Parikka, Mark Changizi, Peggy Hill, John Himmelman, Paul Kahn, Michael Ryan, Hara Woltz, Catherine Chalmers, Charlie Keil, Mark Slobin, Bruno Nettl, Laurie Anderson, Jim Cummings, Pauline Oliveros, Marilyn Crispell, Manfred Eicher, David Abram, Lasse-Marc Riek, Robin Rimbaud, Jefferson Porter, Edie Meidav, Joel Chadabe, Angela Schuster, Halley Harrisburg, and Richard Powers.

Thanks to my wife, Jaanika, and son, Umru, for continuing to put up with ever stranger sounds, and thanks to all those bugs for not biting me too much and instead sometimes being content just to sing, fly, mate, and die.

Notes

Prologue

vii "All depends on your ears" My translation of these lines that appear in Keith Kevan and Vernon Vickery, *Land of the Locusts* part 4, vol. 1 (Montreal: Lyman Entomological Museum, 1998), p. 180.

One: The Seventeen-Year Pitch

3 "a model of the cricket brain" See M. Zorovic and B. Hedwig, "Processing of Species-specific Auditory Patterns in the Cricket Brain by Ascending, Local, and Descending Neurons During Standing and Walking," *Journal of Neurophysiology,* vol. 105 (2011), pp. 2181–94.

7 "We praise thee auspicious Cicada" Louis Figuier, *The Insect World* (New York: Appleton, 1872), p. 102.

8 "They all will die." Bashō. My translation of a poem that appears in Keith Kevan, *Land of the Grasshoppers* (Montreal: Lyman Entomological Museum: Memoir no. 2, 1974), p. 300.

9 "A man wanted to eat a cicada" Keith Kevan, *Land of the Locusts*, part 2 (Montreal: Lyman Entomological Museum: Memoir no. 10, 1983), p. 74.

10 "Here was a thing that cried upon a treetop," Keith Kevan, ibid. pp. 96–97.

11 "a great sort of flyes" William Bradford, *Of Plymouth Plantation 1620–1647,* quoted in Gene Kritsky, *Periodical Cicadas: The Plague and the Puzzle* (Indianapolis: Indiana Academy of Sciences, 2004), p. 10.

12 "They are in great numbers" Paul Dudley, in *Philosophical Transactions of the Royal Society,* 1733. Quoted in Kritsky, p. 16.

13 "It was unbelievable" Pehr Kalm, "Beskifning på et slags Gras-Hoppor, uti Norra Americas (*Cicada septendecim*), *Vetenskaps Akademiske Handling* 17 (1756), pp. 101–16. Quoted in Kritsky, p. 27.

14 "the monotonous, protracted *twang*" Nathanial Potter, *Notes on the Locusta septentrionalis americanæ decim septima* (Baltimore: J. Robinson, 1839). Quoted in Kritsky, p. 45.

15 "languishing notes of true love" D. L. Phares, in the Woodville, Miss. *Republican,* May 17, 1845. Quoted in Kritsky, p. 66.

15 "Of course he won the prize" "The Cicada and Eunomos," *New York Times,* November 12, 1882.

15 "album called *Cicada Summer*" Download here and pay what you wish. Online at http://specialpassenger.bandcamp.com/album/cicada-summer.

16 "There were originally fourteen 17-year broods" All broods and their ranges are described in detail at http://magicicada.org/about/brood_pages/broods.php.

18 "Nervous people who become exasperated" "Wanted: A Use for Cicadas," *New York Times,* editorial page, June 22, 1894.

18 "the quintessence of vegetable juices" "Prof. Riley Eats the Cicada and Praises Its Flavor," *New York Times,* June 2, 1885.

18 "They're soft for just a few hours" "Cicadas: It's What's for Dinner," *Missourian,* May 26, 2011. Online at http://www.columbiamissourian.com/stories/2011/05/26/cicadas-breakfast-lunch-and-dinner/.

19 "1½ pounds of cicadas" Recipes and cicada food photos here: http://cicadainvasion.blogspot.com/2011_04_01_archive.html.

21 "still the most misunderstood insect" Donald Prattie, "Strangest of All Insect Dreams," *New York Times,* May 24, 1936, p. 8.

21 "I felt a *positive* sadness" H. A. Allard, "Some Observations Concerning the Periodical Cicada," *American Naturalist,* vol. 54, no. 635 (1920), p. 551.

22 "To join / To feel" Keith Kevan and Vernon Vickery, *Land of the Locusts,* part 4, vol. 1 (Montreal: Lyman Entomological Museum: Memoir no. 18, 1998), p. 88.

22 "Even Bob Dylan caught a whiff" Iver Peterson, "17 Year Cicadas Answer Cue with a Crunch Across the East," *New York Times,* May 19, 2004.

23 "as opposed to harmless lovers" You can find the lyrics to Bob Dylan's "Day of the Locusts" easy enough online, www.metrolyrics.com/day-of-the-locusts-lyrics-bob-dylan.html.

27 "Only simulated wing-flicks" John Cooley and David Marshall, "Sexual Signaling in Periodical Cicadas," *Behaviour* 138 (2001), p. 841.

34 "How can I leave my body?" Keith Kevan, *Land of the Locusts*, part 2 (Montreal: Lyman Entomological Museum: Memoir no. 10 1983), p. 134.

41 "how come I always know / just when you will arrive" Cicada Boy? That's me.

43 "nature's prime number generators," Clifford Pickover, *The Math Book* (New York: Sterling, 2009), p. 22.

45 "a very rare event" Jin Yoshimura et al., "Selection for Prime Number Intervals in a Numerical Model of Periodical Cicada Evolution," *Evolution,* vol. 63, no. 1, (January 2009), p. 292.

47 "It wears diaphanous silk" Keith Kevan, *Land of the Locusts,* part 2 (Montreal: Lyman Entomological Museum Memoir no. 10, 1983), p. 146.

50 "Who listens any more to me?" Lo Ping-Wang, 658, translated by Witter Bynner, 1920 (Kevan, *Land of the Locusts,* part 2, Lyman Memoir no. 10, 1983), p. 21.

Two: Mr. Fung's Cricket Orchestra

56 "When it is time to sing" The five cricket virtues, quoted in Hugh Raffles, *Insectopedia* (New York: Pantheon, 2010), p. 78.

57 "the most prized competitors" Hugh Raffles, *Insectopedia* (New York: Pantheon, 2010), p. 83.

58 "Cricket in hall, the year runs to its close" Ezra Pound, from "Songs of Tang," *Shih-Ching* (Cambridge: Harvard University Press, 1954), pp. 54–55.

62 "doing some deep listening" Phone conversation with Adam Rudolph, May 9, 2012.

62 "an elephant in a porcelain store" Email from Bengt Berger, May 20, 2012.

65 "We are a hurried, worried people" H. A. Allard, "Specializations Governing Musical Expression Among Insects," *Scientific Monthly,* vol. 27, no. 1 (July 1928), p. 86.

65 *"No cricket needs to chirp himself to death"* H. A. Allard, "Our Insect Instrumentalists and Their Musical Technique," *Smithsonian Report* (1928), p. 567.

67 "I feel the throbbing of life" Jean-Henri Fabre, "The Cricket: The Song, The Pairing," in *The Life of the Grasshopper,* translated by Alexander Texeira de Mattos (New York: Dodd, Mead, 1920 [1891]), p. 350. Online at http://archive.org/details/lifeofthegrass00fabriala.

67 "the rhythm of the repetition" Brian Eno, "Ambient Music," *Book of Music and Nature,* ed. David Rothenberg (Middletown: Wesleyan University Press, 2001), pp. 139–42.

69 "rough, buzzy, scratchy" So he is supposed to have said, but so far I have not found the reference. Actually it seems a rather un-Nettlish thing to say, since the man, like most ethnomusicologists, is not known for passing judgment on the musical qualities of one form rather than another, but emphasizing instead differences in social context. The music itself can often sound more similar than the way it is framed in the midst of culture. Or so ethnomusicologists and

anthropologists like to say. But two of my most trusted ethnomusicological sources, Angela Impey and Ben Mandelson, are *sure* he said it somewhere!

71 "Snowball that likes to sway along with the Backstreet Boys" Aniruddh Patel, Irene Schulz, et al., "Experimental Evidence for Synchronization to a Musical Beat in a Nonhuman Animal," *Current Biology,* vol. 19, no. 10 (2009), pp. 827–30.

72 "great numbers would flash so closely in unison" H. A. Allard, "The Synchronal Flashing of Fireflies," *Science,* vol. 44, no. 1142 (1916), p. 710.

72 "the involuntary twitching of his own eyelids" Philip Laurent, "The Supposed Synchronization of Fireflies," *Science,* vol. 45, no. 1150 (1917), p. 44.

74 "Each firefly contains an oscillator" Steven Strogatz, *Sync* (New York: Hyperion, 2003), p. 13.

74 "a vast Web page containing a huge amount of information on singing insects" Online at http://entnemdept.ufl.edu/walker/buzz/.

74 "an 'inhibitory-resetting, phase-delay' mechanism" Michael Greenfield, "Synchronous and Alternating Choruses in Insects and Anurans," *American Zoologist,* vol. 34 (1994), pp. 605–15.

79 "Why should the tiny cricket's / tune so sway my heart?" My translation of a poem that appears in Keith Kevan, *Land of the Locusts,* part 2, p. 328 in three different translations.

80 " 'Nature makes no noise.' " Henry David Thoreau, *Journals,* vol. 1 (Princeton: (Princeton University Press, 1981), p. 12.

81 "full meaning of that word 'sound' " Ibid., pp. 226–27.

81 "the 'great animal orchestra' " Bernie Krause, *The Great Animal Orchestra* (New York: Little, Brown, 2012).

82 "all of creation is sound" Michael Jackson interviewed by Robert E. Johnson in *Ebony,* quoted in John Jeremiah Sullivan, *Pulphead* (New York: 2011), p. 126.

82 "you may dry out those lonely years" David Rothenberg, *Blue Cliff Record: Zen Echoes* (New Paltz: Codhill Press, 2001), p. 46.

Three: What Makes Them Dance

84 " 'Two Hundred Crickets: A Young Lady Artist's Mania for Capturing the Musical Insects,' " *New York Times,* May 29, 1880.

88 "Music is pure rhythm" Ezra Pound, introduction to his translation of Cavalcanti. Quoted in Anthony David Moody, *Ezra Pound, Poet* [*Vol. 1, The Young Genius*] (New York: Oxford University Press, 2007), p. 154.

90 "curvilinear and fuzzy morphologies" Curtis Roads, *Microsound* (Cambridge: MIT Press, 2004), p. 340.

92 "never needing food or sleep" Plato's myth of the cicadas appears in his dialogue *The Phaedrus,* lines 259a–259d. "Before the birth of the Muses, cicadas used to be human beings. When the Muses came into existence, some people

became so obsessed with singing that they died from forgetting to eat and drink. These people became cicadas, to whom the Muses gave a gift: they begin singing at birth and need neither food nor drink until death. And when they die, they report to the Muses which morals have honored their special kind of music by leading a philosophical life." (259d) Online at http://classics.mit.edu/Plato/phaedrus.html.

93 "nature is full of oscillators" All these exponential time cycles are from Russell Foster and Leon Kreutzman, *Rhythms of Life: The Biological Clocks that Control the Daily Lives of Every Living Thing* (New Haven: Yale University Press, 2004), pp. 38–39.

96 "music must have a beat" Mark Changizi, *Harnessed* (Dallas: Benbella Books, 2011), p. 127.

97 "'*Boooom-da-da-da-da-da-da-da . . .*'" Ibid., p. 134.

98 "listening to birdsong is good for people" Patrick Barkhan, "Scientists to Study the Psychological Benefits of Birdsong," *The Guardian,* December 21, 2011. Online at http://www.guardian.co.uk/environment/2011/dec/21/scientists-study-psychological-effects-birdsong.

99 "the 'fairy bell ringer'" Lines spoken by Rachel Carson in the 2009 film *A Sense of Wonder.* Quoted in John Himmelman, *Cricket Radio: Tuning In the Night-Singing Insects* (Cambridge: Harvard University Press, 2011), p. 1.

100 "those cold, hard facts" John Himmelman, ibid., p. 2.

102 "*the most strident song they could muster*" ibid., p. 5.

103 "stimulated by the typewriter" Richard Alexander, "Sound Communication in Orthoptera and Cicadae," in *Animal Sounds and Communication,* ed. W. E. Lanyon and W. H. Tavolga (Washington: American Institute of Biological Sciences, Publ. 7, 1960) p. 84.

105 "'acoustic startling'" P. A. Faure and R. R. Hoy, "The Sounds of Silence: Cessation of Singing and Song Pausing Are Ultrasound-induced Acoustic Startle Behaviors in the Katydid *Neoconocephalus ensiger* (Orthoptera; Tettigoniidae)," vol. 186 (2000), *Journal of Comparative Physiology,* pp. 129–42.

106 "silence becomes a signal" Amy Dapper, Alexander Baugh, and Michael Ryan, "The Sounds of Silence as an Alarm Cue in Túngara Frogs," *Biotropica,* vol. 43, no. 3, (2011), pp. 380–85.

107 "the structure of its forewings" Jun-Jie Gua, Fernando Montealegre-Z, et al., "Wing Stridulation in a Jurassic Katydid Produced Low-pitched Musical Calls to Attract Females," *Proceedings of the National Academy of Sciences,* 2012. Online at www.pnas.org/cgi/doi/10.1073/pnas.1118372109.

108 "'entrainment' . . . in the domain of ethnomusicology" Martin Clayton, Rebecca Sagor, and Udo Will, "In Time with the Music: The Concept of Entrainment and Its Significance for Ethnomusicology." *European Meetings in Ethnomusicology,* 11, (2005), pp. 3–142.

109 "clouds of midges" Ibid., p. 55.

109 "the upper body can . . . move to an independent meter" Ibid., p. 21.

110 "'lift-up-over-sounding'" Ibid., p. 22. See also Steven Feld, *Sound and Sentiment* (Philadelphia: University of Pennsylvania Press, 1990), p. 119.

110 "the greatness of the groove" Simha Aron, *African Polyphony and Polyrhythm* (Cambridge: Cambridge University Press, 1991), pp. 658–59.

111 "few other primates show much interest in dancing to a single beat" Björn Merker, Guy Madison, and Patricia Eckerdal, "On the Role and Origin of Human Isochrony in Human Entrainment," *Cortex* 45 (2009), pp. 4–17.

111 "an excited bout of loud calling" Ibid., p. 6.

112 "mutual entrainment to an isochronous pulse" Ibid., p. 6.

113 "West African drum languages" James Gleick, *The Information* (New York: Pantheon, 2011), pp. 13–27. See also J. F. Carrington, *Talking Drums of Africa* (New York: Negro Universities Press, 1949).

Four: Listen Outside the Ear

121 "a form of convergent evolution" Simon Conway Morris, *Life's Solution: Inevitable Humans in a Lonely Universe* (Cambridge: Cambridge University Press, 2003), p. 191.

123 "through our hands into our ears" Laurie Anderson's "Handphone Table," Museum of Modern Art, 1978. Online at www.angelika-maschke.de/table.pdf.

128 "jamming of rival signals by male nightingales" Silke Kipper, Roger Mundry, Henrike Hultsche, and Dietmar Todt, "Long-term Persistence of Song Performance Rules in Nightingales," *Behaviour* 141 (2004), pp. 371–90.

129 "*Treeverb*" Peter Marting interviewed at http://blogs.riverfronttimes.com/atoz /2011/05/ptarmigan_free_music_treeverb_nature_sounds.php.

130 "seventy thousand acres of forest" Jim Robbins, "What's Killing the Great Forests of the American West?" *Environment360*, March 15, 2010. On line at http:// e360.yale.edu/feature/whats_killing_the_great_forests_of_the_american_west /2252/.

131 "sixty and eighty percent of all the harvestable forests" Ibid., see also Larry Pynn, "The Environmental Costs of BC's War on Pine Beetles," *Vancouver Sun,* December 5, 2011. On line at http://www.vancouversun.com/technology/ environmental+costs+logging+pine+beetles/5798233/story.html.

133 "*The Sound of Light in Trees*" Extensive information about this recording and its connection to bark beetle infestations may be found here: http://www.acousticecology.org/dunn/solit.html.

134 "'the entire beetle is the ear'" David Dunn, *The Sound of Light in Trees* (Santa Fe: EarthEar Records ee0513, 2005), liner notes.

136 "the beetles keep making all sorts of sounds" David Dunn and James Crutchfield, "Insects, Trees, and Climate: The Bioacoustic Ecology of Deforestation and Entemogenic Climate Change," *Santa Fe Institute Working Paper 06-12-055,* December 2006, p. 10. Online at http://csc.ucdavis.edu/~chaos/papers/ecc.pdf.

137 "'It was not a political statement'" Richard McGuire quoted in Andrew Nikiforuk, *Empire of the Beetle* (Vancouver: Greystone Books, 2011), p. 156.

138 " 'It's just not natural' " Ibid., p. 157.

139 "Females produced low-intensity chirps" S. Sivalinghem and J. E. Yack, "Acoustic Communication in the Pine Engraver Bark Beetle," Conference Presentation, ISV Meeting, June 7, 2011, *ISV Schedule with Abstracts* (Columbia, Missouri: University of Missouri, 2011), p. 82. Online at http://isv2011.missouri.edu/Program_files/Proc_web.pdf.

140 "Acoustic signals varied . . . depending on the behavioral context" Amanda Lindeman, et al., "Sound and Vibration Signals in the Mountain Pine Beetle," Poster Presentation, ISV Meeting, June 8, 2011, *ISV Schedule with Abstracts* (Columbia, Missouri: University of Missouri, 2011), p. 59. Online at http://isv2011.missouri.edu/Program_files/Proc_web.pdf.

142 "don't try this at home" Jerome Sueur, David Mackie, and James Windmill, "So Small, So Loud: Extremely High Sound Pressure Level from a Pygmy Insect (Corixidae, Micronectinae)," *PLoS One,* 6(6). Online at doi%2F10.1371%2Fjournal_pone.0021089.

145 " 'the origin of music' " Tom Lawrence, quoted by Paul Evans in "The Water Boatmen's Song," *Nature Series 5,* episode 2, *BBC Radio 4,* broadcast Jan. 12, 2012. Online at http://www.bbc.co.uk/programmes/b0194mvq.

Five: From *El Grillo* to Das Techno

149 "he sings just for love" Keith Kevan, *Land of the Grasshoppers* (Montreal: Lyman Entomological Museum Memoir no. 2, 1974), p. 200. See also Keith Kevan, *Land of the Locusts,* part 2 (Montreal: Lyman Entomological Museum Memoir no. 10, 1983), pp. 440–42.

150 "the basic, simple chirps" Pungur's notation described in Keith Kevan, *Land of the Locusts,* part 4, vol. 2 (Montreal: Lyman Entomological Museum Memoir no. 18, 1998), pp. 583–85.

152 " 'This stylization of the sounds of nature in Bartóks works' " László Somfai, "Analytical Notes on Bartók's Piano Year of 1926," *Studia Musicologica Academiae Scientiarum Hungaricae,* vol. 26 (1984), p. 6.

153 "abstract rhythmic glyphs" Heiko Bellmann, *Field Guide to the Crickets and Grasshoppers of Northern Europe* (London: Collins, 1988), p. 127.

154 " 'Artikulation,' was given a graphic score" Ligeti's piece scored by Rainer Wehinger. Online at http://www.youtube.com/watch?v=71hN1_skTZQ&feature=related.

155 "the awesome white noise of the cicadas" Louis Sarno, *Bayaka: The Extraordinary Music of the BaBenzélé Pygmies* (Roslyn, New York: Ellipsis Arts, 1996), p. 23.

156 "Mushroom gathering lends itself especially well to lyrical accompaniment" Louis Sarno quoted in *The Book of Music and Nature,* ed. David Rothenberg and Marta Ulvaeus (Middletown: Wesleyan University Press, 2001), p. 240.

158 "they settle in and use their relative acoustic niches" See Bryan C. Pijanowski, Almo Farina, Bernie L. Krause, et al., "Soundscape Ecology," *BioScience,* vol. 61, no. 3 (March 2011), pp. 203–16. Also Almo Farina, Rachele Malavasi,

et al., "Avian Soundscapes and Cognitive Landscapes," *Landscape Ecology* 26 (2011), pp. 1257–67.

160 "ensemble in Ghana" Hewitt Pantaleoni, *On the Nature of Music* (Oneonta: Welkin Books, 1985), p. 284.

161 "the sounds of Indonesian insects immediately after a gamelan performance" See Richard Lerman's CD *Within Earreach*. Online at http://www.allmusic. com/album/within-earreach-mw0000777832.

162 " 'Barbet and cicada calls . . . persistent yet unobtainable' " Marina Roseman, *Healing Sounds from the Malaysian Rainforest* (Berkeley: University of California Press, 1991), p. 172.

163 "the time / of dizziness, whirling, and change" Ibid., p. 110.

163 "to 'intensify longings of the heart' " Liner notes to Marina Roseman, *Dream Songs and Healing Sounds in the Rainforests of Malaysia* (Smithsonian Folkways 40417, 1995). Online at http://www.folkways.si.edu/albumdetails.aspx?itemid= 2351.

164 "longing for a romanticized natural world" Francisco Lopez, "Blind Listening," in *The Book of Music and Nature,* ed. David Rothenberg and Marta Ulvaeus (Middletown: Wesleyan University Press, 2001), pp. 163–68.

167 "fusions of slowly evolving sounds" Michel Chion, *Guide to Sound Objects: Pierre Schaeffer and Musical Research,* translated by John Dack and Christine North (Paris: Éditions Buchet Chastel, 2009 [1983]), p. 148. Online at http://modisti .com/news/?p=14239. A new translation of Pierre Schaeffer, *In Search of a Concrete Music,* translated by John Dack (Berkeley: University of California Press, 2012), has just been published.

167 "hundreds of shimmering pizzicatos" Ibid., p. 152.

168 "machines . . . are not neutral" Francisco Lopez, *Hyper-Rainforest,* concert installation at EMPAC, Rensselaer Polytechnic Institute, 2011. Online at http:// empac.rpi.edu/events/2011/spring/lopez/program.html.

169 "Nightfall by a riverside camp" Robert Curgenven, liner notes to *Silent Landscapes*. Online at http://www.gruenrekorder.de/?page_id=196.

175 "An unforeseen difficulty presented itself" From the liner notes to Graeme Revell, *The Insect Musicians* (Musique Brut, 1986). This CD is not available online, but the complete liner notes may be found here, http://home.scarlet.be /~spk/spktheinsectmusicians.htm.

175 "A poetic technology must satisfy somewhat greater conditions" Ibid.

179 "Airports . . . are intense and overwhelming revealing environments" The Black Dog, *Music for Real Airports* (2010). Online at http://www.musicforre alairports.com/live/.

181 "the freeware synth Automat" You may download the Automat synthesizer plugin for free at http://www.alphakanal.de. Sorry people, this one only works on a Mac.

183 "a synth plug-in by the name of Zebra" Online at http://www.u-he.com/cms /zebra.

Six: Throat-Singing with the Katydids of Glynwood

197 "the visual art of the pygmies" Georges Meurant, *Mbuti Design* (London: Thames and Hudson, 1996). p. 41.

199 "music emerges out of raw sound when it is periodic" Michael Tenzer, *Analytical Studies in World Music* (Oxford: Oxford University Press, 2006), p. 89.

199 "one subsonic pulse exactly every two minutes" David Rothenberg, *Thousand Mile Song: Whale Music in a Sea of Sound* (New York: Basic Books, 2008), p. 199.

201 " 'I like slowly evolving sounds' " Robert Henke, explaining Granulator, http://www.ableton.com/library/granulator.

202 "How I hate those dirty little flies." Robert Henke, liner notes to *Ghosts* (2012). Online at http://www.monolake.de/releases/ml-026.html.

203 " 'After that I decided it was safer to stay home in Berlin' " Robert Henke, talk at the Goethe Institute in Manhattan, April 19, 2012.

207 "It is thought that they produce four distinct varieties of song" Irene Moon, live at the Cornelia St. Café, March 11, 2012.

208 "Science is just really cool." Irene Moon, *The Begonia Society: Residency at the Institute for Electronic Arts* (Alfred, New York: Alfred University, 2009), p. 12. Online at http://www.blurb.com/books/2495556.

Seven: Sax and Cicadas

216 "Now there are websites full of professional and citizens' reports on where the bugs are." Online at www.magicicada.org and www.cicadamania.com and www.insectsingers.com.

223 "the rough, dizzy voice of the ancestors" Paul Berliner, *The Soul of Mbira* (Berkeley: University of California Press, 1978), p. 39.

230 " 'to see in music something beyond itself' " Bruno Nettl, "The Basic Unit," *The Study of Ethnomusicology* (Urbana: University of Illinois Press, 1983), p. 202.

230 " 'The music we like conforms to an ideal' " Ibid., p. 316.

234 "*Desert-silence where they sang.*" Keith Kevan, *Land of the Locusts,* part 2, (Montreal: Lyman Entomological Museum Memoir no. 10, 1983), p. 207.

Index

accumulation, 167–168, 181

Acoustic Communication in Insects and Anurans (Gerhardt & Huber), 71

acoustic startling, 105

Adorno, Theodor, 129–130, 205

Africa, 109–114, 155–157

Alexander, Richard, 23–24, 37, 102–103, 111–112

Allard, H. A., 21, 53, 64–66, 71–72

Allee, Warder Clyde, 45

Allee Effect, 45, 46

Anacreon, 7

analog music, 89–90, 183–184

Analytical Studies in World Music (Tenzer), 199

Anderson, Laurie, 122

animals, 7, 11, 35, 77–78, 123–124

An Anthology of Chinese Experimental Music, 248

Ap, Arnold, 211–212, 248

"Apuse," 248

Arduser, Mike, 18

"Aria Locustae," 248

Ariston, 15, *16*

Aron, Simha, 110

"Artikulation," 154, 248

Arumisore, Hein, 211

"Atmospheres," 154

atonality, 225

Attenborough, David, 28, 35

Australia, 170

Automat, 181–182

automatic rhythms, 68

Bali, 161

"Balinese Monkey Chant 2: Forest Scene," 247

Bartók, Béla, 151–152, 208, 247

Bartók: Out of Doors, 247

Baudelaire, Charles, 220

Bayaka, 155–161

Bayaka—The Extraordinary Music of the BaBenzele Pygmies, 247

Beckman, Ours, 183, 184

bees, 120, 147–148

beetles, 130–131, 252
   chaos effect on, 136–139
   engravings of, 134, *135*
   Ips confusus, 132–133
   Ips pini, 139–140
   mating behavior, 136–139, 139–140
   musical warfare on, 137–139
   recordings of, 144
   sounds/songs, 132–137, 139–140
   water boatman, 141–142, *143,* 144,
      252
Bellmann, Heiko, 153
Berger, Bengt, 62
Bestioles le temps s'étend, 248
biological clocks, 93–94
birds, sounds/songs, 1, 3, 38, 49, 68,
   98, 162
   nightingales, 128, 142
   slowed-down, 59
The Black Dog, 179–180, 248
blindfolds, 165, 168–169
Blunk, Tim, 48–53, 239–241
bone conduction, 122–123
The Book of Crickets (Sidao), 56
Book of Music and Nature, 168–169
Borror, Donald, 35
Boucher, Stéphanie, 9
boyobi ceremony, *157,* 159
Bradford, William, 11
brains, 93–94
Brand, Stewart, 88
Bridie, David, 210, 211, 248
broadband pulses, 121
Bryars, Gavin, 172
Buddhism, 61–62, 82, 189
Bug Music CD, 77, 125, 200, 239,
   249–253
"Bug Nite," 182
Burchfield, Charles, 218, *219*

Cage, John, 3, 81, 166, 168, 187, 204
Calix, Mira, 170–172, 248
Carrington, John, 113
Carson, Rachel, 99–100, 101
Changizi, Mark, 96–99

chanting, 161
chaos, 136–139
"Chaos and the Emergent Mind of the
   Pond," 141
China, 58–59
Chion, Michel, 167
"Chirped to Death," 252
Chou Yuan, 47
"Cicada," 248
Cicada (album), 249
Cicada Summer, 15
cicadas, 15–17, 155–156, 162–163, *217,*
   231
   behavior, 8, 39–41
   collaboration with, 221–223, 250
   in food, 18–19, *20,* 21
   geography and diversification, 33–34
   of Greece, 14
   growth of, *14*
   hearing of, 38
   human awareness of, 33
   hybridization of, 37, 44, 45–46
   Magicicada neotredecim (13-year),
      25, *26,* 42–45, *46,* 47
   Magicicada septendecim, 27
   Maori people and, 22
   maps/locations of, 16, *17*
   morphology, 33
   musicality of, 200
   nervous system, 38
   poems about, 6–7, 9–11, 34, 41–42,
      47, 50
   population, 43–45, *46*
   recordings of, 33–34
   saxophone and, 222, *223*
   species, 25, *26,* 33, 37, 40
   symbology of, 7–8
   Tibicen chloromera, 91
   tredecassini, 25, 29, 37, 41, 219
   tredecim, 25, 37, 219, 237
   tredecula, 25, 228
   in visual arts, 218, *219*
cicadas, broods, 16–17, 42
   I, 236–237
   II, 16–18

X, 22–23

XIX, 21–22, 35, 53, 214–216, *217,*
251–252

cicadas, cycles, 42

Allee Effect, 45, 46

early emergence, 47

human identification with, 48–50

measurement of, 94–95, 240

population and, *46*

predation and, 43–44, 46

prime numbering and, 43–44, 45,
94–96, 220, 229

synchronization and, 108

thermophotoperiod, *96*

cicadas, *Magicicadas* (17-year), 3–5, 69,
171–172

catching, 39

cycles of, 42–45, *46,* 47, 94–95

genus of, 23

in media, 17–18

reasons for, 13–14

sonograms, *24*

sounds of, *23, 24, 26*

species of, 25, 26

studying, 25

cicadas, mating behavior, 26, *27,* 28,
32, 95

Court III, 238–239

group dynamic of, 30, 38, 45

music and, 29–30

wing flick of female cicadas, 30–32,
38, 39, 94, 224, 236, 237–238

cicadas, sounds/songs, 1, 38, 163–164,
167, 218, 227–228

emotions and, 47–48

gender and, 26, *27*

meaning of, 33

nonacoustic anomalies, 28

sonograms of, *24, 91,* 92, *196*

species and, 33

timing of, 237–238

tymbals of, 118, *119*

"Cigales cymbals," 248

circadian rhythms, 93

classical music, 154–155, 173, 205

Clayton, Martin, 108

"Clementine," 161

"Clock of the Long Now," 88

clouds (musical idea), 90–91

Cocroft, Reginald, 123–125, 251

collaboration, 3, 7, 103–104, 164,
171–172, 221–223, 250

communication, 35, 107, 126–127

composition, 67–68, 89, 153–154,
164–167, 185, 187

computers, 173, 205, 232

"Congotronics," 69

Cooley, John, 25, 26–27, 31, 236–238

creative process, 67–68, 208

Cricket Radio (Himmelman), 100

crickets, 3, *85*

aging of, 59

Allonemobius tinnulus, 100

bush, 68

in China, 58–59

concerts, 63–64, 84

drummers and, 61–62

Ensifera, 85

fighting, 56–57, 59, 60–61

hearing of, 122–123

mating behavior, 190–191

nervous system of, 74–75

orchestra, 61, 64, 78

poems about, 58, 79, 82

raising, 54, 56

recordings, 63–64

Say's Trigs, *Anaxipha exigua,* 101

seasons and, 58

simulation software, 76–77

snowy tree, 61, 65, 74, 80, 121, *122,*
252

species, 61, 64

symbology of, 58–59

synchronization of, *75,* 76, *76,* 77

tree, 68, 121, *122*

virtues of, 56, 58

crickets, sounds/songs, 70, 147–150,
163–164, 167

death and, 59, 229–230

geography and, 64–65

crickets, sounds/songs *(continued)*
  locating, 66–67
  lovers of, 57–58
  musical texture of, 69
  notation of, *151*
  overtone singing with, 191–194, *195,*
    197
  pitch of, 60, 61
  reasons for, 65–66
  safety and, 55
  sex and, 65–66
  species and, 61
  stridulation, 118
  temperature and, 207–208
  weather and, 55
Critique of Judgment (Kant), 68
Crutchfield, James, 136
Cultural Entomology, 9
Curgenven, Robert, 169–170

dance, 163, 205–206, 212, 230
Darwin, Charles, 67
Davis, William T., 23
"Day of the Locusts," 23
Deadmau5 (featuring Chris James),
    248
death, 59, 229–230
Desmond, Paul, 49
Despréz, Josquin, 147, 247
digital music, 89–90, 184
The Disc of Music and Nature, 248
dissonance, 152, *153*
diversification, geography and cicada,
    33–34
Doppler shifts, 123
drum machines, 172, 173
drums, 2, 61–62, 113–114
Dudley, Paul, 12
Dunn, David, 130, 132–135, 141, 248

echo, 161
ecology, 130–132
El Grillo (The Cricket), 147–150, 247
electronic instruments, 177–178,
    180–181

electronic music, 172–173, 201–202
  aesthetics of, 184–185, 187–188
  musicians, 70, 125, 181–182
  vintage, 176–177
"The Electrosense of Paddlefish," 215
Elliott, Lang, 100
Eno, Brian, 67–68, 88, 179
entrainment, 108–109, 111–112, 113
Eunomos, 15, *16*
Ever Since Darwin (Gould), 43
evolution, 4, 33, 35, 40, 101–103, 235
experimental music, 153–154, 166
extinction, 45

Fabre, Jean-Henri, 21, 66–67
Fairlight CMI sampler, 174–175, 178
Farina, Almo, 158
Faure, Paul, 105
Feld, Steven, 110
"Final Creatures," 253
Finer, Jem, 88
Finkelman, Jason, 220, 226–227
fireflies, 71, *72,* 73–74, *75,* 76
flamenco, 63
flies, 120, 145
"Flight of the Bumblebee," 147–148, 247
Folds, Ben, 177
folk music, 69
Fonseca, Paulo, 38
Forbidden Planets—Music from the
    Pioneers of Electronic Sound, 248
The Forest Darling, 128–129
forests, 130–132, 155–156. *See also*
    rainforest
Fredriksson, Lars ("Mr. Fung"), 54–55,
    60, 62–63, 248
frogs, 105–106, 162
Fusatai Susume, 34
"Future Delay Thinking," 179–180, 248

Gabriel, Peter, 210
gamelan, 161, 229
gathering, 156, *157*
genggong (jaw harp), 162
geography, 33–34, 64–65, 169–170

Gerhardt, Carl, 71
Ghana, *160*
Ghosts, 202–203, 248
Glass, Philip, 172
Gleick, James, 113
"Glitches'n'Bugs," 248
"Glittering Clouds (Locusts)," 210, 248
global warming, 131–132, 208
Glynwood Farm, 190–191
"Glynwood Nights," 252
Gould, Stephen Jay, 43
granular synthesis, 86–88, 167
Granulator, 201–204
The Great Animal Orchestra (Krause),
    158
Great Bass, 88
"The Great Southern Brood," 15
Greece, cicadas of, 14
Greenfield, Michael, 74
groove, 110–111, 173
Gruenrekorder, 144
Gryllus, 150, *151*
Gu, Jun-Jie, 106
Guide to Sound Objects (Chion), 167

"The Handphone Table," 122–123
harmonic series, 191
harmonic singing. *See* overtone singing
harmonics, 69
Harnessed (Changizi), 96–99
Hazmat Modine, 248
Heap, Imogen, 210, 248
hearing
    aesthetics of, 130
    bone conduction, 122–123
    of cicadas, 38
    of crickets, 122–123
    of insects, 117–118
heart, 76, 94
Henke, Robert ("Monolake"),
    200–203, 205–206, 248
Hill, Kathy, 38
Hill, Peggy, 120
Hill, Timothy, 189, 191–194, *195, 197,*
    249, 252

Himmelman, John, 100, 101
Hofstetter, Richard, 137
Hoy, Ronald, 105
Huber, Franz, 71
Hutchinson, Evelyn, 37
hybridization, cicada, 37, 44, 45–46
hydrophone, 142, 145
Hykes, David, 189–190
Hyper-Rainforest, 168

"The Incomplete Image," 248
information theory, 113
inhibitory-resetting, phase-delay,
    74, *75*
"Insect Chorus," 185
The Insect Chorus, 218, *219*
Insect Drummers (Ossiannilsson), 117
"Insect Drummers 1: Inside the
    Mosquito's Brain," 251
"Insect Drummers 2: The Water
    Boatman's Loudest Penis," 252
"Insect Drummers 3: Your Sound Can
    Kill," 252
insect music, 60, 66. *See also* music
    aesthetics of, 69–71
    age of, 102
    complexity of, 96, 116–117
    composition and, 164–165
    evolution of, 101–103
    harmonics of, 69
    human and, 33–34, 152, 162,
        178–179, 187, 194
    human culture and, 81, 162
    recordings of, 69
    repetition and, 68
    rhythmic glyphs of, *153*
    sex, violence and, 56
The Insect Musicians (Revell), 174–176,
    178, 200, 248
insects. *See also specific types*
    collaboration with, 3, 103–104, 164,
        171–172
    environment and, 55
    hearing of, 117–118
    rhythms and, 173, 200, 233

insects *(continued)*
   rules of music and, 11
   synchronization of, 159–160
"Insects After Gamelan," 247
instruments, 177–178, 180–181
International Meeting on Invertebrate
   Sound and Vibration, 34
intervals, 191
Into a Wild Sanctuary (Krause), 158
"Invaders of the Heart," 176, 248
Invertebrate Sound and Vibration
   Meeting, 139
"Invocation II: Three Harmonious
   Bells," 248
irregular loops, 201
irregular rhythms, 206

Jackson, Michael, 82
James, Harry, 247
Jarrett, Keith, 226
jaw harp, 162
Johnston's organ, *120,* 121
Journal (Thoreau), 80
Jürjendal, Robert, 249
"Just Go Along With It," 82

kalimba, 69
Kalm, Petr, 13
Kaluli people, 110
Kant, Immanuel, 68
Karban, Rick, 95
"Katydid Prehistory," 250–251
katydids, 118
   Archaboilus musicus, 107, 250–251
   Pterophylla camellifolia, 103–104
   sword-bearing conehead, 104–105,
      106
   Uhler's, 251
Kecak from Bali, 247
Keil, Charles, 110
Kevan, Keith, 9
"Kikitara," 252
Kirch, Stefan, 181
Koewenhoven, Frank, 109
Kogoya, Gillius, 211

Konono N°1, 69
Krause, Bernie, 81, 157–158, 211

La Selva, 165–166, 169, 248
ladybugs, 145
language, 11, 99, 113, 230
Laurent, Philip, 72
Lawrence, Tom, 144, 145, 248
leafhoppers, 115, *116, 117,* 118
Lerman, Richard, 161–162, 247
Lewis, Jerome, 155–156
Life in the Undergrowth, 28, 35
Ligeti, György, 154, 208, 248
Ligeti, Lukas, 154
Lindeman, Amanda, 140
Lindsay, Charles, 215–216, 225–226,
   228, 249
"Listen Outside the Ear," 252
listening, 3, 4, 130, 166, 182, 213
Listening to Autumn, 63
Lockett, Pete, 172–173
locusts, 8, 12, 21, 22–23
Loderbauer, Max, 248
Loga, 248
Lomax, Alan, 109, 209
London Sinfonietta, 171
"Longplayer," 88
looping, 171, 185, 199–200
López, Francisco, 164–166, 168–169,
   249
Lo-Ping Wang, 50
Luo Binwang, 50

machines, 2, 77, 172, 173, 194
"Magicicada Unexpected Road," 250
"Magicicada Warm Springs," 253
Malavasi, Rachele, 158
Mandelson, Ben ("Hijaz Mustapha"), 173
Manzo, V. J., 77
Maori, cicadas and, 22
Marlatt, C. L., 15–16
Marshall, David, 25–29, 236
Marting, Peter, 127
The Math Book, 43
Mbuti Design (Meurant), 197, *198*

McGuire, Reagan, 137
Merker, Björn, 111–112
Messiaen, Olivier, 151–152
Meurant, Georges, 197, *198*
Micronecta scholtzi, 141–142, *143,* 144
Microsound (Roads), 86–88
microsounds, 90–91
midges, 109
Mingus, Charles, 80
molecules, 145, 146
Mongolia, 189, 190
Montealegre-Z, Fernando, 106–107
Moon, Irene, 206, *207,* 207–208
Moore, Thomas, 24
mosquitoes, *120,* 121, 145, 204
movement, music and human, 96–97
Mujuru, Ephat, 223–224
Mungolian Jet Set, 248
The Muses, 92–93
Museum of Zoology (Michigan),
    35–36, 37
music. *See also* digital music
    aesthetics, 69–71
    definition of, 199–200, 225
    folk and art, 69
    gathering and, 156, *157*
    human movement and, 96–97
    insects and human, 33–34, 152, 162,
        178–179, 187, 194
    insects and rules of, 11
    language and, 11, 99, 113
    mating and, 29–30
    missing element in, 68
    nature and, 164–166, 206
    noise and, 69–70, 204, 227–228, 242,
        250
    popular, 129–130, 209–210
    sounds and, 81–82, 86, *87,* 88, 231
Music and Trance (Rouget), 163
Music for Airports, 179
Music for Real Airports, 179–180, 248
musical warfare, 137–138
musicology, 109, 223–224
*Musique de la Renaissance au temps de
    Botticelli,* 247

natural selection, 158
nature, 89–90
    evolution and exceptions in, 35
    music and, 164–166, 206
    noise and, 80–81
    oscillators in, 93–94
    sounds, 81–82
    technology and, 250
Nettl, Bruno, 69, 224, 227, 230
New Guinea, 110, 210, 211–212
New York, 17
New York Times, 17–18, 21, 84
niche hypothesis, 157–159
nightingales, 128, 142
"The Night's Music," 151
noise, 11, 12
    desire for, 233
    fear of, 242
    love of, 2, 14–15, 69
    music and, 69–70, 204, 227–228,
        242, 250
    nature and, 80–81
    tone and, 223–224
Noriega, Manuel, 137
Not Drowning Waving, 210
notation, *116,* 150, *151,* 153–154
Nunu, 170–172, 248

O'Grady, John P., 6, 235–36
Oriental rhythms, 109–110
Oropendola, 248
oscillators, 89, 93–94, 104, 108, 250
oscillograms, *117*
Ossiannilsson, Frej, 115, *117,* 251
Out of Doors, 151, 247
Ou-Yang Hsiu, 10–11, 88, 234
overtone singing, 191–194, *195, 197*

Pantaleoni, Hewitt, 160
Papua New Guinea, 211–212
Pavarotti, Luciano, 242
Pedanik, Martin, 220–221
performance, software and, 183, 201
performance art, 206–207
Perkins, George, Jr., 190

Perovsek, Boštjan, 248
"Phaaaroah!", 251–252
Phaedrus, 92–93
Phares, D. L., 15
phase shifting, 77, 110, 201
Pierce, George W., 104, 111–112
pitch, 60, 61
"Pitch Accumulator," 168
Plague Songs, 210, 248
plant hoppers, 121
Pliny & the Poets, 12
"Plush Insect," 172–173
Poinsignon, Jean, 248
"A Political Prisoner to a Cicada," 50
polyphony, 111
polyrhythms, 109, 110–111, *160,* 173
pop music, 129–130, 173, 205, 209–210
"A Portrait of Shunkin," 78
Potter, Nathaniel, 14
Pound, Ezra, 58, 88–89
Powers, Richard, 227
Prattie, Donald, 21
programming sounds, 181–182
Ptarmigan, 128–129
Pterophylla camellifolia, 103–104
Puffin Foundation, 52
Pungur, Gyula, 150, *151*
Putra, I Gusti Putu, 247
puya gathering ceremony, *157*
pygmies, 155–161, 197, *198,* 213, 247

quantization, 77
quasiperiodicity, 110–111
Quin, Douglas, 248

Raffles, Hugh, 57
rainforest, 155–159, 162–163, 168, 198
"Ramifications," 154
Rare War Time Recordings vol. 1, 247
Ratcliffe, Ellie, 98
Re: ECM, 248
Reich, Steve, 172
repetition, 68, 113–114, 172, 185,
    199–200. *See also* rhythms
"Respite," 248

Revell, Graeme, 174–178, 200, 248
rhythms, 2, 105. *See also* cicadas, cycles;
    synchronization
  automatic, 68
  biological clocks, 93–94
  circadian, 93
  composition and, 67–68
  earthquakes, 76
  entrainment, 108–109, 111–112, 113
  of fireflies, 71, *72,* 73–74, *75,* 76
  glyphs of insect, *153*
  groove, 110–111, 173
  human heart, 76
  human love of, 71
  human movement and, 96–97
  human synchronization, 108–109
  insects and, 173, 200, 233
  irregular, 206
  meter, 109
  Oriental, 109–110
  overlapping, 89, 94, 110–111, *160*
  phase shifting, 77, 110, 201
  polyrhythms, 109–111
  quantization, 77
  quasiperiodicity, 110–111
  sound and, 199–200
  time scales, *87,* 88
  walking gait and, 96–97
  West African drum languages,
    113–114
"Riddim Bugz," 251
Riley, Charles, 15–16, 18, 23
Riley, Terry, 172
Rimsky-Korsakov, Nikolai, 147–148
Roads, Curtis, 86–88, 167, 201–202
Robert, Daniel, 107
Robinson, Richard, 240, 251
Roché, Jean, 203–204
Rodriguez, Rafael, 126
Rolling Stones, 226
Roseman, Marina, 162, 171
Rothenberg, David, *223, 228, 234,*
    249
Rothenberg, Umru, 239, 249
Rouget, Gilbert, 163

Royal Society of London, 12
Rudolph, Adam, 61
Rumbiak, Jacob, 211
Russolo, Luigi, 3, 90, 204
Ryan, Michael, 105–106

Sager, Rebecca, 108
sampling, 176–183
Sarno, Louis, 155–156, 159, 162,
    198–199, 210–211
saxophone, cicadas and, 222, *223*
Say's Trigs, *Anaxipha exigua,* 101
Scanner, 172
Schaeffer, Pierre, 166–167, 168, 181,
    204–205
Schoenberg, Arnold, 225
Science, 72
Search for Extraterrestrial Intelligence
    (SETI), 215
seasons, 2, 58, 233
seljefløyte, 252
"Sentient," 129
Serious Tam, 210, 248
SETI. *See* Search for Extraterrestrial
    Intelligence
"Seven Springs," 248
sex, 56, 65–66, 102
sharawadji effect, 193
Shocked, Michelle, 209–210, 248
Sidao, Jia, 56
silence, 2, 105–106, 168
Silent Landscape No. 2, 169–170
Simon, Chris, 45
sine waves, 175
Sivalinghem, S., 139–140
"620," 248
Socrates, 92–93
software, 76–77, 181–187, 200–201
Sokolov, Igor, 145
solitary confinement, 51
Somfai, László, 151–152
"Song of the Cicada," 10
"Songs of T'ang," 58
Songs of the Humpback Whale, 144
sonic illusions, 193–194

sonograms
    of cicada sounds/songs, *24, 91,* 92,
        196
    of Ghana percussion ensemble, *160*
    of overtone singing, *195, 197*
    of puya gathering ceremony, *157*
    of treehoppers, *124, 128*
sound art, 166–167
The Sound of Light in Trees, 133, 248,
    249
sounds, 68
    categorization of, 168
    clouds of, 202
    composition with, 166–167
    music and, 81–82, 86, *87,* 88, 231
    nature, 81–82
    programming, 181–182
    rhythms and, 199–200
    transmission of, 125, *126*
    wave-oriented view of, 90
"The Sounds of Silence," 105
SPK, 174
stethoscopes, 146
"Still in Love in 2024," 15
*Strange Birds in Paradise: A West Papuan
    Soundtrack,* 211, 248
Stravinsky, Igor, 205
stridulation, 118
Strogatz, Steven, 73–74, 104
Subotnik, Morton, 90
Suneur, Jérôme, 142
Survival of the Beautiful, 142
Sync (Strogatz), 73–74, 104
synchronization, 108, 111–112, 163
    of cicadas, 108
    of crickets, *75,* 76, 77
    of fireflies, 73–74, *75,* 76
    human, 108–109
    of insects, 159–160
    of katydids, 104–105
synthesizers, 181, 186

Tabaran, 210
Tanaka, Yumi, 45
Tanizaki, Junichiro, 78

technology, 2, 175–176, 182, 213, 232, 250
Telek, George, 210, 248
Temiar people, 162–163
Tenzer, Michael, 199
Texas Campfire Tapes, 209, 248
texture, 69, 192–194, 200–201, 213
"The Theatre of Eternal Music," 88
Thoreau, Henry David, 80
Thousand Mile Song (Rothenberg), 1
3 Commissions, 248
Tibet, 190
timbre, 192–193
time scales, *87,* 88
time signatures, 49
timing, 237–238
Ting Qiu: Mr. Fung's Ensemble of 108 Singing Crickets, 248
Tingqiuxuan Presents, 63
"Toku," 248
"Tolili," 248
tone, 177–178, 223–224
    overtone singing, 191–194, *195, 197*
Touchings, 248
Tracey, Hugh, 69
trance, 163
Treatise on Musical Objects (Schaeffer), 167, 205
tredecula, 228
"Treehop," 251
treehoppers, 120, 123, *124,* 127, *128,* 129, 251
Tu Fu, 79
Turnbull, Colin, 155–156, 161
Tuva, 189
Twain, Mark, 42
"Two Hundred Crickets: A Lady Artist's Mania for Capturing the Musical Insects," 84
Tylopelta gibbera, 127
tymbals, 116–118, *119*

underwater, 141–145

Varèse, Edgard, 3, 204
"The Veldt," 248
The Veldt EP, 248
Vibrational Communication in Animals (Hill), 120
Villalobos, Ricardo, 248

Waley, Arthur, 10
Walker, Thomas, 74
Walsh, Benjamin, 15–16
Water Beetles of Pollardstown Fen (Lawrence), 144, 248
"The Way of the Old Woman Cicada," 162–163
"We, the Forest," 129
We Gave It All Away . . . And Now We Are Taking It Back, 248
weather, 55, 72
weft, 168, 181
Wehinger, Rainer, 154
weta, 122
Whale Music, 168–169
whales, 1, 3, 142, 144, 168–169, 230
"What Makes Them Dance?", 251
Why Birds Sing (Rothenberg), 1, 49
"Why Do You Keep Me Up at Night?", 15
Will, Udo, 108
Wilson, E. O., 125, 208
Windmill, James, 142
Within Earreach, 247
"Women Off to Gather Payu," 156, 247

Yack, Jayne, 139
"The Year of Insect Thinking," 253
Yoshimura, Jin, 45
Young, La Monte, 88

"A Zene Hangjegyekben-*Notae stridorus*" ("The Chirp Notation"), 150, *151*
Zimmer, Hans, 174